Growing Up with
Bootleggers, Gamblers and Pigeons

Growing Up with Bootleggers, Gamblers and Pigeons

Patrick M. Canfield

Interlude Enterprises
Wilmington, Delaware

Library of Congress Catalog Card Number: 92-73193

ISBN 0-9633952-0-3 $7.95

This Interlude Enterprises first edition is printed and bound in
the United States of America.

Contents

Acknowledgments

The information in this book is based on personal reflections, interviews and public records.

The following people have contributed time and information vital to the completion of this manuscript: Joseph Holden, Eddie Kelly, Lamar Lurwick, Vince Lurwick, James Bergen, Willie Murray, Eddie Delker, Rocco and Pete Petrole, Reed Middleton, Katie Koperna, Jack Mulhall, Mickey Puzauskie and Sam Russell.

A special thanks to Florence Prusmack, Bruce Bew and the members of the creative writing class at the Indian River Community College, Port St. Lucie, Florida, for their patience, constructive criticism and encouragement.

Matthew Abbate, an editor at the MIT Press, Cambridge, Massachusetts, did the final editing of the manuscript. His editorial advice and suggestions are greatly appreciated.

The *Pottsville Republican*, Schuylkill County Historical Society and Pottsville Public Library were most helpful in furnishing germane materials.

I am indebted to David Camoirano, Wilmington, Delaware, for working so diligently to recover many chapters of manuscript I had lost in the computer.

To Dr. Carlos X. Villarreal, of Pottsville, Pennsylvania, who successfully performed two emergency operations on my wife during the writing of this book, I will be ever grateful.

To the people of New Philadelphia, relatives and friends for their contributions and support.

Finally, my heartfelt thanks to my beloved wife Rose, whose love, enthusiasm and supportive strength gave me the will and determination to complete the manuscript. To her I dedicate this book.

Introduction

This is a story about pigeon shooting as a sport, but more than that it is a saga about coming of age in a lusty, brawling Pennsylvania mining town during the years of the Great Depression. When I compare the surrounding poverty of my youth with the considerably more affluent life in later years at Rosemount, the mountain I bought for my wife, I feel poignant doubts as to which were the happier times. But in retrospect, adversities tend to lose much of their trauma, while nostalgic memories seem to intensify with the passing of the years.

Schuylkill County, located in the western tier of the anthracite coal region, is the setting for this story. It is the county where John O'Hara, the literary giant, roamed the streets of Pottsville in his youth, and famous musicians of the big band era, Tommy and Jimmy Dorsey and Les Brown, had their roots. Joe Boley, a member of Connie Mack's Philadelphia Athletics immortal "million dollar infield" during the twenties, romped and played his teenage baseball in the rough and tumble area of Shenandoah.

Religious bigotry, ethnic turmoil and violent conflict between the large coal companies and the miners were rampant in the region from the time of the Civil War until World War II. The Civil War years saw the emergence of the Molly Maguires, a band of Irish Catholic miners who terrorized the coal fields. The coal company owners branded them as hoodlums and murderers, but the miners and their sympathizers idolized and honored them as the champions of the working class.

Pigeon matches and pigeon shooters may be added to the list of events and individuals who contributed to the violence. Gamblers, bootleggers and tavern owners were the driving force which arranged, manipulated and promoted the sport.

In spite of its reputation as a "tough" area, this was a wonderful place in which to grow up.

* * *

The day I bought my wife a mountain, my life was changed forever. On December 31, 1962, New Year's Eve, my Rose and I were returning to Wilmington, Delaware, after spending a few days with my parents in New Philadelphia, Pennsylvania. I was hired to play a music engagement for a New Year's Eve celebration at the Hotel Dupont.

We were listening to the radio and by chance tuned in a station where a man was interviewing Skitch Henderson, who at that time was the music director of the Johnny Carson show. The interviewer asked Skitch, "What did your wife give you for Christmas?"

He answered, "She bought me a mountain in Vermont."

At that moment my wife said, "That's what I want you to do for me, buy me a mountain!"

A few months later I bought my wife Rose a mountain and I called it Rosemount, Rose's Mountain.

Rosemount consisted of 150 acres located in the Lewistown Valley, three miles from my hometown of New Philadelphia. It was situated at the extreme eastern section of the Pennsylvania Dutch country, which extended to the west and encompassed the famous Amish area in Lancaster County. The valley, nestled between the Sharp and Second Mountains, its rolling hills planted with corn and barley in the traditional Pennsylvania State University contour farming plan, presented the local residents and tourists a panoramic view of one of Schuylkill County's most beautiful scenic areas.

Known as the P.Q. Pheasant Farm during the forties and fifties, the property had been owned by Ralph Peters, a prosperous strip-mining contractor. He operated the pheasant farm initially as a hobby, but within a short time it became a thriving enterprise. Peters took great pride in the estate, keeping a staff of five men to maintain and repair the property. Special emphasis was placed on the upkeep and beautification of the grounds and picnic grove. By the late thirties, the P.Q. was the showcase of the Lewistown Valley.

The picnic grove, encircled by twelve-foot-high honeysuckle bushes, overlooked a ten-acre lake. Between the honeysuckle and the lake was a beautiful manicured lawn, one hundred feet in depth. The lawn was adorned with seven massive evergreens, which stood ten feet high and had a diameter of twenty feet and, as in the case of the honeysuckle, extended from the entrance of the lane to the grove.

The picnic area featured all the necessities for barbecues, family picnics, wedding receptions and sporting events; a small dance pavilion, large picnic tables, a refreshment stand, horseshoe and barbecue pits, badminton court, and two latrines. Wedding receptions and picnics were a common occurrence during the summer and fall. Peters entertained his friends and business associates in these peaceful and beautiful surroundings.

Summer brought to the valley its loveliest scenes and fragrances; flowers in bloom, the mountains showing their numerous shades of green, intermingled with Pennsylvania's famous mountain laurel. The exceptional beauty of the farmland at the height of its productive cycle, boats leisurely drifting on the lake, family groups relaxing and enjoying the picnic area, music and laughter resounding across the lake, all presented a beautiful and nostalgic sight, which for some would be stored in their memory capsule for future remembrances of happier days.

After the war, Peters sold his coal company and the pheasant farm. By 1960 the new proprietor, his health failing and business in a downward slide, put the property up for sale. The property had deteriorated during his tenure. The buildings were in deplorable condition for lack of maintenance and repair, the picnic area was overgrown with weeds and high grass, the property was in complete disarray. Because of the existing conditions, I was able to buy the estate at a very advantageous price.

It was an exceptional piece of real estate with great potential. It consisted of two homes, a four-car garage, a large, well-built storage building, the lake and the picnic grove. We now owned one hundred fifty acres of prime land, located in a most beautiful and picturesque setting. What were we going to do with it? We spent nearly a year investigating the various options available to our situation. After much deliberation, we decided to build a camping resort, which we believed would present a challenge and an interesting endeavor. I can assure you, it was both!

The northern section of the property was mountainous, part of the Sharp Mountains. It was in this area that we decided to build the camp. I contacted Professor Joseph Cardenuto, a recreational specialist from Penn State, seeking his help in developing and designing the camp. He and I surveyed and analyzed the mountainous terrain very carefully. He drew up a plot plan which he believed was appropriate for the heavily laden terrain of oak and maple trees. Joe Pattay, my brother-in-law and a foreman in my dad's construction company, helped me with the layout of the camp. We followed Cardenuto's plot plan to the letter. With the help of my father, we completed forty campsites, each provided with water, electric and sewage hookups. We opened for business in June 1964.

Ignorance is bliss. I had never camped a day in my life, yet I was instrumental in designing and constructing a camp in the heart of a mountain. I called it Rosemount Camping Resort, in honor of my wife, Rose. By the end of eight years, the camp had grown to two hundred and ten camping sites, with all the amenities of a first class resort. Rosemount received a four-star rating in the Woodall Camping Guide, America's leading camping magazine and rating book. Only six camps in the state of Pennsylvania received such a superior rating.

Our venture into the camping business changed our lives. In time I became president of the Pennsylvania Campground Owner's Association, serving two terms, followed by two terms as president of the National Campground Owner's Association. My wife and I conducted eight state conventions and three national conventions in Pennsylvania, South Carolina and Colorado.

In 1986, Rose and I sold the camp to my nephew Michael Canfield and his wife Marigrace. At the conclusion of the 1989 camping season, our active participation in the resort ended.

During the months of May through October, our activities are confined to Rosemount and Wilmington, Delaware, where we maintain a residence. The remaining time is spent on Hutchinson Island, Florida, the Sunshine State, which affords us the opportunity to mingle with people of our age and enjoy life at a slower and more casual pace. Golf, walking and attending creative writing classes at Port St. Lucie Community College occupies most of my time. Rose has her art, flower arranging and jewelry classes.

Our generation has survived the Great Depression and World War II. At this point in life, in the vernacular of the National Football League, "We're in the two-minute drill and no timeouts."

We pray for the best and endeavor to lead good and healthy lives. As my old friend Tata Foley used to say, "Lead a good life and you'll get the good rewards."

Rose and I have been blessed with many of the good rewards.

* * *

Johnnie Rice, a gentle and patient man, worked for us at Rosemount for twelve years. In his youth he spent fifteen years working at the Silver Creek coal breaker, but in 1923 he retired from the mines and opened a bar in his home in Middleport, about three miles from Rosemount. When the United States entered World War II in 1941 he closed his bar and went to work as a carpenter at a shipyard in Baltimore, Maryland. At the war's end he returned to Middleport and reopened his bar and continued at carpentry work on the side. He retired again in 1965, still in good health, with nothing to occupy his time.

Lew Stutzman, an old friend of mine and a mining buddy of Johnnie's, had worked for us at the camp since 1965. One evening he and Johnnie were having a beer in the American Legion, located next to Johnnie's home.

"Lew, do you think Patty needs any more help at the camp?" Johnnie asked. "I know I'd feel better if I had something to do."

"I don't know," Lew replied, "but there's no harm in askin'. I'll mention it to him tomorra when I go to work."

When Lew broached the subject of hiring Johnnie I was delighted. Johnnie's daughter, Mary, was in my high school class, and I had met him on numerous occasions during those happy carefree days. I discussed the matter with Rose and she agreed that Johnnie would be an asset to our staff, so he was hired.

Johnnie and Lew were good friends and worked well together, keeping our camp in tip-top condition during our expanding years. Because of poor eyesight and advancing age he retired in 1977.

One Sunday afternoon as I was sitting in the recreation room watching a baseball game on TV, my sister-in-law Helen, who was manning the front office that day, entered the room. "You'll never guess who is here to see you," she announced, "you'll really be surprised."

I lifted myself from my chair and proceeded to the office. There, to my great delight, stood Johnnie Rice. He was stooped with age, his tanned face lined with deep creases from mining and outdoor carpentry, and he was almost blind. With him was

Eddie Canfield, my first cousin, and William Murray, an old friend. Eddie and Willie were about ten or twelve years older than I. We grew up in the same area but I had not seen them in years.

"What the hell are you guys doin' around here?" I said gleefully as I shook hands and hugged each one. "Are you lost?"

Willie's tiny voice squeaked. "Eddie and me heard you had a great camp, so we thought we'd give the place the once-over. Johnnie came along to show us the way." Then he added "We'll give our report to everyone over town." ("Over town" was a reference to my hometown, New Philadelphia, better known to the locals as "New Phillie.")

Eddie lived in Silver Creek, a small mining patch with about thirty homes, located one mile north of New Philadelphia. Willie made his home in Valley Furnace, a patch of ten homes, made up of the Murrays, McGoverns, Russells, McDonalds and the Subloskys. It was situated a half-mile northeast of town. The townspeople used to say, "When you live in the Furnace, you're in the suburbs."

I gave the trio the cook's tour of the facilities and they were greatly impressed. "Holy Christ, this is some camp you have, Patty! I can't believe what you did ta this place. I hunted in this area a lotta years and it was nothin' but brush and trees. I'm amazed."

I smiled. "I'll tell you this, Willie, building this camp was the joy of my life, but it was no picnic. It was a lot of hard work. Ask Johnnie, he knows."

We made our way to the parking lot and were saying our good-byes when on impulse I asked, "Do you guys ever get to see any pigeon matches?" Their faces lit up.

"We go nearly every Sunday," replied Willie. "There's plenty of good matches, but the shooters ain't that hot. Hell, Patty, you could even win a few matches, and you weren't that good a shooter." All nodded agreement with his statement. Eddie and Willie recalled incidents from past matches, and my own memories flooded my brain.

During my youth, in the thirties and forties, my family was involved in pigeon-shooting matches. I had looked forward to Sunday mornings when, after mass and a hearty breakfast, we would travel to Willie Murray's Golden Rod Gun Club on Murray's Hill where I would watch my father and my brothers John, Tom and Bob shoot pigeons. I also did some shooting. Dad was an above-average marksman, and old-timers like Brock Murray, Bill McGowan and Bill McDonald enjoyed watching him shoot.

"Let's see you drive one, Pat" (my father), Brock would yell. "Show these young guys how ta shoot."

My dad was not a quick shooter, he let the birds go near the forty-yard boundaries before firing. He usually killed eight out of ten birds. My brothers were pop shooters, they shot before the birds had flown fifteen feet from the trap. Tom and Bob shot about ten birds at each outing. Brother John, an affluent doctor, would shoot as many as fifty. Because of my tighter finances, my limit was five.

Usually about fifty people would show up for the Sunday outings, all ready and eager to make wagers on every shot. Beer, soft drinks and food were available and the atmosphere was one of good fun and fellowship. Each fan had his favorite shooters and backed them with his bets.

"Well, Patty, it was great seein' ya." Willie squeezed my hand. "You have a mighty good-looking camp. If ya want ta see a pigeon match, just give me a call. You can always get me on Sunday mornings, I always leave the house about 12:30."

Willie positioned himself behind the wheel with Eddie seated beside him. I helped Johnnie into the back seat with a final pat on his cheek.

"Be good and watch those two birds in the front seat. If they fly too far, they'll get in trouble." With mixed joy and sadness I watched them drive away.

After the usual noisy, boisterous bingo games that evening Rose and I returned to our home by the lake, tired and ready to retire. But sleep wouldn't come to me. I rolled and tossed for what seemed like hours, my mind flooded with long-dormant nostalgic memories brought back by the visit of my friends.

Eventually I drifted into a sound sleep, not realizing at the time that the visit of my friends would ignite a curiosity within me, a curiosity that would lead to five years of research and the writing of this book.

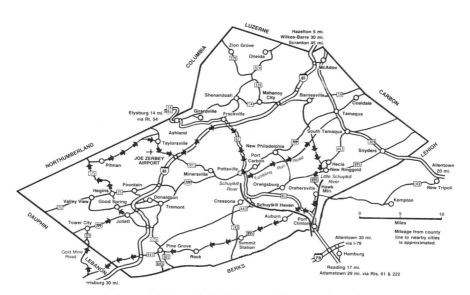

Map of Schuylkill County, Pennsylvania.

Part I

Bootleggers, Gamblers and Pigeons, 1890s to World War II

Breaker boys picking slate, Silver Creek Colliery.

Silver Creek Colliery, on the outskirts of New Philadelphia, Pennsylvania.

1 County History: The Molly Maguires

Schuylkill County is located in the southeastern part of Pennsylvania. It is a blend of Pennsylvania Dutch, Polish, Lithuanian, Irish, Welsh and Slovaks. The west end of the county is overwhelmingly Pennsylvania Dutch, mostly Protestant and Republican.

During my youth, Pottsville, the county seat, had a population of thirty thousand and was a conglomeration of all ethnic groups, evenly divided politically and religiously. The Jewish community was rather small, but many of the leading merchants were Jewish. The blacks lived on Minersville Street, which was one block long. They numbered no more than fifty residents. This was also the red light district.

The southeastern section of the county was also Pennsylvania Dutch, Republican and mostly Protestant. Our camp was located in this area. Catholics and Democrats were few and far between. On election day, the Democrats could always count on a few choice votes; my wife and I plus the monks at St. Mary's Monastery, which was located three miles south of the camp.

New Philadelphia, my hometown, had a population of fifteen hundred and was almost completely Catholic. The ethnic mix was Lithuanian, Irish, Slovak, Polish and a few families of Pennsylvania Dutch and Welsh.

Because of the ethnic and religious make-up of the region, it was evident that a person seeking political office had to be of a specific nationality and religion if he or she hoped to be elected. A Catholic had about as much chance of winning an election in the western and southeast districts as Jimmy Carter had being reelected President. Likewise, if a candidate aspired to be a winner north of the Frackville Mountain, he had better be Irish or Lithuanian and Catholic.

Schuylkill County is located at the western end of the anthracite coal region. It reached its peak of productivity and prominence during the years between 1860 and 1929.

The Irish began emigrating to America about 1850 because of the potato famine in their country. They settled in the large cities along the east coast, especially Philadelphia, New York and Boston. Seeking employment, many found their way to the coal region and settled in Schuylkill County and other areas as far north as Scranton.

With little or no education, and lacking the skills of the trades, they became miners. Boys, as young as ten years of age, worked as slate pickers in the coal breakers, which cleaned and sized the coal before it was shipped to the large eastern cities for consumption.

Six large coal mines were located within five miles of my home. During the years between 1850 and 1929, the scenario for the working class was one of turmoil, ethnic clashes, discord, weariness, murder and a continuous struggle to progress above the level of poverty.

Conditions at the mines were deplorable. The miners worked ten hours a day with little protection from the lethal gases and penetrating coal dust. Because of these conditions, many miners died at an early age of black lung disease. Wages were low and the mines were controlled by two large coal companies, the Reading Company and the Lehigh Coal and Navigation Company, known as the LC&N. I heard my father say many times, "Those dirty thieves came in and stole the land at the expense of the poor."

The Welsh held all important jobs inside and outside the mines. Most of the miners lived in company houses, received low wages and were actually held in a kind of feudal bondage. Money was never exchanged. They were paid in scrip, which was exchangeable only at the company stores. The threat of losing their jobs was another form of intimidation. Loss of a job in the mines could put a family on the street, homeless and penniless.

Under the prevailing conditions, much bitterness and strife existed between the Irish and the Welsh. The Welsh were at the top of the economic ladder and they intended to keep the Irish at the bottom. Religion played an important part in the struggle: the Welsh were Protestant and the Irish were Catholic. Not only were conditions at the mines in turmoil, but the religious differences added fuel to the fire. All that was needed was a spark to plunge the county into a bloodbath.

That spark was provided by the emergence of the Molly Maguires, a secret Irish society whose main purpose was to provide protection for the Irish against the brutality and tyranny of the Welsh bosses, the Reading Company, and the LC&N.

There was much violence in the coal region at that time. Murders, riots and damage to the large coal companies' mine property were rampant. Franklin Gowen, president of the Philadelphia and Reading Railroad, took advantage of the turmoil and blamed the trouble on the Molly Maguires. This became one of the rallying points Gowen needed to pressure and prosecute the Mollies. The other was the rise of unionism among the miners.

In 1868, John Siney of St. Clair organized several hundred miners at the Eagle Hill colliery in a strike against wage cuts and deplorable working conditions. The strike was successful and the miners rallied around Siney, their new-found hero.

He founded the Workmen's Benevolent Association (WBA), which was the first miners' union in the coal fields. At its peak it had thirty thousand members. The rise of unionism in the anthracite region was brought to the attention of Gowen. From that moment, the union and the miners had problems.

In 1873, Siney became president of the newly formed Miner's National Association (MNA). However, Siney's involvement in the national union was the turning point in his career. The union had much success in the southern fields, which were dominated by individual coal companies. In contrast, it had little success in the northern fields, which were controlled by the large coal companies. He found it difficult to bring miners from different sections of the country to act as one. It was this isolation which helped defeat the anthracite miners in their quest for higher wages, improved mine conditions and better housing.

The miners in Schuylkill County never joined the MNA because they believed Siney had betrayed them by devoting too much time and money to the national union.

On April 8, 1876, Siney resigned as president of the MNA and returned to his hometown of St. Clair. He died of tuberculosis on April 16, 1880, a broken and bitter man. Shortly before his death, he said: "I care nothing about my enemies, it never troubles me for a moment, but the ingratitude of the workmen cuts deep into my heart."

Gowen, an Irish Protestant, was the man who orchestrated the demise of the Molly Maguires and the temporary destruction of the labor movement in the anthracite coal region. He was born in Philadelphia, the son of a merchant, and educated at the prestigious private John Becks School in Lancaster County. He rubbed shoulders with the sons of the elite Pennsylvania Dutch and Quaker families of that area.

At age thirty-three, he became president of the Philadelphia and Reading Railroad, which controlled the coal lands and the transportation of coal from the anthracite region. Gowen convinced the English bankers, who controlled the Reading Company, that if they wanted to control and dominate the coal fields, they had to control the railroads and coal lands. Between 1871 and 1875, Gowen bought, with the bankers' cooperation, one hundred thousand acres of coal land. He vowed he would break the miners' labor movement and destroy and hang the Mollies. He accomplished both goals. He was quoted as having said, "I will turn Schuylkill County into a wilderness before I'll give in to the miners."

He laid his plans well. He strengthened the Coal and Iron Police, which was the private police force of the Reading Company, and hired Alan Pinkerton's National Detective Agency to infiltrate the Molly Maguires organization.

Pinkerton sent James McParlan, alias James McKenna, into the coal region as his agent. It was McParlan's task to gather information, which Gowen hoped would send the Mollies to the gallows.

Only two men would see the secret memos which McParlan sent to the Philadelphia office. They were Pinkerton and Superintendent Franklin of the Philadelphia office. Not even Gowen knew the identity of the informer. The liaison between Pinkerton and McParlan was Captain Robert Linden of the Coal and Iron Police, who were headquartered in Pottsville.

Gowen was a genius in public relations; his manipulation of the local and national press was a work of art. He molded the media into a powerful anti-Molly machine, to which he supplied all the needed and tainted information. His close and friendly relationship with the hierarchy of the Catholic Church in Philadelphia paid unbelievable dividends. Archbishop Wood was the most visible and outspoken foe of the Mollies. He repeatedly denounced them from the pulpit: "The Mollies are the disgrace of Irishmen and the scandal of the Catholic Church!"

Father Daniel McDermott of St. Ignatius Church in Centralia was another outspoken critic of the secret Irish society. His sermons from the altar on Sunday mornings were torrid. He refused to extend the holy sacraments to any member of the Mollies or their families.

One day three masked men took him to a cemetery where they gave him an unmerciful beating. "If you continue with the same type of sermons, it'll be worse the next time."

The priest replied, "Wait till you hear my next sermon. It, too, will be worse!"

McParlan traveled and broke bread with the Mollies for three years. Father O'Connor of Pottsville, sympathetic to the Mollies' cause, concluded, after much investigation, that McParlan was a spy. He reported the facts to John Keho, the reputed head of the secret organization, who, in a face-to-face meeting with McParlan, repeated the priest's charges. McParlan was outraged, denied the allegations and demanded a trial.

While the trial was being arranged McParlan disappeared from sight.

The information he had secretly gathered during the past three years was turned over to Pinkerton. The information was accurate and conclusive. It included the names and addresses of suspected murderers who participated in the alleged crimes, detailed information pertaining to secret meetings, dates and places where the meetings were held, membership lists, and names and addresses of the officers.

Gowen was proud of his accomplishments. As he neared the end of his mission, he proclaimed, "We have all the information we need. And now, in the vernacular of the Mollies, we're gonna hang those Irish Pope-lovin' bastards."

The trials began in Mauch Chunk in January 1876. In the first trial, four Mollies, Edward Kelly, Jack Donahue, Michael Doyle and Alexander Campbell, were convicted of murder and sentenced to die by hanging.

The second trial began in Pottsville on May 4, 1876. Six men, James Carroll, Thomas Munley, James Boyle, Hugh McGeehan, Thomas Duffy and James Roarity, were convicted of the murder of Tamaqua policeman Ben Yost. All were sentenced to hang.

On March 21, 1877, these six men were hanged in the Pottsville prison courtyard, and the other four were hanged inside the prison at Mauch Chunk. On March 25, 1878, at Bloomsburg, the last of the Mollies were hanged. Pat Hester, Pat Tully and Pete McHugh paid the price for the murder of Alex Rea, thus bringing an end to the bloodiest and most controversial era in the history of the anthracite region of Pennsylvania.

In 1889, at the age of fifty-three, his company in bankruptcy, Franklin B. Gowen committed suicide.

2 Schuylkill County (Shades of Chicago)

Prohibition, the 18th Amendment, was adopted on January 16, 1919, and became effective one year later. The new law had little effect on the way of life in Chicago, Illinois, or Schuylkill County, Pennsylvania.

Al Capone ruled Chicago with an iron fist. He controlled the rackets, the distribution of liquor and beer coming in and out of the Windy City. He was in charge of every illegal operation which took place within the city limits.

Monk Miller didn't control Schuylkill County and all of its rackets with an iron fist, but he did control the distribution of liquor and beer throughout the county. He was the county's most renowned bootlegger, and he was also a great gambler. He would bet on anything; however, he was not a bookie. He never took a bet. Like the song said, "It's just one of those things." He simply had an insatiable desire to gamble.

The county was wide open. If you wanted a drink, you could find one in any town in the region. Monk placed money in the proper hands, state and local politicians, state and local police, judges, and county dignitaries. Because he took great care to touch all bases, he encountered no trouble distributing his illegal beer and moonshine throughout the area.

One of the prominent figures at most of the pigeon matches since the twenties was Big Bill Yeasted of Pottsville. He was a huge man who had played tackle on the Pottsville Maroons football team. After his football days were over, Bill bought a farm near Pottsville and lived there until his death in 1975.

With prohibition in full swing and Schuylkill County caught up in the roaring twenties hectic lifestyle, Bill obtained a job with Monk Miller. Monk's home was located on the outskirts of Ashland, in a section called Fountain Springs. Monk and Joe Spittack, from St. Clair, ran an illegal brewery behind Monk's home. It was from this brewery that most of the beer in Schuylkill County flowed.

Bill was Monk's right-hand man and was in charge of all deliveries, whether during the day, night, or the early hours of the morning. Most of the night deliveries were made by large trucks in a two-man operation, a driver and a helper.

The daytime deliveries were on a much smaller scale. Most of the time they were emergency calls, to tide the regular customers over until a night delivery could be made. Bill was the only one in Monk's organization who handled the daytime part of the operation. He made his deliveries in a ten-passenger black Cadillac with some modifications. He removed the back seats to make room for at least twelve half barrels of beer. After making the deliveries, he took a hose, washed out the back of the car, and replaced the seats.

At pigeon matches it was a common sight to see his huge frame along the sidelines, making bets, bellowing epithets in his usual loud and thunderous manner. Besides making his own bets, he also laid large sums of Monk's money on the betting line. He never engaged in shooting a match but played an important part in the outcome of many of them, especially when the big money was on the line. His immense size and penetrating voice had a telling effect on many shooters.

The slot machines in southern Schuylkill County were controlled by Eddie Stapinsky of Valley Furnace. In 1935, he and his wife Lizzie were the owners of the Wonder Bar in Middleport, which was the hub of the operation. Eddie was an astute businessman, and like his friend Monk Miller he put in place all the right connections.

Once the state police were in on the take, all the lights were green. Eddie controlled the area from Coaldale in the east to

Hegins in the west. He never ventured into the northern section of the county because that area was controlled by the Hazleton boys.

Everyone was happy with the arrangements. Most of the social clubs, bars, country clubs, fire companies, and Moose, Masonic, Elks, and Knights of Columbus lodges had the slots. They were operating in the black, paying their bills, and business was flourishing.

There was an understanding throughout the county. There would be raids, but everyone would be taken care of by those in the know.

Jack Edwards, whose father owned a bar, recalls the so-called raids. "Whenever a raid was scheduled to take place the clubs and bars were notified and the machines were hidden under lock and key. We hid our machines under the steps leading to the second floor. The raids were a joke. I knew where the machines were and so did the raiding party. After a round of drinks, they made their departure. About every six months, the machines remained in the bar and we'd have to pay a fine, something like twenty-five bucks. Within a few days we were back in business!"

Eddie's brother and his nephews Duke and Boots Zelonis ran the operation, which was smooth and profitable. The Wonder Bar was one of the best-known spots in the region. Business boomed and it was the place to be if you wanted excitement and pleasure.

Eddie died in 1944 and the operation was taken over by his wife Lizzie. She knew the business, and after a shaky start, she outperformed her husband in the management of the slots and the operation of the Wonder Bar.

A resident of Valley Furnace gives a glimpse of the attitudes of their neighbors in the small mining village. "Eddie and Lizzie were wonderful people. They helped their family, relatives, and also many poor families in the Furnace. They never forgot where they came from!"

In 1947 there was a statewide crackdown on slots and gambling. The pipeline to the state police was closed and the operation was spearheaded by the Internal Revenue Service, whose purpose was to apprehend the people who controlled the slots and bring them to trial for income tax evasion.

The crackdown was a huge success, and within six months the slots industry was just a memory. Not a slot machine was operating in the county. As a result, almost all the clubs began operating in the red and many closed their doors.

The manager of a social club lamented, "When we had the slots, we had a thriving business. We paid our bills and hired many people in the club. I think it was a mistake by the state not to let the clubs have the slots. They may be right, but they sure as hell made a lot of citizens unhappy."

New Philadelphia, with a population of 1,500 people, had thirty-five bars and was a favorite haven for those seeking fun and relaxation. The four favorite bars in town were Bartashus and Gatavatkus, located on Water Street, and John Callery's and Van Alexander's, located in the center of town at Valley and Water Streets. At that intersection were four bars, one on each corner. New Phillie was the only town in the U.S.A. having such a distinction.

The bars opened at 6 a.m. and remained open into the wee hours of the morning, seven days a week. It was a wide open town, and as Mooney Finley used to say, "It's the only western town in the east." In spite of its free-spirited reputation, it held steadfast to one of the town's unwritten laws: On Sundays, no bars opened until after the nine o'clock mass!

John Callery's bar was favored by the Irish and Slovak miners. The door was never locked. When Callery closed up for the night, he always left the side door open. Many miners on their way to work at 5:30 a.m. dropped in and helped themselves to anything they wanted, usually a shot or two of whiskey and a few beers. Because the working conditions were so horrible and dangerous, this procedure put them in a more positive mood to face the realities of the day. Whatever they drank was marked on a tab and paid for when they returned from work.

The atmosphere of the roaring twenties, low unemployment, speakeasies, an abundance of money, the golden era of sports with celebrities such as Babe Ruth, Jack Dempsey, Ty Cobb and Bobby Jones, the ethnic clashes between the Irish and the Welsh, the Lithuanians and the Irish, the Polish and the Lithuanians, the religious rifts between the Protestants and Catholics, produced the setting for exciting, hectic and chaotic events throughout the county.

Baseball and football occupied much of the free time of the male residents. However, there was another form of recreation which took the fancy of many people, pigeon shooting and pigeon matches.

The sport was unique because it affected only about ten thousand people. Its followers ranged from the lowest on the economic and social ladder to the more affluent members of society. Doctors, lawyers, judges, police officials, affluent businessmen, gamblers and bootleggers enjoyed the sport. It fulfilled their urge to gamble, and at the same time it was a diversion from the drudgery of their everyday lives, jobs and professions.

3 Rules and Regulations of the Matches

Pigeon matches are conducted under the strictest of rules. A contract, or agreement, is drawn up for each match. Included in the agreement are the following: the site, date and time of the match, number of birds, type of match (straight match or trap and handle), purse, time of arrival of the shooters, elbow down and gun below the elbow until the bird takes flight, and boundaries.

A coin toss decides who will shoot first. Loser of the toss has the option of changing the setting of the trap at the halfway mark of the match or leaving it in its original position for the remainder of the match. The procedure to be followed if the match ends in a tie is spelled out. The agreement is as holy as the Bible. The referee is chosen the day of the match and his decisions are absolute and final.

The trap is located twenty-one yards from the shooter and out of bounds is forty yards from the center of the trap. If a hit bird lands beyond the forty-yard boundary, it is considered a missed bird.

Once the agreement is signed, the contestants prepare for the event at least a week, and in some cases as much as a month. They practice four or five days a week, shooting between thirty and fifty birds a day.

There are two types of matches, a "straight match" and "trap and handle." In a straight match, the trapper cannot tamper with the bird in any way when he puts it in the trap. He is observed by a judge at all times to see that he abides by this rule.

During my active days as a shooter, all matches held in the central section of the county, which included the towns of Minersville, Port Carbon, St. Clair, New Philadelphia and Tamaqua, in addition to towns north of the Frackville Mountain (Frackville, Ashland, Mahanoy City, Shenandoah, Gordon and Girardville), were straight matches.

In a trap and handle match, the trapper can manipulate or tamper with the birds in any way he deems necessary as long as he does not mistreat or abuse them. Since World War II, all matches have been trap and handle.

The practice of "brushing" the birds, another way of saying the training of the birds, is a highly skilled operation and plays a decisive part in the outcome of many important matches.

Individuals who handle and place the birds in the trap during a match are know as "trappers." Most trappers have, in their home pens, as many as three or four hundred birds at all times. For each match they select twenty or thirty pigeons and brush them.

Many devices are used in this procedure. Typical of these is a "rig" tied to the bird. A rig is a small wire five inches long with a small bell attached to the end. A bright piece of crepe paper sticks out of the bell. The rig is tied to the middle feathers of the bird's tail with string and extends to either side of the head or above the head of the bird. The sound of the bell and the fluttering of the crepe paper cause the pigeon to perform many spectacular and unpredictable maneuvers.

If the trappers want the bird to fly to the right, the rig is placed on the left side of the bird's head, and vice versa. If the bird is to fly low and straight, the rig is placed directly above its head. However, the birds do not always adhere to the predicted flight pattern, and some matches are won and lost because the pigeon does not perform as programmed.

In the early stages of brushing, firecrackers were often used to frighten the birds so they would take flight as soon as the trap was opened. This practice is now outlawed. During the middle thirties, Rocky Petrole, of Tresckow, had the unflattering distinction of burning his neighbor's garage to the ground as a result of using firecrackers during the brushing of his birds.

It was a hot summer afternoon, rain had not fallen in nearly a month, and the wooden roof was extremely hot and dry. One of Rocky's birds, firecrackers attached, flew out of the trap and landed on his neighbor's garage. When the bird flew out of the trap, the firecrackers did not ignite. Within a few seconds after landing, however, the firecrackers exploded and the bird took flight. Some sparks from the firecrackers ignited the roof, and in a matter of minutes the structure was engulfed in flames.

Before the fire company arrived on the scene, the garage burned to the ground. The residents of Tresckow voted Rocky "Honorary Fire Chief of the Month" for his outstanding example of "How to start a fire without trying!"

Rocky and his brother Pete were famous for their black pigeons. The birds won many important matches because of their ability to leave the trap at a high rate of speed. The Petroles used all the customary methods of brushing, with one distinct innovation. If a bird was slow in moving out of the trap, Pete would whistle as loud as he could and at the same time Rocky would release a small terrier dog about five feet from the trap. The dog was released a split second before the trap was opened and was at full speed as the trap was sprung. Many times the dog almost caught the bird before it took flight. As a result, after three or four such episodes the birds went out of the trap as though they were shot out of a cannon.

Jim "Shorty" Bergen, an outstanding shooter in the late forties, recalls a match he saw at Phil Laudeman's gun club in Minersville. "I was watching a match between Eddie Kelly and Cletus Coyne for a thousand dollars a side. It was a seventeen-bird match, and with two birds remaining, the match was tied. Eddie killed his two birds and Cletus killed his first bird, with one shot left in the match.

"Pete Petrole put a black pigeon in the trap as Cletus came to the mark and prepared to make his final shot. When the trap was sprung, the bird took off to the right and was rising. Cletus was a fast shooter and usually fired at the bird within the first ten feet. However, he let this one fly until it was just ten yards from the out-of-bounds marker.

"Cletus' shot grounded the bird just five yards from the out-of-bounds marker. Each side has an official bird catcher, and it is his job to catch the downed bird before it goes out of bounds. As the bird catcher raced to gather the bird, Pete began to whistle.

"The bird, with all the energy left in its small body, struggled toward the marker. It reached the safety area just before it was picked up by the catcher. It was declared a missed bird and Eddie Kelly was declared the winner."

Later, Jim approached Pete. "Your whistling act did it again, Pete. When the bird heard you whistle it really moved."

"No, I don't think it was the whistlin' that did it," Pete replied, "I think the bird heard the dog comin'!"

A promoter was a person who arranged the matches for his shooters, who could number as many as ten or as few as one or two. In most instances, promoters were owners of bars or shooting clubs. They were close to the action and were in contact with outstanding shooters and the best trappers. They also had ties to the gamblers who had the capital and influence to finance the purses, which could amount to thousands of dollars.

A rule of the sport states, "The gun must be held below the elbow at all times until the bird takes flight." In the central area of the county and "north of the mountain" (a term used to identify the towns located above St. Clair and the Frackville Mountain), the shooters let their arm and elbow hang at their side in a natural position and placed the gun below their elbow; they were said to hold a "fair gun." The western part of the county, which included the towns of Pine Grove, Tower City, Tremont and Hegins, was the home of the "high gun" or "high elbow" shooters. Their interpretation of the rule was somewhat different. They executed the terminology of the rule to the letter. The arm was raised approximately ten degrees above the shoulder, so that the elbow was above the shoulder, and the gun was then raised into position to shoot. The gun was aimed at the trap and on the command of "pull" the trap was opened. The shooter did not have to move his gun, he just pulled the trigger. The bird rarely moved more than six inches from the trap, resulting most often in a kill.

The westenders were known as "pull bang shooters." Sammy Lehman, a westender and owner of the Ten Pin Shooting Club, gave his interpretation of the rule. "The rule states that gun must be held below the elbow. We're holdin' the gun in that position, therefore we're not breakin' any rules. What the hell's all the shoutin' about!"

The westenders held a distinct advantage over the fair gun shooters. Finally, after years of controversy some adjustments had to be made. When a contest between the westenders and an opponent from another part of the county took place, specific language was written into the agreement as to the position of the elbow and the gun.

The referee had the final word. If he declared a shooter held an illegal gun position, it was counted as a missed bird. The rule was a judgment call; in fact the referees rarely, if ever, called a missed bird because a man held a supposedly illegal gun.

All activities involved in pigeon matches revolved around bars, gamblers, booze and promoters. Most matches were initiated and finalized in bars amid the atmosphere of smoke, pool tables, loud conversation, juke box music, darts, cards, crap games, chicken fights (many chicken fights were held in bars) and the continuous flow of the bubbly.

Often, as the night wore on and the drinks flowed, the stakes became higher. The shooters got better, trappers were not only good but they became magicians at the trap. These conditions often produced negative results such as mismatches and overextended capital.

Every shooter had a backer or promoter who was constantly looking for an edge. It could be the location of the match, the amount of birds to be shot, securing the best trappers, and a very important point, the amount of the purse. If it was high enough, it could intimidate some shooters. All matches were even up and many shooters believed they were God's gift to the shooting world.

The greatest and most famous pigeon shooter in the history of the sport was Fred Coleman of Hegins, Pennsylvania. He made his first appearance as a shooter in 1894, at the age of twenty. Coleman's shooting career was confined to Schuylkill County for the first three years. In 1897 he entered the professional ranks and in 1900 won the state championship shoot at Chambersburg, killing thirty straight birds. In 1903, at the state shoot-off, he won all three championship cups: targets, live birds, and individual marksmanship.

Touring Europe, in 1905 he beat William Piccles of Lightcliff, England, the champion shot of the British Isles. His fame spread throughout Europe, and as a result of his achievements he was courted and entertained by British royalty.

In 1908, Coleman won the Pennsylvania state championship at Lebanon, the last championship contest of his career. He killed 250 out of 252, a world record.

Fred Coleman, born 1874, reproduced from the *Pottsville Republican*.

4 Charlie Simons and Big Bill Yeasted

Jake Lurwick, of Port Carbon, was one of the outstanding shooters and trappers during the twenties and thirties. His bar was the headquarters for the pigeon and dart shooters in Port Carbon and the surrounding area. How many agreements were discussed and signed in Lurwick's bar!

For sixty years the Lurwick name was synonymous with pigeons and pigeon matches in Schuylkill County, whether for raising, trapping, training, promotion or participation in matches. Jake began his shooting career in 1915 and retired in the fifties. Lamar, his eldest son, was an outstanding shooter and an excellent trapper. He concluded his stint in the shooting arena in the early sixties, after thirty years. Vince, Larry and Jack continued the tradition, participating in the sport from the mid-forties to the mid-seventies.

Vince was the most successful of the three. He began his career in 1946 by beating Dr. John Canfield, my brother, in two matches and Al Edwards of New Phillie in three matches. He was off to a great start. During his twenty-two years as a shooter he compiled a record of thirty-five wins and thirteen losses. Jack, the last of the Lurwicks, shot his last match in 1975.

Jake operated the Lurwick bar from 1933 until 1959, then turned the business over to Vince and Vince's wife, Mary. They sold it to another pigeon enthusiast, Nick Bennett, in 1970. The bar was still in operation until Bennett's death in 1990.

When Lamar Lurwick was thirteen years old, Charlie Simons, a restaurant owner from Girardville, north of the mountain, picked him up Thursday afternoons during the summer months and traveled to the Pine Grove Gun Club. At that time, Thursday afternoon was half-holiday for the doctors, lawyers and businessmen. Each had his own form of entertainment and relaxation. Some played golf, others went to the gun clubs to shoot and wager on pigeon shooting and matches. In addition to the professional men, the gamblers and promoters made their appearance. Their presence was a welcome sight to Sammy Lehman, the owner of the club. It meant more activity, excitement and more money in his coffers.

Charlie had money to spare, and two of his greatest passions were gambling and shooting pigeons. He was a good-looking man with an outgoing and pleasing personality, a muscular build and a weight of about 180 pounds.

When Charlie arrived on the scene, the excitement and betting rose a few notches higher. He was always greeted with open arms. As Eddie Kelly once said, "Why the hell shouldn't they greet him with open arms, they can't wait ta take his money!"

He was a good shooter, and as long as the money lasted he'd shoot against anyone and for any amount. Quoting Lamar, "When Charlie shot, the sky was the limit. Some days he went home with a bundle of dough and other days he'd go home broke and in debt. He was famous for his diamond rings. When he was having a bad day and needed money, he could always get two thousand or twenty-five hundred dollars from the gamblers, or his close friends. Monk Miller, Phil Laudeman, my dad or Sammy Lehman were always good for a touch. His rings were his collateral and his word was as reliable as the Bible."

His wife was heard to say on numerous occasions, "Some day I won't buy those damned rings back." When Jake Lurwick reminded him of his wife's remarks, Charlie replied, "You mustn't mind her, Jake, that's just some of her Irish humor."

Whenever Charlie made an appearance at a match, he added glamour and pizazz, and his presence made things happen. Many people took him lightly because of his outgoing and unassuming manner, but not the gamblers. They knew he was an above-average shooter, and when he was having a good day he could make a dent in their winnings, or, if they were backing him, win them large sums of money.

Although beer was plentiful and the whiskey flasks were in evidence, most of the Thursday afternoons at the Pine Grove Gun Club were subdued and peaceful. A small town carnival atmosphere seemed to prevail: have a few drinks, make your bets, and enjoy the friendly surroundings.

On one occasion things were a bit different. One of the spectators was giving Charlie Simons a rough time. Charlie was full of fun and took a great deal of kidding as he took his turn at shooting or along the sidelines making bets. Lamar Lurwick recalls the incident. "This guy was really on Charlie's back. Maybe it was because he was losing money or had too much to drink. Bill Yeasted was along the sidelines making bets and enjoying the afternoon fun. He didn't like the remarks the stranger was making to his friend Charlie."

Bill was a professional football player who had played for the Pottsville Maroons. The team was owned by Dr. John Striegel, a prominent physician and surgeon in Pottsville. The Maroons entered the National Football League in 1924. The 1925 season was a dream come true for the doctor and the Pottsville fans. They were leading the league going into the final weeks of the season. On December 6, the Maroons played the Chicago Cardinals for the NFL title; the final score was Pottsville 21, Chicago 7. The Maroons arrived in Pottsville as national heroes and were acclaimed the NFL champions.

The Maroons were scheduled to play an exhibition game against the Notre Dame all-stars, which included the famous Four Horsemen. The game was scheduled for December 12, at Shibe Park in Philadelphia. Dr. Striegel was notified by Joe Carr, President of the NFL, that he was suspending the Pottsville team because they were playing in the protected territory of the Philadelphia Frankford Yellow Jackets. Dr. Striegel protested, claiming there was no such rule on the NFL books. The Maroons were disqualified and stripped of the title. Although the Pottsville sports fans protested and spent many years appealing the ruling, the title was never restored.

"Bill approached the loudmouth," Lamar continued. "'What the hell's the matter with you, buddy? Why don't you get off Charlie's back and let him alone?' Bill tipped the scales at 275 pounds and was six feet five inches tall. The heckler was no midget; he matched Bill pound for pound.

"He whirled around, put his face about two inches from Bill's nose, and in a loud and defiant voice roared, 'Drop dead, you no good son of a bitch, keep your big mouth shut and mind your own business.'

"Before he could utter another word, Bill took a step backward and nailed him with a terrific punch to the side of the head. As he was swaying backwards, Bill delivered a left hook to the middle of his nose, dropping him to the ground. The man lay on the turf writhing in pain, blood streaming from his nose and mouth. His friends intervened and carried him to the rear. He was finished for the day! Within a short time the festivities resumed with no further interruptions."

The birds that were used at the gun clubs in those days were barn birds, which means they were untrained, heavy and slow. Under those conditions, it was logical there would be more kills than misses. Knowing these facts, the gamblers always bet on the kill even if they had to lay odds. Most of the time they were on the winning side. If they lost a large amount, there was always tomorrow to take the money from the "suckers."

For the professional and business men, it was just another day at the club. The shooting stopped at dusk and many called it a day and headed for home. But for others, it was the beginning of an evening of good times and excitement. After the shooting came the cards, craps, and, in the early morning hours, the chicken fights. There was always an abundance of food, beer and moonshine, and most often the gamblers ended up with the money.

The most notable gamblers in the county were the Sophy brothers, Jit, Bill, Joe, and their uncle Matt, Big Bill Heck, Joe,

Dave, Mike and Johnnie Hallahan, Petie Joseph and Jack Jefferson from the Pottsville area. North of the mountain the contingent included Monk Miller and his sidekick Big Bill Yeasted, Charlie Simons, Battler Delago and Cletus Coyne.

From the New Philadelphia area, Joe Piel, Joe Tobin, Jim McGowan, Al Edwards and Josh Daukshus were the heavyweights. The Hazleton area was represented by Georgie Breen, Paul Ferry, Bill Seager and J.J. Maguire. The west end had its share of gamblers, including Sammy Lehman, Fats Umbenhauer, Les Felty, Billie McCue, Bully Boyer and Chick Fetteroff.

Jake Lurwick shooting in a match at the Tremont ballpark in the 1920s.

Jake Lurwick at a match at a local ballpark in Schuylkill County in the 1920s. While the shooter stands and loads his gun, the onlookers behind him try to avoid the cold wind.

5 Jake Lurwick versus Norman Erbe: The Biggest Match of the Twenties

Jake Lurwick won many matches in the twenties. The purses varied with each encounter, ranging from three hundred dollars to several thousand dollars a side. A group of betters from Mount Laffee, known as the Mount Laffee gang, backed Jake on many occasions. However, they also backed other triggermen, especially if they believed these shooters could win them some money.

When matches were arranged between shooters from the same area things got a little touchy. Everyone hoped to secure the services of the same trappers and birdmen.

In 1924, Jake took the Mount Laffee boys to the cleaners when they backed Sun Kelly in two matches at the Minersville ballpark. Jake won both matches. As Jake's reputation grew, so did the demand for his services. He could pick and choose as to where he would shoot and with who.

Charlie Simons and Monk Miller backed Tommy Mariano, from Shamokin, in a match against Jake at the Ashland ballpark in early October. Jake killed 17 out of 21 and beat Tommy by one bird.

Billie Biscunis, of New Philadelphia, fell by the wayside two weeks later, as Jake killed 12 out of 15 birds and pocketed an easy five hundred dollars.

The Mount Laffee gang, still smarting from Sun Kelly's two defeats the year before, thought they had a winner in Dave Smith, a Pottsville native. He was a good shot and ten years younger than Jake. Birding for Dave were three outstanding trappers, Dodger Loftus, Willie Hall (the dummy) and Sun Kelly.

His money backers were the Hallahans and the Raring brothers. Birding for Jake were his son Lamar, Clyde and Jack Mills, Phil Laudeman and Brock Murray. The Pottsville gamblers put their money on Jake. The match took place in the Minersville ballpark in October 1925, one thousand dollars a side, twenty-one birds. The Sophy brothers once again picked the right man, as Jake beat Dave by one bird.

It looked as though the Mount Laffee gang would never be able to settle the score with Jake. Only time would tell.

Jake Lurwick and Jake Erbe were good friends and drinking buddies. They traveled to many matches together and supported and birded for each other when one or the other was engaged in a match. They fell out over a silly argument regarding pigeons, and things were never quite the same after the disagreement.

Lamar Lurwick, Jake's son, recalls the meeting of the two men at a match. It wasn't long before they were in a heated conversation.

"Maybe you should give up shootin' and let your son Lamar take over. Yer gettin' old and yer eyesight ain't what it use ta be."

"Look, you old bastard, I might be gettin' old but I can still beat anybody in your family including yer son Norman. What do ya think of that?"

"Well, if ya think yer that good, we'll tie a match and ya can put yer money where yer mouth is."

"It's OK with me. It'll be a pleasure ta shut yer big Dutch mouth once and fer all."

Three days later, a meeting at Lurwick's bar took place and the agreement was signed. The match would be held in the Tamaqua ballpark at 2:00 p.m. on Sunday, November 21, 1925, twenty-five birds and two thousand dollars a side. The referee would be chosen the day of the match.

Norman Erbe was in his middle twenties and considered one of the premier shooters in the county. He shot most of his matches in Tamaqua and seldom signed agreements to shoot outside his hometown. That was one of the sticky points which held up the signing of the agreement. The Lurwick forces eventually gave in to the Erbe demands that the event be held in Tamaqua. The Lurwicks had the privilege, however, of determining the purse and the number of birds in the match.

Norman was a boss in one of the local coal mines. He didn't drink, smoke or swear and was well respected in the community. His father and three brothers also worked in the mines but didn't lead the same monastic life as did Norman. They regularly drank and caroused with their mining buddies. At a match, after being fine-tuned with illegal booze, they could be extremely tough and no one ever saw them back away from a confrontation. Jack, the oldest son, had been a professional boxer in his younger days, and it was he who wore the family colors when it came to fighting or defending the family honor.

Norman's father, Jake, was his manager and promoter. He was very particular as to who Norman would engage in a match. The Erbes had a vast following headed by the Dutch Hill gang, a rough and tough bunch of Pennsylvania Dutch, Irish, Lithuanians and Poles who were great football and baseball players, great drinkers, and were ready for a fight at the least provocation. They had a reputation which could intimidate many of their adversaries. If they were losing a match, they made certain the match broke up in a fight or mini riot.

The Dutch Hill gang were renowned for the breed of pigeons they produced, a breed known as archangels. John Bergalis, Norman's brother-in-law, explains how they produced this special breed of pigeon. "We crossbred the birds until we came up with a breed that was fast and scary, had big wings and small bodies and was built for speed and stamina. Let me tell ya, they were the greatest pigeons that ever took flight!"

Although the Erbes had their Dutch Hill gang, the Lurwicks also had their big guns and would not be intimidated when they arrived for the showdown in Tamaqua. Included in the Lurwick entourage was Big Bill Yeasted and his brother Honey. Both were in the battleship class, but their ace in the hole was Dominic Valent. He worked in the mines with Jake and was his closest friend. He was built like a Mack truck and could hit like the kick of a mule.

The Lurwicks felt very comfortable knowing they had first class protection. Before departing for the trip to Tamaqua, Dominic met with the Lurwick faithful at the bar and gave them a parting thought. "If those Dutch Hill bastards think they're gonna scare us taday, they have another thing comin'. The first son of a bitch that lays a hand on any of us, they'll pay a price! Remember, we don't back down an inch from them Dutchmen and their Irish and Lithuanian buddies!"

The gambling fraternities of the Sophy brothers, Monk Miller and Charlie Simons were backing the Lurwicks, while the Hazleton contingent of Georgie Breen, Paul Ferry, J.J. Maguire and Bill Seager choose the Erbes.

The event received much publicity in the local newspapers. Jack Richards wrote a daily column "Rod and Gun" for the *Pottsville Republican*, in which he gave the match an unusual amount of print. The additional coverage helped enlarge the gate and kept interest at fever pitch.

Many people who were not among the usual pigeon crowd planned to attend the match because of the reputation of the shooters, who were the best in the area. If there was going to be trouble, what better way to spend a Sunday afternoon than to watch some of the county's best brawlers in action? It promised to be a great spectacle.

November 21 was a beautiful autumn day. Huge white clouds made their way through the dark blue sky. The sunshine occasionally broke through, bringing a warmth that penetrated the slight autumn breeze. It wasn't just a pigeon shoot, it was a showcase for the shooters, where fame and fortune could be had in a day.

It was the biggest match of the twenties. Five thousand people arrived to gamble, eat, drink and cheer their favorite shooter. The vendors were having a field day. Prohibition was still the law of the land, but the booze was flowing like the Mississippi River. Monk Miller, Schuylkill County's famous bootlegger, was extremely happy. The crowd was drinking his beer and whiskey, and even if Lurwick lost the match, he would end up in the black.

The usual tactics were being employed throughout the contest: shouting, swearing, and crude and vile epithets which were meant to unnerve the shooter. Because of the size of the crowd, ropes were erected to keep them as far away from the shooters as possible. As the match progressed, the crowd slowly closed in upon the shooters, leaving only a small opening for them to shoot at the birds.

Erbe won the coin toss and chose to shoot first. The match progressed to the twentieth bird, at which point he was losing by one. As Lurwick stepped to the mark, Dominic Valent, his rope puller, was in a kneeling position looking at his friend and awaiting the command to open the trap.

Directly behind Jake and a little to his left was old man Erbe, yelling and swearing at the top of his voice. He was doing his utmost to distract Lurwick and disrupt his concentration. Occasionally he touched Jake's right shoulder, as though he was brushing some light material from his clothing.

Jake turned to the referee for some relief from his tormentor. "Tell that man to keep his hands off me. He can say anything he wants, but tell him to keep his hands to himself." The referee's response was total rejection. He continued to look straight ahead as though Jake had never uttered a word.

Jake took his stance, took two practice sightings, a quick glance at Dominic, then turned his head and concentrated on the trap. A few moments' pause and the familiar word "pull" resounded through the boisterous crowd.

The trap opened, and within a split second the archangel was airborne, flying low to the ground along the right side, twisting and turning as it sped for the out-of-bounds marker and safety. As the bird began to rise at a fantastic rate of speed, Lurwick fired. His shot was low and behind the archangel. It was a missed bird!

The moment Jake missed the bird, old man Erbe hit him in the middle of the back and yelled, "You missed the archangel!" The force and suddenness of the blow knocked Jake to the ground. As he hit the hardened turf, he was momentarily stunned and the gun was jarred loose from his hands.

Erbe was six years older than Lurwick, but about the same size and weight. Jake jumped to his feet, leaving the gun on the ground. He lunged at Erbe and hit him a right hand blow to the side of his head, knocking him to his knees. At that moment, Jack Erbe came charging out of the crowd and hit Lurwick with a vicious left-handed punch, knocking him into the crowd, where he slipped to the turf.

Dominic Valent was still in a kneeling position with the rope in his hand. In an instant he was on his feet, ready to enter the fray. All his years of experience as a barroom and street fighter would come into play. He approached Jack from the left side, stepping in front of his opponent. He grabbed him with both hands as he turned him around and threw him to the ground.

Jack was taken aback by Dominic's swift and ferocious attack. As he tried to right himself, Dominic was on top of him like a charging bull, raining swift and powerful blows to the head and an occasional hit to the midsection.

Jack was trying to protect his face from further damage; with a sudden surge of strength he gave a powerful lunge to his right and managed to throw Dominic off his battered body. Within moments he was in a standing position over Dominic, who was making an effort to get to his feet.

Jack raised both his hands over his head and with all the strength he could muster brought them down on the base of Dominic's head and shoulders. The blow dropped him to the turf. Without looking up, Dominic plunged his powerful body into Jack's midsection, driving him to the ground. He continued to batter Jack's face and body, with many powerful blows finding their mark.

Dominic was at his best in this type of a fight, rough and tumble, no holds barred, no Marquis of Queensberry rules, just an old-fashioned street brawl. He was also demonstrating to his drinking buddies that he was backing with action the words he had delivered at the bar before they departed for the match. Someone had laid a hand on a member of the group; now that someone was paying the price.

Jack's face was a mass of blood, swollen beyond recognition. He tried to protect himself but couldn't hold off the vicious attack of his powerful and brawling opponent. At that point the fight was halted to save Jack from further harm.

It took about fifteen minutes before order was restored. The referee gave the Erbe forces twenty minutes to put a bird in the trap or Lurwick would be declared the winner. Erbe killed four out of the next five birds but it wasn't enough to offset the strong finish of his opponent. Lurwick killed the last five birds and the match was his, thus ending one of the wildest and bloodiest matches of the twenties.

Erbe and Lurwick never faced each other again. They went their separate ways and both compiled records which would designate them as among the greatest pigeon shooters of the twenties. During the years between 1926 and 1929, Jake Lurwick competed against the best shooters in the county, Sammy Lehman, George Starr, Jake and Luke Hand, Georgie Breen, Klate Hartman, Danny Kessler, Harry Hoover, Charlie Simons, Harry Beech, Dutch Reigle, Brock Murray and Eddie Kenna.

After that it was time to turn the shooting mantle over to a member of his family, his oldest son, Lamar. Jake continued in the pigeon business as one of the outstanding trappers in the county. He had the pleasure of trapping for his five sons until his death in the early sixties.

6 Harry Beech versus Jack Long: The Riot at Ashland

The last notable match of the twenties took place in the Girardville ballpark on December 1, 1928. The money people from north of the mountain, Monk Miller and Charlie Simons, wanted to tie a match with Jake Lurwick with the understanding that it would take place in Girardville. Not many shooters from the Pottsville area or the west end relished the idea of shooting a match in that section of the county. Sammy Lehman was heard to say, "It's not too damned safe up there when those Lithuanians, Polish and Irish miners get a few drinks under their belts. You're lucky if you get out alive!"

Monk and Charlie had a young hot-shot shooter by the name of Jack Long from Mount Carmel, located just beyond the county line. He was twenty-five years old, a good shooter who was reportedly cool under pressure.

Lamar Lurwick describes the scene as Monk and Charlie walked into his dad's bar. "It was about two o'clock on a Wednesday afternoon when the two lads from north of the mountain walked in. My dad and I were having a sandwich at one of the tables. Dad looked up and acknowledged the pair: 'You guys are outta your territory. What's wrong, is the mob after ya?'

"'It's not that bad,' quipped Charlie, 'but we might be interested in takin' some of yer money, and from all reports you got plenty.'

"'I wish the hell you were right,' replied my dad.

"As they pulled their chairs up to the table, I went behind the bar and brought each a beer. 'Here ya are Monk, here's some of your fresh brewed beer that Big Bill dropped off yesterday.'"

Monk sipped his beer and took a quick glance at Lamar. "At least you're serving the best beer in town."

Jake settled back in his chair, spread his feet full length under the table and said in a modulated voice, "What's on your mind?"

Charlie paused a few moments. "We'd like you ta shoot a match with Jack Long, someplace north of the mountain for a thousand dollars a side, twenty-five birds in a trap and handle match."

Jake hesitated a few moments before answering. "Well, I'll tell ya, fellas, I'm glad ta hear of yer offer, but I decided ta give up shootin' any big matches. From now on I'll stick ta trapping. If there's gonna be any more shootin' in the family, it'll be done by Lamar. At this point I don't think he's ready fer a big match." Jake continued, "How would you boys like ta back Harry Beech from Hazleton in the same match? You know he's a good shot and it would be a close contest. I can call Georgie Breen and he can find out if Harry is willing ta shoot against Long. If they go fer the arrangements, all of us will back him. What do ya think of the idea?"

Monk was quiet for a few moments. "We'll think about it, we'll get back ta ya in a day or so. In the meantime, see if Beech wants ta take the match. But remember, it must take place north of the mountain!"

Within three days, the match was set. Beech versus Long at the Girardville ballpark, 1:00 p.m., December 1, a thousand dollars a side, trap and handle, twenty-five birds.

All shooters had their followers, who were known as crews. Eddie Kelly explains, "Every shooter had a crew. They were men who followed him ta every match. You must remember that they had other things ta do besides looking at the match. The other things were drinkin' and raisin' hell. They drank mostly beer, moonshine and wine.

"After a few hours of drinkin', they didn't know or care who was shootin'. In fact some of them never saw a match. They were more interested in drinkin' and havin' a good time."

The crews looked forward to the Sunday afternoon festivities. It was a great way to top off the weekend before going back to the mines, where they worked ten hours a day under extremely difficult conditions.

Jack Long's crew was especially rough and tough. They were a bunch of hard-drinking Lithuanian miners from Mount Carmel. They were ready to defend their honor, or anyone's honor, and they reveled in a good brawl.

As expected, a large crowd assembled for the event. It was an exciting match, and closer than the gamblers and the average fan had expected. After twenty-three birds the match was tied, each having killed twenty.

With two birds to go, dusk was fast approaching and it was becoming overcast. A cold breeze brought a chill to the large crowd and dark clouds began to engulf the area. If the contest ended in a tie, there would be a shoot-off. The first shooter to miss would be the loser.

For the gamblers everything was going their way. Things couldn't be better even if they wrote a script for the event. They were betting on the kill even though they had to lay as much as three-to-one odds.

Long was shooting first. Although he was always an excellent marksman, he was shooting better than expected. His attitude and outward appearance hadn't changed throughout the match. His piercing eyes, his determined and sober facial expression portrayed a man of confidence. He was killing birds which flew in any direction, high or low, and any pattern of flight. There was no doubt that he was having a banner day.

The Beech forces held a brief meeting to agree on the strategy to use for the last two birds. It was decided, because of the fast approaching darkness, that Jake Lurwick would fly a black pigeon and hope for the best. Before Jake made his trek to the trap, Brock Murray, an excellent trapper in his own right, offered a few words of advice: "Keep the bird low, Jake, if it stays low it'll be harder fer him ta see the bird." Jake nodded in agreement.

Long approached the mark, took his customary two sightings and yelled "pull." The bird took flight quickly and, as planned, flew low and to the right. Long was normally a fast shooter; however, he let this bird fly at least twenty yards before firing. He expected the bird to rise at any moment so he aimed his shot slightly above the moving target. The bird never moved out of its flight pattern, and Long missed the bird. The Beech supporters were ecstatic as they collected their bets.

Long was surprised and disheartened. He turned to Bully Boyer, his rope puller. "I can't believe I missed that shot. I knew it was gonna fly low and I was waitin' fer it ta rise, but it never did. I made a dumb mistake!"

It was Harry's turn to face the pro-Long jeering mob. As he made his way to the mark the noise was deafening. You could read his mind, "I've been in this position before, it's nothing new. They can yell and swear all they want but it won't shake me."

He turned to his rope puller, Brock Murray. "Don't worry about this bird, Brock, I'll blow the son of a bitch ta kingdom come!"

"That's the way ta talk, Harry. We'll show them Lithuanian bastards how ta win a match. Hit him with the full load."

"I'm not gonna waste much time, so get ready fer a quick pull."

Brock nodded. "I'll be watchin', Harry, just give me the word."

After arriving at the mark, Harry took one practice sighting, a quick glance at Brock and yelled "pull." The trap opened and within a split second Harry pulled the trigger and hit the bird with the full load. He blew the pigeon in half. The bird hadn't moved more than a foot from the trap. The match was over!

Lamar Lurwick recalls the events which took place immediately following the conclusion of the contest. "We were seated in the stands and had an excellent view of what was happening. Honey Yeasted and about ten of his cronies from Pottsville were among the spectators lined up along the left side of the shooters.

"They had been making bets all afternoon along with members of Long's crew. The match was over and they were now ready to collect their winnings. Both groups were feeling no pain because of the amount of booze they had guzzled during the match. As they were payin' off their debts, one of the Lithuanians made a derogatory remark and the gloves were off. A riot ensued.

"Honey's brother Bill and his buddies joined the free-for-all; it was a sight to behold. About fifty people became involved. Out of nowhere appeared eight state troopers on horseback. They had been alerted to the possibility of trouble. They charged into the middle of the riot, swinging their billy clubs at will; they weren't too particular who they were hittin'.

"Being in the stands gave us a great view and at the same time we were pretty safe. One of the state troopers was hitting Bill Yeasted over the head and arms. Blood was streaming down Bill's face making it almost impossible for him to get a clear view of his enemy, which at that time was the trooper.

"He pulled the trooper off his horse, wrestled him to the ground and beat him with his own billy club. It was a bloody and scary scene."

After twenty minutes, peace was restored. Twenty-five people were arrested, and six received medical treatment at the local hospital.

No one is ever declared the winner in such a situation. Both sides took a beating and had the entire winter to lick their wounds and lay plans for their next encounter.

As 1929 was nearing its end, prohibition was still was still the law of the land. Monk Miller and Al Capone were still the kingpin bootleggers in their respective territories. The rich were getting richer, the poor would always be with us, so what else was new?

The good times would last forever! The stock market was telling the rich to keep the party alive; to hell with tomorrow, now is the time to live. No one realized that the great party was nearing its end. Looming on the horizon were two events which would change the world: the stock market crash of 1929 and the Great Depression that followed.

7 Rol Holley the King

The Depression brought about many changes, not only to the economy but to all phases of the American way of life. The anthracite coal region of Pennsylvania was devastated. Most of the mines closed and the unemployment rate was extremely high. Throughout the country the rate was about eleven percent, but it ran much higher in Schuylkill County, about seventy percent.

Many people lost businesses and homes, and those who had been living in a comfortable style before found themselves with nothing but their life savings on which to live. After much trial and error, the only temporary solution to the situation was government intervention.

The local public schools became the prime centers for the distribution of food to the masses. Only the basic necessities of life were issued: flour, cheese, sugar and canned goods. Those items helped to sustain life at the poverty level in the communities.

Prohibition was still the law of the land. Al Capone ruled Chicago with an iron fist, and speakeasies were in full swing and still the center of entertainment and relaxation. Football, baseball and pigeon matches continued to hold the attention of the sport enthusiasts and golf was still a rich man's game.

Doctors, lawyers and businessmen controlled most of the money. The working class, including the miners, found itself at the lower end of the economic and social ladder with little hope for the future.

Despite the dismal outlook, life went on, and the years between 1929 and the outbreak of World War II produced some of the most interesting pigeon matches in the history of the sport.

Rol Holley was king. He headed into the thirties with all the cockiness and determination of a shooter who could beat anyone in the world. His self-assured manner and a touch of arrogance brought a feeling of uneasiness to his opponents. Not only was he the most renowned shooter, he was also the most imposing. He stood six feet tall, with a robust figure. His handsomely designed features plus a pleasing personality produced a shooter with great charisma.

Rol had little education and worked most of his life on the farm. From 1935 to 1943 he worked on the WPA, a government work project instituted by President Roosevelt to alleviate the unemployment situation. He enjoyed the night life! He spent many hours in the local bars and on numerous occasions he partied far into the wee hours of the morning. Because of his admiring following and popularity, he seldom had to buy a drink. He was toasted and treated like a celebrity. In spite of his love for the night life, he never missed a day's work or a pigeon match in which he was involved.

His manager and confidant was Tom Casey of Seltzer City. They were boyhood buddies and the greatest of friends. Tom arranged Rol's matches and took charge of every detail: who he would shoot, where, when, the amount of the purse, the referee, the trappers and bird handlers.

Casey was wary about tying a match with any of the west end shooters. They held a high gun, which created turmoil. Casey also believed the referee could be intimidated by the westenders and could not call a fair match. In spite of his misgivings, he arranged two matches with Klate Hartman in 1932. Both matches were a thousand dollars a side, twenty-one birds, trap and handle, on a home and home basis. The first match took place in early September at Pine Grove, where Klate beat Rol by one bird,

17 and 18 out of 21. A month later, they met in the Minersville ballpark and Rol beat Klate by two birds.

In November of the same year, Casey tied the match with Joe Hand of Hegins for a thousand dollars a side, seventeen birds, trap and handle. The match was to be held at Hegins. Tension was running high because Joe Hand held a high gun and Holley supporters were going to insist that the referee call a fair match. Casey was expecting trouble; therefore, he came to the match with a crew that was ready for any event that could mar the match.

Before leaving the local bar in Seltzer City for their trip to Hegins, Casey assembled his crew. "There might be trouble at the match taday, so we better be ready. We arrive together and we leave together. If anybody gets in a fight, we all get in the fight! We'll beat their heads in!" Cheers and catcalls echoed through the bar as they made their way to their cars. A spirited crowd of three thousand people showed up for the match.

Sammy Lehman and his followers were prepared to meet the challenge; they were backing Joe with their presence and their money. If any disturbance took place, they were also ready to shed a little blood for the good of the order.

The score was tied after ten birds. Rol killed the eleventh bird and Joe approached the mark. The usual shouting, taunts and yelling prevailed. Dominic Valent's booming voice pierced the autumn afternoon bedlam. "Keep that gun down or we'll nail your Dutch ass ta the barn." Joe never moved a muscle. He took his practice sights and in a firm voice yelled "pull."

The bird didn't move more than six inches from the trap before Joe hit it with the full load. Dominic bolted toward the referee. "It was a missed bird. He held a high gun."

The referee never moved. He looked directly at Dominic. "It's a killed bird."

"You no-good Dutch bastard, you're afraid to call a fair match!" A minor brawl broke out with the customary yelling, cursing and shoving. But order was restored after about ten minutes. Rol went on to win the match, and Casey and his

Seltzer City crew made their way to their cars as a unit. They were thankful for a peaceful exit and a safe trip home.

In 1935, Rol once again ventured into the west end territory. Casey tied a match with Link Hand, a brother of Joe, for a thousand dollars a side, trap and handle. Sammy Lehman, the Hartmans, Bully Boyer and the Umbenhauers were going to use any method, within the law, to upset Rol.

Eddie Kelly recalls the match. "The westenders knew it was gonna be a tough job ta beat Rol. They put twenty-seven sitters in a row to upset him." When a bird sits for over five seconds and does not take flight, it's called a sitter. The referee can bar the bird and another bird must be put in the trap.

In spite of all the tricks and maneuvers at the trap, Rol took the measure of Link in an easy fashion, killing 13 out of 15 while Link killed 10 out of 15.

If there was any trouble at the matches, it usually took place between the opponents, or between their supporters. However, there were always exceptions to the rule. At the halfway mark the match between Rol and Link was interrupted by a fight between Bill Yeasted and Paul Sweat, supposedly good friends.

Lamar Lurwick, who was trapping for Rol, describes the altercation. "Bad blood had been building up between the two during the past three or four months. Bill had been winning money from Paul and kept needlin' him as to his bad judgment on picking a winner.

"As Bill was taking money from one of the bets, I heard him say to Paul: 'I don't know why the hell you ever bet on a match, I ain't seen you win a bet today! As a matter of fact you ain't picked many winners in the last three months.'

"I could see that Paul was as mad as hell, but he turned around and took his place among the crowd. Big Bill and Paul were about the same age and size. Bill, along with his boss Monk Miller, had stepped back from the crowd about forty feet and were standing on the crest of a hill overlooking a meadow.

"Bill was crouching down, sitting on his honkers, doing nothing in particular. Paul left his place in the crowd, walked nonchalantly up to Bill and hit him with a right hand blow which landed squarely on his left eye and nose. The blow knocked Bill down the hill. He rolled at least fifteen feet and landed in a sitting position, facing the top of the incline. He was momentarily dazed and raised his hand to his face. He was bleeding profusely and had no vision in his left eye. He didn't have too much time to evaluate his situation because Paul was standing over him ready to deliver another blow to the head.

"Instinctively, Bill grabbed Paul by the legs and wrestled him to the ground. From that point on it was a rough and tumble fight. Each man took turns being on top and administering blows to the head and body of the other, yelling and swearing at the same time. After two or three minutes they were pulled apart and order was restored.

"Paul Sweat got the better of the fight; getting in the first blow gave him a decided edge. Even though Big Bill got the worst of the skirmish, it didn't alter his personality or mannerisms. Within a half hour he was along the sidelines making bets and his booming voice was as crisp as ever." As Lamar recalls, "He was holding a big handkerchief over his eye. He had a beautiful shiner!"

Rol Holley was in the twilight of his career as the forties were ushered in. His last big match took place on August 31, 1940, at the Salem Hill ballpark in Port Carbon against Reed Middleton of Gordon.

The young upstart from north of the mountain had won twelve out of fifteen matches and his backers, Monk Miller and friends, believed he was the best shooter in the county. Monk was eager to arrange a match with Holley and it took some lengthy meetings with Tom Casey to arrange the details.

Though Rol was near the end of his career, he would be no pushover. Whoever beat him would have to be at his best. When anyone participated in a match against a man who had the reputation of a legend, the pressure could be unbelievable. Only time would tell if the young shooter was capable of handling the situation.

Most of the people north of the mountain were backing Reed. They believed he was a winner who could stand up under pressure and not fold down the stretch. They were coming to Port Carbon with a confident young shooter, the best birds and trappers north of the mountain, and plenty of money to bet.

All the money people in and about Pottsville were behind Rol. Eddie Kelly, Willie Murray, the Hartman brothers and the Petrole brothers were his trappers. They were the best; now all Rol had to do was win the match.

Pigeon matches were receiving much publicity in the local newspapers. Jack Richards of the *Pottsville Republican* devoted much space to the upcoming match between Middleton and Holley. Newspapers in Philadelphia, Scranton and Harrisburg were showing a great interest in the event. The *Philadelphia Record* sent Bill McGraw, one of the leading sportswriters at that time, to cover the match.

The agreement called for twenty-five birds, trap and handle. In case of a tie the first one to miss in the shoot-off was the loser. The purse was a thousand dollars a side. The Sophy brothers and Petie Joseph had a side bet with Monk Miller and Cletus Coyne for five thousand dollars. It was a match with no holds barred, and no one, including the gamblers, was sure of the outcome.

August 31 was a terrible day. It rained Saturday night and throughout the Sunday match. The agreement stated that the event would take place rain or shine. At the conclusion of the twenty-fifth bird the match was tied and the shoot-off was in force, the first one to miss to be the loser.

Thousands of dollars had been bet on each bird, but in the shoot-off many of the bets were doubled. The gamblers were betting heavily; one miss and the winner went home with a bundle of cash.

After Rol and Reed both killed the twenty-sixth and twenty-seventh birds, the pressure on the shooters was mounting. Who was going to break? The king, or the young man who wanted to be king?

Reed had trained hard and was as cool and calm as if he was shooting a practice round. Earl Middleton, Reed's father, often repeated the story about Reed preparing for a match. "Whenever Reed was gettin' ready fer a match, he never took a drink or a cigarette, he was always in bed by 10:00 p.m. Every night he'd take the gun upstairs and sit on the edge of the bed for about ten minutes and practice putting it to his shoulder. After a few weeks it was automatic and beautiful."

Rol never changed his daily routine. As Bill Sophy, a great admirer of Rol's, said, "Why the hell should he change his habits? He always wins! He kin beat most of these clowns anytime of the day or night, drunk or sober."

Reed stepped to the mark, took one practice sighting and yelled "pull." The bird got no more than two feet from the trap before Reed blew it apart. Pete Petrole's black pigeon never had a chance.

Rol Holley, the king of the shooters since the twenties, a man who wore the crown so proudly, stepped to the mark. He was calm and collected, confidence just oozing through him. He had been here before, this situation was nothing new, he knew how to cope.

He took his customary two practice sights, halted just a moment and yelled "pull." The bird was fast out of the trap and flew to the right. Rol followed the target and after about twenty feet pulled the trigger. The pigeon was about ten feet above the ground and in a straight line of flight.

Rol shot behind the bird, which was hit with a few pellets. It faltered momentarily and was having difficulty maintaining its altitude. The bird dropped to within two feet of the ground and appeared as though it would never make the out-of-bounds marker. Suddenly, as if it had been given a shot of adrenalin, the pigeon regained its momentum and flew to safety. It was a missed bird!

Rol stood motionless for a few moments; he couldn't believe he had missed the moving target. Slowly he came to the realization that he had lost the match. His reign as king was over. With a bit of luck he could still have been the reigning monarch. But it wasn't to be.

The winners were wild with joy as they collected their bets. Monk Miller and Cletus Coyne gathered their side-bet winnings and departed for a victory celebration at Monk's home. Among the invited guests was Rol Holley.

Reed Middleton was the new king, but he tipped his hat to his friend Rol Holley. "Rol was always my idol. He was a great shooter and I was lucky ta beat him. The scales were well balanced, but they happened ta tip my way taday." Rol shot a few more matches but his glory days were over.

8 Lamar Lurwick

Jake Lurwick was past his peak and the time had come to turn the shooting mantle over to his oldest son, Lamar, who had been around birds all his life. By the time Lamar was fifteen years old, he was considered an excellent shot and trapper. When the Lurwicks shot a match the best trappers in the region worked for them: Dave Smith, the Mills brothers, Willie Hall (the dummy), Willie and Brock Murray, the Barnhardt brothers, the Felty brothers, Allie Sublosky and the Petrole brothers.

Lamar started his career by tying a match with his old buddy Charlie Simons of Girardville, who was backed by Monk Miller, Jackie McDonald, Battler Delago and Cletus Coyne. The Sophy brothers were well aware of the shooting powers of Charlie. However, they were backing Lamar because he was younger and they believed he was a better shooter. They shot five matches and Lamar won four.

Joe Bugeye owned a bar in Middleport, located about four miles east of Port Carbon along Route 209. He and his backers were eager to tie a match with Lamar. Bugeye was young and an excellent shooter. Old Jake held off as long as possible because he wasn't too sure Lamar could handle Bugeye. They finally tied a match for seven hundred dollars a side, twenty-one birds, trap and handle, a home and home arrangement. The first match was in Port Carbon on October 1. Lamar won. The second match was won by Bugeye.

The biggest match in Lamar's career took place at the Salem Hill ballpark on September 25, 1934. Prohibition had ended in December 1933 and all the bars opened their doors to legitimate customers. Lamar recalls this scene in his dad's bar.

"My dad and I were sitting at one of the tables having a sandwich and a cup of coffee on a Wednesday afternoon about 2:00 p.m. when in walked Bill and Joe Sophy and Big Bill Heck.

"'Hello fellas, what brings you to these parts?' asked Dad.

"'Hello Jake, we thought we'd like to have a few beers and chew the fat, any law against that?' retorted Bill Sophy.

"'Naw, I guess not. It's still a free country. Lamar, bring the boys a few beers.'

"I went behind the bar, got the drinks and returned to the table. Bill Sophy took a sip of beer and wiped the foam from his lips. He leaned forward in his chair as he spoke to Dad.

"'Do you think Lamar can take Tony Antonelli?'

"Dad turned his head and stared at the floor. 'Lamar can beat him, if we shoot seventeen birds and make the match late in the afternoon.'

"'What the hell does late afternoon have to do with the match?' asked Bill.

"Dad never lifted his head or changed his expression. 'Because that Wop can't shoot when it's gettin' dark. If we can get the Petrole brothers from Hazleton to fly their black birds, we'll tie the match.' Everyone agreed if those conditions could be met, the match should be tied. A week later, the agreement was signed, seventeen birds, a thousand dollars a side, 3:00 p.m., trap and handle, on September 25, 1934, at the Salem Hill ballpark.

The Antonelli group thought they held the edge. Tony was a veteran trap and handle shooter, whereas Lamar's strong suit was a straight match. In spite of the apparent advantage, the Sophys signed the agreement.

Sammy Lehman and the westenders were backing and trapping for Tony. It would be a close match and both sides were ready to back their shooter to the limit. Both were excellent shots. The money moguls knew everyone would be betting on the kill. Therefore, they placed large sums of money on the outcome of the event. They were hedging their bets!

The westenders thought they had a sure thing; they were going to take the Sophys and the north of the mountain boys to the cleaners. Monk Miller and Charlie Simons sent word to the westenders. "We'll cover all your bets, so bring all that moldy Dutch money to the match."

A crowd of more than a thousand people showed up at the ballpark. It was a balmy and warm autumn day, and the sun was shining brightly. It was a perfect setting for an important encounter between two excellent shooters. The crowd was in a festive mood, plenty of booze, moonshine, wine and the usual hot dogs and beer available. The contestants were ready, both mentally and physically. They looked good in practice and each arrived at the park with his confidence at its highest level.

After shooting at ten birds, Antonelli was leading by one bird. The score remained the same as they prepared to shoot the sixteenth bird. Lamar killed the sixteenth bird. It was now Antonelli's turn to approach the mark amid the jeers and thunderous noise.

As old Jake had said, "He can't shoot when it's gettin' dark, especially against Pete's black birds." It was agreed beforehand that if this particular situation arose, Pete would put a black pigeon in the trap, fly it to the left and low to the ground. Because of the approaching darkness and the shadowy dark background, it made for a very difficult shot.

Pete approached the trap from the right, the bird tucked inside his heavy, oversized coat. He didn't want the opposition to get a look at the bird. Pete slipped the bird snugly into position, fitted the rig to the pigeon and carefully closed the trap.

Before leaving, he rattled ten bottle tops, which were tied to a string, on the top of the trap, making as much noise as possible. And for good measure, like the baker's dozen, he banged them against the side of the trap. This procedure was designed to scare the bird so it would take flight the instant the trap was opened.

As Pete made his way back to his place along the sidelines, he held a twenty dollar bill high over his head and yelled, "Twenty bucks on the miss." Antonelli backers were eager to accommodate him.

Darkness was closing in and Antonelli wasted little time approaching the mark. Excitement was running high among the crowd. Everyone was getting his bets down; however, they had to lay two-to-one odds on the kill. The patrons were getting their money's worth. They were observing two fine shooters and the outcome was up for grabs.

It was the usual custom for the shooter and his gun handler to go to a four-door car parked about thirty yards to the rear of the shooting mark. This gave the shooter time to relax and get away from the shouts and taunts of the crowd.

As Tony headed for the mark, Lamar looked at his dad. "Let's go up and see how Tony's gonna do. Pop, I have a feelin' he's gonna miss."

"OK, let's go."

They took their place among the crowd about thirty feet to the right of Tony. They had a good view of the shooter and could watch his every move and expression.

"Look, Pop, he's sweatin' and squintin', I think the darkness is gettin' ta him. I tell ya Pop, that son of a bitch is gonna miss, he's gonna miss!"

Jake, looking intently at Tony, nodded his head. "I think you're right, he looks nervous."

True to the plan, the bird flew to the left and low to the ground twisting and turning, exacting every ounce of energy to save itself from extinction. Tony fired high and missed the bird completely. The match was tied and the scene was set for the final shots.

Lamar killed the next bird. Now it was Tony's turn to face the jeering mob. There was great gloom among Sammy Lehman and the westenders that evening. Tony missed the last shot. In Port Carbon the scene was quite different; a boisterous and joyous party took place at Lurwick's bar. Lamar and the Petrole brothers were the heroes and were toasted with many a drink far into the night.

The gamblers, especially the Sophys, Petie Joseph and the north of the mountain boys were happy as hell and much richer.

9 Gamblers and Gun Clubs

Petie Joseph was shooting craps at Phil Laudeman's on a Thursday evening in the early thirties. Eddie Kelly was standing next to him observing the action. Things weren't going too well for Petie, and after an unsuccessful roll of the dice he turned to his friend. "They might break Petie Joseph at the crap table, but they'll never break Petie Joseph! Remember that, Edward, they'll never break Petie Joseph!"

In 1933, at the depth of the Depression, President Roosevelt, in an effort to reorganize banking and place it on a more sound and stable basis, recalled all the paper money. The paper money was known as "gold certificates" because of the gold emblem printed on each bill. New money was issued to each person as he or she surrendered the old money. The new edition was smaller in size and no longer carried the gold emblem. After a prescribed date, the gold certificates were no longer acceptable as legal tender. This presented something of a problem to the gamblers, who kept large amounts of cash on hand.

On a brisk November morning in Pottsville the trolley came to a halt in front of the railroad station at precisely 7:50 a.m. This gave the passengers enough time to report to work at the nearby shops, or, for those making the trip to Philadelphia, time to board the Reading Railroad's famous Trail Blazer. The Blazer made its departure at 8:00 a.m. seven days a week. After making stops at Reading and Pottstown, it arrived in Philadelphia at 11:15 a.m.

Petie stepped off the trolley, made his way to the station and boarded the Trail Blazer. His attire was noticeably different from the baggy pants, white tee shirt, and tattered brown hat he wore while attending pigeon matches and chicken fights. But his usual attire was not for today. Today was different! He was making an important trip to Philadelphia to consult with his bankers. It was imperative that he make a good impression.

It was 1934, and Petie looked as though he stepped out of the pages of *Esquire*. His attire included a new Stetson hat, a dark blue Hart Schaffner and Marx suit, a new Arrow shirt and a pair of Florsheim shoes, all purchased at Bohorad's, Pottsville's leading men's store. As Scape Hanford would say, "He's the cat's meow!"

When he alighted from the train, Petie was carrying a black satchel containing two hundred and fifty thousand dollars, the money he had stashed away from his gambling winnings during the twenties and early thirties.

He entered the bank and asked to see one of the vice-presidents. Within a short time he was greeted and escorted to the vice-president's plush center city office.

"Now Mr. Joseph, how can I accommodate you?"

"I'd like to make a deposit of some money."

"Our bank is most appreciative of new accounts. We'll do everything in our power to be of service."

Petie placed the bag on the desk and showed the banker the contents.

"How much money do you have, Mr. Joseph?"

"I think it's about two hundred and fifty thousand dollars, give or take a few bucks."

Petie's remark brought a slight smile to the face of the usually unemotional banker. "It will take us a little time to take care of this matter. Meanwhile, why don't you take a seat and make yourself comfortable?" He motioned to one of his assistants. "This young lady will take care of you if you need any assistance. Perhaps you would like some refreshments."

Petie raised his hand. "No thank you, I don't need anything right now."

The banker nodded to a young man who removed the satchel from the desk, placed it on a table and began counting the money. The vice-president excused himself and walked to another section of the building.

Within a half hour he returned accompanied by two men. "Mr. Joseph, these men would like to ask you a few questions."

The men were from the Secret Service. They escorted Petie to an adjoining room for a conference. Within two hours he was released. However, they confiscated the satchel and its contents.

Eventually, Petie was convicted of income tax evasion. The money in the satchel contained bills with gold emblem markings which could no longer be used as legal tender. He received a two-year suspended sentence and was fined $5,000. Throughout the county the episode became known as "Petie Joseph's Moldy Money Caper."

Phil Laudeman lived in Minersville, a small community of seventy-five hundred people located four miles west of Pottsville, the county seat. He was one of Schuylkill County's most renowned sportsmen. He was a slight, rather sickly man, and throughout his adult life he never enjoyed robust health. Because of this condition, he rarely participated in sporting events. However, he organized baseball and softball games for teenagers and adults during the Depression and helped a number of churches and several community groups organize their sports activities.

In 1933, he opened his shooting club, Strawberry Mansion, to the public. Located one mile east of Minersville, it was an immediate success. Within a year it was the most popular shooting club in the county and remained so until his death in 1972.

The clubhouse was adequate. It consisted of a kitchen, where light items such as soups, hot dogs and hamburgers were prepared, a bar with ten stools, and tables which could seat twenty people. There also was a card room with a craps table and dart board.

Phil displayed his gun collection in the card room. Among the collection were military pieces dating back to the Civil War and World Wars I and II, and an array of sporting guns which would thrill most gun collectors and enthusiasts.

The front of the building had an overhang about eight feet deep and thirty feet long to shelter observers of the shooting. If inclement weather prevailed it never interrupted the shooting; all activities continued rain or shine. He had at least two thousand birds on hand at all times, most of them shipped by rail from Oklahoma and Nebraska.

His customers began shooting at 9:00 a.m. and continued until dark. The busiest days were Thursday, Saturday and Sunday. Thursday afternoon, half holiday for the professional people, was the busiest of all, with at least two hundred customers participating in the shooting activities.

The price of a bird and a shot was twenty-five cents. Wagers, ranging from five dollars to five hundred dollars, were placed on each shot. Many small matches of five or seven birds were arranged as the day progressed, the purses ranging from twenty-five to a hundred dollars a side with the loser paying for the birds.

Special guests, such as Progie Deegan, Pottsville's chief of police, were given preferential treatment. Progie arrived promptly at noon and was extended the privilege of shooting one hundred pigeons at Phil's expense.

Other favorite shooters were many of the leading citizens of the county; Dr. Shore, the Raring brothers, Dr. Dolbin, Dave Smith of Pottsville, Dr. Gwinner of St. Clair, Dr. Alimenti from Hazleton, P.S. Canfield (my father), Bim Feeley, Eddie Kenna, Jimmy Hill from New Philadelphia, and Jimmy Ryan from Coal Castle. The gamblers, the Sophys, Bill Yeasted, Petie Joseph, Bill McGowan, Bill Heck, Jack Jefferson, the Hallahan brothers, Joe Piel and Josh Daukshus were on the premises to satisfy the betters.

Laudeman's was a favorite place for shooters who were preparing for a straight match. The pigeons were barn birds, not brushed or trained, taken out of the crates and put in the trap. For a shooter who was preparing for a trap and handle match, in which rigs were placed on the birds, it was not the ideal situation. The birds were untrained, heavy, and slow; they offered no challenge.

When Charlie Simons or Georgie Breen arrived on the scene, things began to happen. The action picked up and the area was alive with excitement. Phil was delighted when this happened. "Whenever those two guys show up, my profits are assured for the day. I should send them a Christmas present every year."

Georgie Breen's constant companion was a short one-armed man, about five feet tall, who carried Georgie's money in a black satchel. Whenever a bet was made, the one-armed man took charge. Georgie made the bets but never handled the money.

Lamar Lurwick said, "When George Breen comes on the scene, the sky's the limit."

The gamblers had a field day when Georgie and Charlie were shooting. Bets were heavy and plentiful, and if they were having a bad shooting day the gamblers did rather well.

When darkness engulfed the surroundings and the shooting came to an end, the gamblers took over and practiced their chosen profession. Food and booze were plentiful, and no one was in a hurry to get home. There was much to whet the appetite of those who wanted to participate in the extracurricular activities: cards, craps, darts, pool and chicken fights. It was a gambler's paradise!

Other shooting clubs made their appearance during the thirties and forties. In the west end, Sammy Lehman was king. His club was known as the Ten Pin Gun Club. The Orwin Gun Club in Tower City, Willie Murray's Golden Rod Club in New Philadelphia, Jim Bergen's Island Gun Club in Heckshersville, Jake Lurwick's Twilight Club in Port Carbon, the Ashland Gun Club, John Starr's North American Gun Club in Middleport, the Seltzer City Gun Club, Jackie McDonald's Brandonville Country Club, and Joe Tobin's Gun Club in Tucker Hill all prospered in this period.

Each club had its following, but Phil Laudeman's drew the largest crowds. As the years passed, the activities and stories relating to the famous club became legendary. The old-timers recalled and retold the tales with nostalgia.

10 Reed Middleton

The gamblers north of the mountain were continually looking for a young shooter with potential. Word got back to the boys that a young man from Gordon, a small town located about five miles west of Ashland, was an outstanding shooter. To everyone's knowledge he had never shot a match, and his name was Reed Middleton. A name to remember!

Monk Miller and Bill Yeasted were talking to Battler Delago while attending a match in St. Clair.

"Battler, do you know anything about a kid by the name of Reed Middleton, from Gordon?"

"I never saw him shoot, but some of the fellas say he's pretty good. Maybe ya oughtta see him, Monk, and maybe he'll make us a few bucks."

"Yeah, maybe you're right. Me and Bill might drop over and see his old man."

Monday afternoon, Monk and Bill drove to Gordon to seek out Earl Middleton, Reed's father.

Eddie Kelly remembers Earl. "He was a feisty son of a bitch! He was always needlin' somebody, especially if he was gassed up with booze. He was in many a fight at the matches. He couldn't fight his way out of a paper bag, and usually ended up losin' most of his fights."

They proceeded to the house, knocked on the door and were greeted by Earl. "What's up Monk, do ya want me ta drive one of your beer trucks?"

"No, nothing like that, Earl. If ya have a few minutes, we'd like to talk to ya."

"Sure, come on in."

Gordon was a small mining town with a population of about one thousand people. Earl's home was located on one of the side streets. It was a single home, enclosed with a white picket fence.

Earl ushered his guests into the living room where they remained standing.

"Take a seat, fellas, and I'll get ya a drink."

"No thanks, Earl, we just wanted to talk to ya about Reed. We hear he's a pretty good shot. Why don't we take a ride back to my place. We'll have a few beers, and maybe we can tie him to a few matches, if it's OK with you. What do ya say?"

Not too many local people were afforded an opportunity to visit the famous bootlegger's home, therefore Earl jumped at the offer. "It's OK with me, Monk. Do ya think Bill can drive me back? My car's not workin' too good."

"Sure, he'll be glad ta do that. Let's go."

Any motorist driving north on Route 61 and entering Ashland passed Monk's residence. It sat back from the highway about one hundred and fifty feet, beautifully landscaped with an abundance of flowers and shrubbery. It was a large four-story building with a very distinctive roof, for which it was famous, a roof of deep blue Spanish clay tiles.

"There's Monk Miller's home" was a familiar phrase among passing motorists. Almost everyone knew where Monk Miller lived! As you entered the grounds, there was a circular driveway which wound its way to the front door. At the right side of the house was another paved road which led to the rear of the house. Here was the entrance to the bar and game room. It was to this area that Monk conducted his guest.

As Earl entered the room, his eyes and face lit up in amazement. It seemed as though he had stepped into a movie scene, depicting a speakeasy owned by a Chicago mobster during the roaring twenties. It resembled a miniature casino. It was approximately forty-eight feet by twenty-four feet, with a ten-foot ceiling supported by dark, one-foot-square solid oak beams spaced six feet apart. At the far end of the room was a spectacular mirrored bar made of hand-carved dark mahogany. Indirect lighting reflected the beauty of the wood.

The back of the bar was lined with an array of whiskeys, wines, liquors and champagne. The eight bar stools were covered with bright red leather, to blend with the plush red carpet.

To the right was a quarter-sized pool table made of dark mahogany, matching the color of the bar. On the opposite side was a large card table covered with emerald-green felt. A large drop shade was hung over the middle of the table, hovering about eighteen inches above the cloth, just high enough so as not to interfere with the game.

Beyond the pool table were five slot machines, three quarter machines and two dollar slots, which were for the enjoyment of Monk's guests. To the left and opposite the slots were enough stuffed sofas and chairs to accommodate fifteen people.

The walls were covered with dark red tapestry, with indirect lighting encased along the borders of the ceiling, which added to the beauty of the tapestry.

As they stood at the far end of the room, Monk looked in Earl's direction. "What do ya think of the place, Earl?"

Earl stood with his hands on his hips, slowly moving his head from side to side. "Holy Christ, Monk, it's beautiful, I never seen anything like it in my life! How the hell did ya ever decorate this place? Wait till I tell Edith about this!"

Monk touched Earl's shoulder. "I'm glad you like it. Come over and sit down. We'll have a few beers and talk." Without looking up he yelled, "Hey Bill, get us a few beers."

After about ten minutes of idle conversation Monk got around to business. "Earl, how good a shooter is Reed?"

"He's damned good! He has one hell of an eye, he kin really shoot."

"If it's OK with you, we'll tie a match. Tell the kid to get ready. Here's twenty bucks for you and ten for Reed. Maybe it would be a good idea if he laid off the booze."

"You don't have ta worry, Monk, he's no boozer and he'll be ready. I'll give him the word!"

Reed was on his way. He had a backer who was loaded with money and had all the right connections. As Big Bill walked out the door, Monk winked and nudged him in the ribs. "I think we got a winner!"

Reed's first match took place on July 31, 1938, at the Frackville ballpark against Tom Griener. The purse was a thousand dollars a side, seventeen birds and a straight match. They were tied after seventeen birds and proceeded to have a five-bird shoot-off. Reed killed three out of four and Tom missed three in a row. Reed entered the shooting arena as a winner.

Monk and his associates now had a shooter who would compile one of the best records in the history of the sport. Reed won forty-two out of forty-nine matches and made a small fortune for Monk.

Francis Ryan was the only individual who ever beat Reed twice. Reed won the first match and then lost the next two to Ryan. At the conclusion of their final match, Francis turned to Monk. "I'll never shoot that kid again. I was damned lucky to beat him taday and I'm gettin' too old to face that kind of pressure. I took ya for a few bucks, Monk, but no more matches."

Monk was a real professional, he never boasted when he won and never cried when he lost. "OK, Francis, ya shot a good match, but I'm sure I'll get the money back, one way or another."

"You old bastard, I know ya'll get it back, that's why I'm quittin' when I'm ahead. Maybe I'll be a little lucky and hold on ta some of the money." True to his word, Reed never again was his opponent.

An important match in Reed's career took place on September 14, 1941. He engaged Norman Erbe, of Tamaqua, one of Schuylkill County's most renowned pigeon shooters. The match took place at the Tamaqua High School stadium, thirty-five birds, the purse of a thousand dollars a side. To the surprise of many, Erbe won the match with ease. The match was concluded after the thirty-second bird. Erbe had eight misses, while Reed had thirteen. Reed expressed his feelings after the match. "It was one of the biggest disappointments of my shooting career. I never believed anyone could beat me so easy."

The event attracted more than fifteen hundred spectators. Betting was heavy as the Dutch Hill gang flew their famous archangels against Middleton. Johnnie Bergalis flew six archangels for misses and was the reason Erbe took the honors in such an easy manner. The gamblers from the Pottsville area were on the losing side and took quite a bath.

Harry Hoover, from Ashland, was one of the better shooters in the county during the thirties and forties. In the late thirties he had lost two matches to Reed Middleton, and in 1940 he again engaged Middleton in two matches and lost both.

Harry made a point to see Reed off at the railroad station when Reed left for his stint in the army during World War II. Harry extended his hand to his old shooting buddy. "I can never understand how you beat me four matches, so I'll be waitin' for ya when the war's over. We'll have one final match! Good luck to ya, Reed. I have a feelin' the good Lord will take good care of ya. You'll be back!"

"Thanks, Harry, I'll be back and I'll give ya one more chance ta change things, but I think you'll be on the losin' end." Reed did survive the war, and in 1945 returned home. True to their mutual promise, Harry and Reed did shoot a final match against each other. The match was scheduled for Sunday, October 15, 1946, at the Minersville ballpark, twenty-five birds, trap and handle, for three thousand dollars a side. Harry and Reed were from the Ashland area, therefore Minersville was a neutral site.

Monk and his cronies were backing Middleton, as were Willie Murray, the Lurwicks and the Sophys. The westenders, Sammy Lehman, Phil Laudeman, the Rumbergers and the Hartmans, were putting their money on Hoover.

Harry was a quiet man, calm and reserved at all times. He spoke very softly and never lost his temper or raised his voice in anger. When at the mark and preparing to shoot, he gave the impression of having ice water in his veins. He was oblivious to any remarks or distracting actions by his adversaries.

Sammy Lehman once gave this description of him: "Nobody kin rattle Harry. When he goes to the mark he acts like he's deaf and dumb." On this beautiful crisp October afternoon, everyone, including Sammy, was in for quite a surprise.

Harry was seated in an automobile approximately fifty yards from the shooting mark. He was relaxing and gathering his thoughts as to how he was going to react under pressure and at the same time outsmart his old nemesis. The match was tied after twenty birds, and the crowd of three thousand people were witnessing a match that would be talked about for years to come.

As Harry got out of the car and headed for the shooting mark, his handler and rope puller, Fats Umbenhauer, yelled in a booming voice, "OK Harry, uff and druff," which was a Pennsylvania Dutch expression meaning "up and down," an expression of confidence that the shooter would kill the bird.

Harry slowly walked toward the mark. The roar of the crowd was deafening and it reached its climax when he was about twenty yards from the shooting area. The opponents spat out their usual taunts, but one voice, that of Eddie Kelly, stood out above all others.

"You could never shoot when the big money was on the line, when the trap opens you'll choke, just like your old man did." Harry looked straight ahead, never changing his facial expression. His mouth was set in an absolute, defiant line.

For a few seconds, Harry's thoughts were not on the match but on Eddie's epithet. "Why does that no good son of a bitch keep talkin' about my family, especially my father. I'd like to put a shot right between that Irish bastard's ears! If he'd only shut his big mouth."

When Harry and Fats finally made their way to the mark, Eddie continued to besmirch Harry's father with growing intensity. As the final seconds ticked away, Harry's self-assured manner masked his anxiety. As he took the gun from Fats, he heard Eddie's high-pitched voice fling his final insult. Nervous beads of perspiration clung to his upper lip and wrinkled brow. He took his final practice sighting, steadied himself and yelled "pull."

The bird was out of the trap at a blinding rate of speed, flying to the right, twisting and turning with every ounce of strength it could muster as it made its move toward the out-of-bounds marker and safety.

Harry seemed surprised when the bird went to the right, because that was his strong point. If he missed a shot it was usually to the left. As a result, he hurried his shot and missed the bird. He stood motionless as if in a trance; he could not believe he had missed the shot. He put the safety on the gun, but for some unknown reason he did not turn the gun over to his handler, Fats Umbenhauer. He turned and began the trek back to the safety and quietness of the car.

After walking about twenty yards, with his head lowered and eyes cast downward, he heard the familiar voice of Eddie Kelly. "I told ya that you couldn't shoot when the big money was on the line. You're like your old man! I'm bettin' a bundle that you'll miss the next two birds."

Eddie was standing at the edge of a puddle of black muddy water which measured about eight feet feet, and about eight feet from Harry and his handler. In one sweeping motion, Harry took the safety off the gun, pointed it downward and fired directly into the middle of the water. When the shot hit the water it caused a great splash of mud and debris to hit Eddie in the face. He put his hands to his eyes and screamed in pain as he fell to the ground.

"Maybe that'll shut your big Irish mouth, ya lousy Mick. Next time, don't talk about my family or you'll get more of the same, you no good son of a bitch. I hope you and yer father both rot in hell."

Harry lost the match, and his great desire to beat Reed Middleton was never to be. "Reed, I did my best to beat you, but it just wasn't in the cards. You're a fine man and a great shooter. My hat's off to ya!"

From that time forth, Harry was never the same shooter. His career took a downward turn, and within a short time he retired as an active participant in the matches.

In his encounter with Eddie Kelly, he had committed the cardinal sin of pigeon shooting. Never, under any circumstances, let your opponents know you hear their insults or disparaging remarks as you prepare to shoot.

The secret was out. "Harry Hoover has rabbit ears. He hears everything!"

Reed Middleton displays a "fair gun"
position.

11 Eddie Kelly

The most colorful figure ever to grace the pigeon scene in Schuylkill County was Eddie Kelly, from New Street, a small mining patch one-half mile from Seltzer City and two miles north of Pottsville. He was born in 1915, the youngest of a miner's eight children. He had five brothers and two sisters, and he quit school after completing the fourth grade. From that time hence, at the age of ten, he was on his own.

Eddie's father was incapacitated as a mine worker at the age of thirty; he was hurt in a mine accident which left him a cripple.

"My father received a small pension from the coal company that helped us survive. When I was ten years old my brother Joe and me got up at 5 o'clock in the mornin' and walked a mile to my uncle's farm and helped with the chores. We ate our breakfast and then went home, that made things a little easier fer the family.

"During the summer months my father always had a half a barrel of beer on tap, thanks to my brothers Joe and Jack. During prohibition, Monk Miller always moved his illegal beer durin' the wee hours of the mornin'. A short distance from our house, there was a steep hill that we called Quality Hill. The truck had ta go up this hill that was about a half mile long and it was loaded with about fifty half-barrels of beer. Because of the heavy load and the pitch of the hill the truck moved very slow, about five miles an hour. It was equipped with hard rubber tires and at two o'clock in the mornin' you could hear the sound of the truck a mile away.

"The family would be asleep and all at once I would hear my father banging on the wall and yelling. 'Joe, the truck is startin' up the hill, get Jack and hit the truck.' In about a minute, my brothers were out the door and jumpin' inta Joe's model T Ford. They caught up ta the truck about halfway up the hill. They parked the car along the road and climbed up on the back of the truck. It wasn't long before they moved the tarpaulin that covered the beer and threw a half-keg alongside the road. They replaced the tarpaulin and in fifteen minutes they were back in bed.

"The next day my father, with the help of a few of his cronies, moved the half-keg up in the bush and buried it in the side of the hill, to keep it cool, and now they were ready to enjoy themselves. Whenever Pop ran out of beer, Joe and Jack robbed the truck. Pop never got greedy; he always told Joe: 'Remember, Joe, never steal more than one keg or Monk might get wise.'

"About once a week, either me or my brothers would go to the nearby farms and steal a few chickens. We even stole a few from my uncle! Pop and his friends would have beer and chicken soup all summer long."

Eddie's career in pigeons and pigeon matches was hectic, boisterous, heartwarming and at times dangerous. He was respected and admired among his peers and was one of the most popular men in the history of the sport. Despite his encounter with Harry Hoover, over the years he was known as a peacemaker. He broke up many fights at the matches and gun clubs.

Eddie describes the situation: "I was usually three sheets to the wind at most matches, so when a fight broke out, I stepped in and broke it up. I was friendly with all the lads so no one ever hit me. They knew if they punched me, all hell would break loose, so I was lucky and never got hit."

He would become an above-average shooter and participate in hundreds of matches, with purses ranging from twenty-five dollars to thousands. His greatest claim to fame was not as a shooter but as a trapper.

As early as the forties, Johnnie and Klate Hartman, from Pine Grove, were considered to be outstanding trappers. Jake Lurwick, Willie Murray, Steve Salamander, the Petrole brothers and the Dutch Hill gang were considered to be on the same level as the Hartman brothers.

Whenever Eddie had an opportunity to observe them at work in a match, or at a private gun club, he did so with intense interest. "Everything I know about trappin' I learned from Johnnie and Klate. They were the best. When I was young, they always treated me like a prince. I used ta run errands and do little chores for them, and they always gave me something for my trouble. It was either a hot dog or a beer. They were great!"

After Eddie quit school, his constant companion was John Reddinton, the youngest of a family of six boys. Eddie and John were too young to work in the mines, because the minimum working age was thirteen years. They usually walked to Pottsville and ended up at Hallahan's Saloon on Center Street, in the heart of the city's business district.

The speakeasy was owned and operated by Mike, Dave, Johnnie and Joe Hallahan. They had an excellent business and their clientele encompassed the entire length of the social ladder; miners, gamblers, doctors, lawyers. The bar was busy from its opening at 7 a.m. until closing at 2 a.m. the following morning. Between 4:30 and 5:30 p.m. was when businessmen gathered to socialize before beginning their homeward trek. If any unfinished business had to be completed, Hallahan's was the place.

Not only were the Hallahans in the speakeasy and bar business, they were also great gamblers. You name it and you had a bet, and they backed many shooters in pigeon matches. Cards, craps, darts and pool were available to their customers, and many impromptu chicken fights were held in the bar.

When you operate a successful speakeasy on the main street of a city of forty thousand people, somewhere along the line someone has to be paid off. The Hallahan brothers were streetwise and put the money in the proper places. They bought their illegal booze from the people with the right connections, none other than Monk Miller and associates. As a result of those business transactions, they had a free pass to operate above the law.

Eddie and his pal, slowly but surely, worked their way into the confidence of the Hallahans and were doing daily chores of cleaning up the bar, running errands and removing the trash. Eventually John dropped out when he obtained a job in the mines. Eddie continued his daily tasks until he also secured a job in the mines as a laborer, at the age of fourteen.

Saturday and Sunday were not working days at the mines, therefore Eddie was once again working for the Hallahans. After his chores were finished, he usually had a sandwich and a soda. Well, not always. "When I was cleanin' the bar early in the mornin', I always snuck a few beers. At the age of fourteen, I could go to any speakeasy in Pottsville and drink at the bar, as long as I drank the beer and kept my mouth shut. I've been drinkin' since I was thirteen years old and makin' my own way. Why do ya think they call me Fast Eddie!" Drinking at an early age set a pattern which would continue throughout his life.

His association with the Hallahans continued through his youth and into his shooting career. When he began shooting in 1938, the brothers backed him in many of his matches. He started trapping birds in 1932, and by 1935 he was considered such a competent trapper that his services were sought by many of the outstanding shooters in the county.

A few years down the road, Eddie was working as a laborer in a bootleg coal hole called the Hurry Up. "I started to work at seven o'clock in the mornin' and finished at three-thirty in the afternoon. By the time I got home, washed and ate supper, it was six o'clock. I was out drinkin' every night. I didn't spend much time with my family. I'm ashamed ta say it, but my wife raised my two kids, a boy and a girl.

"I'd leave the house on Friday night and I'd get home Monday morning, just in time ta go ta work. I'd spend the weekend drinkin', shootin' craps, playin' cards, shootin' pigeons, trappin' and goin' to the chicken fights. I always had a drink in my hand but I never got sick. Ya know what my secret was? I always ate when I drank! Not many people know this, but if ya eat when ya drink ya'll never get sick. In all my years of drinkin' and boozin', I never missed a shift at work. Now that's sayin' somethin'!"

After World War II, Eddie would come into his own as a shooter and trapper. He would become involved in some of the most controversial and questionable matches in the history of the sport.

Drinking buddies: Reed Middleton and Eddie Kelly.

Eddie Kelly displays a "high gun" position.   Eddie Kelly

12 The Hartman Brothers Even the Odds

Dutch Reigle was one of the busiest shooters of the thirties and probably the most controversial. Whenever he shot a match, there was the probability that the match would be interrupted by a heated argument, a fight or a riot.

He held a high gun, a procedure which drove his opponents and opposing betters into a frenzy. He raised his elbow high above his shoulder and aimed the gun directly at the trap, and when the trap opened he did not move the gun more than an inch before firing. The bird never flew more than six inches from the trap: Dutch was a "pull bang shooter." Many followers of the sport considered that type of shooting illegal. As a result, most shooters in the Pottsville and Tamaqua area and north of the mountain were reluctant to tie a match with him because they believed he had too great an advantage.

In 1935, Dutch tied a match with Sammy Lehman for a thousand dollars a side, seventeen birds, trap and handle. Sammy was the best shooter in the west end and he, too, was a high-gun shooter. When two high-gun shooters squared off it was logical that there would be more kills than misses. The gamblers had an excellent opportunity to make a killing by betting on the kill. However, they had to lay high odds, such as four to one on the kill.

The westenders put their money on their idol, Sammy. The Sophys and Monk Miller believed Reigle was the better of the two, and they were correct. Reigle beat Lehman, killing 14 out of 17 to Sammy's 13. The match was decided on the last bird.

In September of 1938, a match between Reigle and Grant Whitcomb was scheduled for Minersville ballpark, seventeen birds, a thousand dollars a side, trap and handle. Whitcomb held a fair gun. He was an excellent shooter, but the smart money boys didn't give him much of a chance of winning. The Sophys and Monk were set to make a killing.

The westenders, especially the Hartman brothers, thought Whitcomb had a good chance of winning. Two weeks before the match took place, Eddie Kelly met Johnnie and Klate Hartman in Pottsville.

"How the hell can ya beat a guy like Reigle? That son of a bitch can't miss a bird the way he holds a gun. I don't think Whitcomb has a chance."

Klate put his arm on Eddie's shoulder. "When Dutch takes on Grant, he's in for one hell of a surprise. Put your money on Whitcomb and bet all you have. You come out to the ballpark, and Johnnie and me, we'll show ya something new." Eddie didn't press the point, but he knew that something was in the wind.

As expected, a large crowd turned out for the match. Most of the spectators were aware that Reigle was the favorite; therefore, if they wanted to make a bet on the kill, they had to lay odds. All the smart money, Monk Miller, the Sophys, the Hallahan brothers, Charlie Simons, Battler Delago and the Hazleton boys, headed by Georgie Breen and Dr. Frank Alimenti, were on Reigle.

The Lurwicks, Willie Murray, Phil Laudeman and Joe Piel were birding for Reigle. If he was going to lose, it wouldn't be because he had poor trappers. Trapping for Whitcomb were Sammy Lehman, Al Rumberger, the Hartman brothers and Eddie Kelly, who switched sides after talking to the Hartmans.

Whitcomb killed the first bird and the match was off to a rousing start. Klate was scheduled to put the first bird in the trap. A good trapper never exposes the bird to the spectators or the opposing shooter. Everything is secretive, especially the color and size of the bird. When the trap opens, everything that happens is expected to be a surprise to the opposing shooter.

Klate had the bird tucked under his red checkered hunter's jacket. He knelt down in front of the trap with his back to the shooting mark. As he huddled, his face was six inches away from the trap. He opened his coat and placed the bird in its proper position.

Reigle stepped to the mark, took his customary two practice sights and yelled "pull." As expected, he shot as soon as the trap opened, but to everyone's surprise the bird never took flight.

Klate had placed the pigeon on its back, and when the trap opened instead of taking flight it rolled out of the trap. In that split second, Reigle fired and missed the bird. He fired over the trap where the bird usually flew. To his as well as the spectators' great surprise, the bird rolled to the right and never left the ground.

Reigle and the bewildered crowd had never seen anything like that in all their years of attending matches. Because of Klate's unorthodox procedure at the trap, the spectators were confused as to how to bet. Many of them switched their bets. The gamblers, who were backing Reigle, weren't too upset. They were certain Dutch would adjust and be on his way to another victory. But Klate's new maneuver so unnerved him that he missed the next five birds.

Whitcomb won the match in a breeze. The west end boys made a killing and the Hartman brothers added a new dimension to the sport. The Sophys and Monk took a bath, but as seasoned gamblers they took it in stride. Bill Sophy put the situation in perspective as he and his buddy departed the scene: "Come on, Monk, maybe we kin win it back at the crap table or the chicken fights. After all, them suckers must win sometime!"

Eddie Kelly won a few bucks, enough to buy the Hartman brothers a few rounds of drinks at the bar. But more importantly, he learned a new trick at the trap. "Ya really showed me somethin' taday, Klate. From now on those high-gun bastards will be on even terms with everybody else."

A big grin broke out on Klate's face. He looked at Eddie and said in a soft voice, almost a whisper, "You're right, Eddie, you're right."

A match for a thousand dollars a side, seventeen birds, trap and handle, took place at Laudeman's in the late summer of 1939, between Dutch Reigle and Uni Fessler from Pine Grove. Reigle had his usual money backers, because they still believed him to be a good shooter and a winner.

Phil Laudeman, the Lurwicks, Willie Murray, Joe Piel and Al Edwards from New Phillie were backing Uni, and Eddie Kelly was his main trapper. He learned his lesson from the Hartman brothers well. He flew nine birds away from Dutch, and Uni won in a walk.

Later as Monk and Cletus Coyne were having a beer in the bar, Eddie walked by their table. Monk turned his head and looked up. "Eddie you Irish bastard, you're killin' us! Why don't you go up to that coal hole of yours and take a six months vacation? I'll furnish you with all the booze you need."

Eddie looked down at Monk and winked. "I like your money and your booze. Keep bettin' against me."

Everyone at the table joined in the laughter. Monk turned to the bartender. "Give this Irish renegade a drink, and I hope he chokes."

"Thanks, Monk, you're a great loser."

December 7, 1941, the day the Japanese bombed Pearl Harbor, would change the American way of life and the world forever. Most of the outstanding shooters in the county joined the armed forces. Despite the rationing of food, gasoline and other vital materials, pigeon matches continued, but on a limited basis. Because of the gasoline rationing, most people stayed close to their local gun clubs. However, some high stakes matches did take place.

George Starr, of Llewellyn, was the most outstanding shooter at Laudeman's during that period. His main backers and trappers were the Barnhardt brothers. Willie Murray, owner and operator of the Golden Rod Gun Club in New Philadelphia, was also an active shooter. He shot a match with Bill Sharp, the manager of the Kaier Brewery in Mahanoy City, for a thousand dollars a side. The match ended in a tie and Willie won in a shoot-off. He beat Battler Delago of Girardville, lost to Joe Shulp of New Phillie and Steve Salamander of Ashland. Pete Marchetti of New Phillie lost four out of five matches to Willie. Most of the gun clubs had small matches on the weekends. But there was very little action during the week.

My father, together with Bill McGowan, Willie Murray, Josh Daukshus and the Lurwicks, backed my brother Tom in a match with Jake Linabach of Ashland for a thousand dollars. Jake, who was an above-average shooter, must have had a bad day, because Tom won the match.

After the event was over my father took Tom aside. "Thomas, you were a lucky shooter today. You're not a great shot and before you lose money for your backers, I think you had better retire." Tom took Dad's advice and ended his career as the only undefeated pigeon shooter in Schuylkill County.

Within months after the end of hostilities, the boys were on their way home from all parts of the world, ready to make up for the years away from their loved ones. Those who were married were looking forward both to resuming their careers and to raising their families.

In any case, the veterans came home ready to face the world. After winning the war and putting up with all the chicken shit of the armed forces, nothing was impossible. Life was just a bowl of cherries and they were now ready to eat and enjoy the fruit. The years between 1946 and 1960 were the vintage years for the veterans. They were out to change the world. They produced the baby boomers, who not only changed the world but nearly burned it to the ground in the sixties.

Part II

*Growing Up in New Philadelphia,
1920–1943*

Patrick S. Canfield
of New Philadelphia, Pennsylvania.

Sister Helen Marie
Holy Family School
New Philadelphia, 1930.

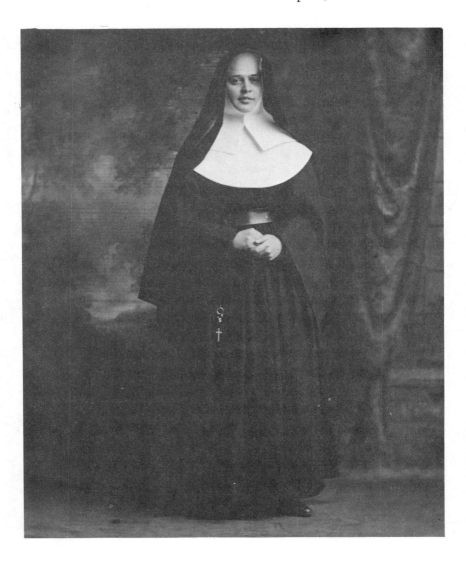

13 New Philadelphia, a Wide-Open Town

I graduated from West Chester State Teacher's College on January 8, 1943, and came back to my home in New Philadelphia to spend a few weeks with my mother and father before my induction into the army on February 8. My brothers John and Bob (Butts) were in the service, and my sister Mary Frances was a freshman at Immaculata College. My brother Tom was married and had six children, therefore he was not subject to call to the armed forces.

I didn't do much socializing because most of my friends were in the military. Consequently I had time to reflect on the past, especially my early days in New Phillie. It seemed such a short time ago that I was roaming the streets of our town with my boyhood chums, Tata Foley, Mickey Doyle, Slim and Eddie Berrang, Alex Pautenius, Francis Kollessor, Jessie Whalen and Brother Feeley. The town was a wonderful place to spend our youthful and carefree years.

There wasn't much auto traffic, so it was safe to play on the side streets without fear of being run over by a motor vehicle. The first recollections of my youth seemed to center around small and noisy parades in honor of our heroes Jack Dempsey, Babe Ruth and Ty Cobb. Bobby Jones, Knute Rockne and the Four Horsemen of Notre Dame added to the mystique and glamour of that immortalized decade.

Dempsey was not always the idol of the American public that he became in the twenties. During the First World War (1917–1918) he didn't enter the army and was labeled a "slacker" and a "draft dodger." He didn't receive too many compliments or accolades in the sports pages prior to his fight with Jess Willard, the reigning heavyweight champion at that time.

Willard weighed 245 pounds and stood 6 feet 6 inches tall; Dempsey weighed 187 pounds and stood 6 feet 1 inch tall. He was given little chance of dethroning Willard. They were scheduled to fight on July 4, 1919, in Toledo, Ohio. Dempsey destroyed Willard in three rounds. Willard had done little training as he regarded Dempsey as an easy opponent. As a result, he received a terrible beating, one of the worst in the history of boxing. Dempsey had attained his lifelong ambition of becoming the heavyweight champion of the world. From that time on, he was an American sports idol.

He lost his title to the fighting marine Gene Tunney in a bout held at the Sesquicentennial Stadium of Philadelphia in 1926. Tunney was never a popular champion, mostly because he had beaten one of the immortal legends in the world of sports. The return match was scheduled at Soldiers Field, Chicago, September 22, 1927. It will always be remembered in the annals of boxing as "The Battle of the Long Count." It was the thinking of our juvenile brain trust that no one could defeat the great Dempsey twice, an opinion shared by the local gamblers, who were laying 8 to 5 odds that Dempsey would regain his title.

We decided to hold a parade honoring our hero, after carefully deciding on the instrumentation of our ensemble: tin cans, old dish pans, bells (of any sort or description) or any object which would produce a cacophony of sounds. My mother and Mrs. Whalen (Jessie's mother) made us soldier hats of paper and a sign tacked on a three-foot pole which read "Dempsey Will Win." After much preparation we were ready for the formal parade. The starting point was Flanagan's garage across the street from our house. We marched a half block to McGovern's corner, made a left turn, crossed the street, made another left and in a high-stepping formation made our way to the terminal point of the parade, the sidewalk in front of our house.

Though the parade lasted only about three minutes, it was a huge success. Mrs. McGovern and her daughter Catherine gave us a rousing round of applause, as did Willie Reagan and the customers in his barbershop. Our next-door neighbor Mrs. Whitacunis, my mother and Mrs. Whalen ended the applause and treated the members of the ensemble to cookies and lemonade, a fitting tribute to a great parade and a great day.

Our enthusiasm and support didn't help our hero; Dempsey was defeated in his quest to regain the title. When Dempsey dropped Tunney to the canvas in the seventh round, he refused to obey the orders of the referee, Dave Barrys, to go to the farthest neutral corner before he would begin the count. How long Tunney was down was never determined, but some ringside observers estimated it to be somewhere between 12 and 16 seconds. Because of his refusal to obey the referee's orders, Dempsey failed in his quest to regain the championship.

Many years later Dempsey admitted that because of the long count he became the darling of the American sport fans. "I know that because of the long count my New York restaurant flourished. Without the long count I would have been just another ex-champ."

We were destined to hold two more parades honoring heroes of the day. Our second parade was in honor of Charles Lindbergh, "Lucky Lindy," after he made his famous nonstop flight across the Atlantic from Roosevelt Field on Long Island to LeBourget Field in Paris on May 27, 1927. Our final parade, at the urging of everyone on Kimber Street to make it our last, was for Al Smith, the presidential candidate of the Democratic Party, in the 1928 election. As in the case of Dempsey, Al Smith was defeated. Herbert Hoover, the Republican candidate, scored a landslide victory.

During the twenties, New Phillie was a wide-open town. Live and let live and don't rock the boat was the underlying theme of most of the town's citizens. In 1928, there were fifteen hundred people in a borough with thirty-five bars, which were open from 7:00 a.m. until 2:00 a.m. seven days a week to quench their thirst.

If anyone was in need of a drink, or wanted to entertain friends, it was easy. Just point their car in the direction of New Phillie and all their drinking problems were over. They were as safe as if they were drinking in the town hall with the chief of police serving the drinks. Before Monk Miller moved booze into a town, the proper connections had already been made. Local and county politicians in addition to the local and state police were paid off. Lo and behold, all the lights were on green! Let the booze flow!

The town is located on Route 209, five miles east of Pottsville and eleven miles west of Tamaqua. The population at that time was made up of Irish, Lithuanians and Slovaks and was mostly Catholic. The Irish worshiped at Holy Family church, and Sacred Heart was the Lithuanian church. The Protestants attended the Methodist church, located three doors from my home on Kimber Street.

The town was divided along ethnic lines. Route 209, which was Valley Street, and Kimber Street were parallel to each other and ran the length of the borough in an east-west direction. Those two streets were inhabited by the Irish and Slovaks and a few Lithuanians.

When you entered the town from the west along 209, the first four blocks were known as the "patch." The next two long blocks on Valley Street were the business center of town. On the right side of the street was the large Feeley complex which housed two rented apartments, the post office and the Feeley residence. Hughie Feeley was the postmaster; his chief assistant was his sister Kate. The Holy Family church and the rectory completed the block.

Across the street from the church, at the beginning of Clay Street, was the Holy Family Elementary School, grades one through eight. A large fenced-in playground bordered the school on the left, and the nuns' living quarters, which were part of the school.

Opposite the school, on Clay Street, was the residence of Dr. Stein, the most impressive and opulent home in town. It was built in the massive and grandiose style of the twenties. The property encompassed, lengthwise, one entire block from Valley to Kimber Streets.

The Stein home was a hundred and fifty feet in length and fifty feet wide. A large yard held an array of beautiful flowers, birdbaths, sundials, rock gardens and a small but well-manicured lawn. In the spring and summer Mrs. Nan Stein was in her garden, puttering and tending to her beloved flowers and plants. Across the front of the house was a large enclosed glass porch comfortably furnished and with the ever-present plants and flowers.

Behind the porch was a large living room at the end of which was a wide dark mahogany staircase, measuring six feet across, ascending about ten steps to a landing. At this point the staircase made a 180-degree turn and continued to the third floor, where five bedrooms and three baths were located.

Beyond the living room on the first floor was a spacious dining room which seated twelve people. It was here that the family ate all their meals. The kitchen and pantry, large and well-lighted, were equipped with the latest in kitchenware, designed to make working in the kitchen as comfortable and pleasurable as possible. A back stairway led from the kitchen to the second floor.

Dr. Stein was an impressive figure. He was six feet tall and muscularly built. He was a quiet man who didn't waste words on idle talk. Politics and community affairs were of little concern, and within the community his lifestyle was low-key. He and Dr. Paul Boord were the family doctors for most of the townspeople. Dr. Stein was our family doctor and delivered our family members into this world.

The children, John, Helen, Bob, and Nancy, added to the image of the ideal American family. John graduated from the University of Pennsylvania and Bob was a graduate of

Muhlenberg College. Helen and Nancy, both charming and beautiful, went to finishing schools and married well.

Before the stock market crash in 1929, the Steins had upstairs and downstairs maids and a chauffeur. They were a typical example of a prestigious, affluent family of the roaring twenties. Most of their money, however, was on paper, and when the stock market hit bottom everyone, rich and poor, was affected. To the Steins it was a crushing blow. The maids and chauffeur were discharged. However, they were still one of the pillars of the community. Their social life was uninterrupted and they continued to enjoy an elegant manner of living as though nothing had happened.

The Silver Creek Bank was located next to their residence. Dr. Stein was president and had controlling interest. The Methodist church, located diagonally across the street from their four-car garage, was controlled by the Steins. They were the dominant force in all aspects of their church community. They selected the minister, who had to conform to the standards and guidelines set up by the leading family.

The Steins never socialized with the residents of the town, but they were an integral part of the social register of Schuylkill County. They belonged to the Schuylkill Country Club, which in the twenties and thirties was the meeting place and playground of the rich. A list of the club membership revealed few Catholics, and no Jews, blacks or residents of eastern European heritage. It was the social haven for the rich WASPs and Pennsylvania Dutch.

One block east was the town square, at Valley and Water Streets. In this area there was a bar on each corner. On the east and west corners of Water Street were the bars of Van Alexander and Jim Kenna. The other two corners were occupied by the bars of Al Edwards and John Callery. These establishments overlooked a small memorial park which fronted on Water Street and extended back one block from Valley to Kimber Streets.

This clean and well-manicured tract displayed a large plaque, erected in front of the park at Valley Street, listing the names of the soldiers of World War I who made the supreme sacrifice defending their country. The nation honored the war heroes of the Spanish-American War and veterans of World War I on May 30, Memorial Day. This was a national holiday, and the U.S.A. was caught up in the fervor of patriotism, pride and love of country. It was a day of relaxation and fun, political speeches, band concerts, baseball games, family picnics, fireworks displays, parades and dances. It wouldn't be too many years in the future that another group of war veterans would be added to the list of heroes on the memorial plaque.

During the twenties the population of New Phillie was divided equally between the Irish and the Lithuanians. When the Depression began in 1929, about twenty percent of the Irish families moved to Philadelphia, where the future seemed much brighter than in the coal regions.

At this time the familiar social and economic inequity which brought about the rise of the Molly Maguires in the 1860s raised its head again. It wasn't as violent or deadly, but it was ugly and vicious. Tension between the Irish and Lithuanians was running high. The Irish working in the mines were first-generation Irish-Americans. In contrast, the Lithuanians were immigrants who arrived between the years 1900 and 1920, and they had many handicaps to overcome. They didn't speak the language and had great difficulty adapting to the ways of the new world. They continued to rely on the traditions, customs, dress codes and food preparation of the old country, attending their own schools and churches and seldom marrying outside their nationality.

Because of their unusual behavior and customs, the Lithuanians weren't readily accepted by the Irish, who believed them to be mysterious, clannish, old-fashioned and untrustworthy. They were often referred to as "Hunkies" or "Brollies." The Lithuanians had their own contempt for the Irish, calling them "Jelly Beans." Lithuanians of fifty and above didn't trust the Irish, mostly because they couldn't speak the language and couldn't understand what the Irish were saying, be it good or bad. In any case, their estimation of their rivals was one of suspicion and mistrust.

The younger generation, especially the unmarried men, had no time for each other; both sides were ready to fight at the least provocation. Many people in town, both Irish and Lithuanian, were aware of the situation and dreaded the day when these festering animosities would lead to unthinkable consequences.

14 The Riot of 1929:
Irish versus Lithuanians

One summer evening in late August of 1929, some members of our gang and I were playing in the street in front of the McGovern residence. About 8:30 we heard loud screams and yelling emanating from the second floor of the home. It sounded as though someone was bashing something against the walls or breaking the furniture. Amid the confusion were heard the screams of Catherine and Brigitte McGovern.

Within a few seconds, we heard the sound of breaking glass. We cast our gaze at the lighted room on the second floor, which was the bathroom, and saw both window panes come crashing to the ground. Catherine came running out of the house, crossed the street and fled into our house, screaming for my father. Within a matter of seconds they were running toward the McGovern home.

Mickey McGovern, the oldest son, had been on a drinking binge and was in the process of making a shambles of the household. My father entered the premises at the height of the melee, and within a short time order was restored and quietness once again prevailed.

My dad was well respected in the community and was a close friend of the McGovern family. He had known Mickey from the day he was born. About ten minutes after assuming the role of peacemaker he made his exit. As he made his way across the street, I ran beside him and took his hand.

"What happened, Pop? What happened at McGoverns?"

He looked straight ahead, never breaking stride or showing any emotion. "I think it's time for you to go to bed, Patrick." That meant the incident was over, and forgotten!

While this episode was unfolding, an event was taking place at Van Alexander's bar on Valley Street which would change the attitudes of New Phillie for years to come, possibly forever. This bar was a favorite watering hole of those people, during the roaring twenties, who enjoyed the exhilaration of being served illegal booze in a small, dimly lit, illegal speakeasy. It was not a beautiful room by any stretch of the imagination, and did not possess the ambience of many of the accessible speakeasies located throughout the county. It was a small bar with a capacity of no more than forty people, and was located in the center of town, facing the town square. Many of Van's customers came to hear him play the organ. He was an exceptionally fine musician and gave very professional renditions of the songs of the past and present.

Van had owned a bar in the crime-ridden city of Chicago. It was common gossip in town that he was asked to continue his career in another section of the country because of a misunderstanding with a certain underworld crime figure. He picked New Phillie because it was located in Schuylkill County, which possessed many of the virtues of Chicago: bootlegging, speakeasies, political and police payoffs, slot machines, prostitution, freewheeling attitudes and a lifestyle which catered to those citizens who wanted to partake of the roaring twenties night life.

Van's bar was located on the left side of the entrance. Four people could sit at the end, near the door, and fifteen could sit comfortably along the bar lengthwise. Van's new Wurlitzer organ rested on an elevated platform a foot higher than the top of the bar, at the end of the room. He played the organ with his back to the wall and sat facing the patrons, which made it easier to hear the requests and comments of his customers.

When someone asked Van why he played the organ with his back to the wall instead of facing the wall, which would make the organ sound better acoustically, he was quick to respond. "In Chicago it was an unwritten rule among those in the know to never sit with your back to the door. If you're gonna get shot at least know who's doin' the shootin'."

On this particular Thursday night, Fumbler Martin, Al Edwards, Greg Norris, Scape Hampford and Big Jim Cavanaugh were enjoying a few beers. They were seated at the far end of the bar just below the organ. It was about 9:30. A few couples were seated at the tables along the opposite wall, and about ten people sat at the bar, including Tony Griggs and three of his Lithuanian companions who were seated near the entrance.

During the early part of the evening the music and conversation were soft and subdued, but as the evening progressed and the alcoholic intake increased, both music and conversation increased in volume from a pianissimo to a forte.

As Van concluded one of his tunes, Greg Norris raised his right hand and gestured to him. "Hey Van, how about playin' an Irish tune, somethin' like 'My Wild Irish Rose'?" Someone at the other end of the bar interrupted in a loud raucous voice. It was Tony Griggs: "The hell with the Irish songs, how about playin' a good Hunkie polka."

Al Edwards turned his head toward the booming Lithuanian voice. "If ya want a polka, go up to Shlackie's bar on Water Street, maybe he'll sing ya a polka. Go ahead, Van, let's hear the Irish tune."

Without missing a beat in the rhythmical verbal barrage, Tony persisted: "Never mind, Van, just play the polka. Ta hell with the Irish!"

Van realized the situation was getting tense and could easily get out of control. "Look, I'll play both tunes, and then everyone will be happy."

Greg was determined not to give in to his antagonist. "It's OK with us, Van, as long as ya play the Irish tune first."

At that instant, Tony bolted from his stool and leaped toward Greg, who was taken by surprise at Tony's accelerated pace and belligerent attitude. Instinctively, he rose from his seated position to face his charging adversary. He stood erect, their faces just inches apart. How they loathed and despised each other! Greg was determined to put this crude dumb-talkin' Brollie in his place, once and for all.

For Tony, all the humiliations, resentments, snide remarks and belittlement of the past decades were focused and reduced to the confines of his scowling face and sweaty and beaded brow.

His voice, trembling with emotion, boomed forth. "Who the hell do you guys think ya are? You think ya own this town! Every time ya say somethin' we're supposed to roll over and play dead! Well I got news fer you, you loud-mouth son on a bitch, them days are over!"

Big Jim Cavanaugh, Greg's brother-in-law, edged his bulky frame beside Greg. "Why don't you Brollies get the hell outta here and go up ta Water Street and do yer drinkin', we'll take care of Valley Street!" Big Jim's words didn't impede Tony's desire to continue his heated dialogue with Greg.

Tony and Greg were both born in New Phillie. They were raised on the hate and disrespect each nationality had for the other. This attitude was accepted and perpetuated in their homes and was carried over into the streets and their everyday lives.

Tony knew Greg's fighting credentials. He talked as tough and boisterous as Al Capone and possessed all the qualities of Jack Dempsey. That is, until he threw the first punch. Then all the comparisons to Dempsey ended; he was one of the worst fighters in town. Tony quickly continued: "You Irish are a pain in the ass, ya talk big, but ya never back it up with action."

Greg had placed himself in a position from which he couldn't retreat. "OK, big mouth, let's go outside and see how tough ya are!" Everyone inside the bar headed for the door and assembled on the pavement.

Greg Norris stood about six feet tall and weighed 170 pounds. He was good looking, and one of his greatest assets was the fact that he was a great conversationalist. He was at his best when he was surrounded by his admirers in a bar. Howard Feeze, a close friend of his, was heard to say, "Most of the time I don't know what the hell Greg's talkin' about, but it really sounds good."

Greg possessed a cocky and aggressive attitude that got him into quite a bit of trouble, such as the situation he was now facing. On numerous occasions his determined look of confidence and cockiness, in addition to his physical attributes, made his adversaries back down.

The Irish had a distinct advantage. It was five against four and it was taking place in the Irish section of town. The fight was going to be rough and tumble, anything goes, but no matter how rough the fight got, it would be a fair fight. One on one, no brass knuckles or knives, just bare knuckles.

As expected, Greg was taking a terrible beating, at which point Big Jim entered the fight. Greg retreated to the sidelines.

Mickey Puzauskie and five of his friends were sitting in front of Lucas' garage when Mickey's sister came running toward the group. Her face was flushed and she was gasping for breath.

"Mickey, there's a big fight at Van's bar. It looks like a riot!" Within seconds Mickey and his buddies were running toward the brawl. Mickey was fifteen years old and a little too young to become involved in the events that were beginning to unfold.

He describes the mob scene. "When we arrived, a small riot was in progress. Four fights were taking place and about fifty people had gathered. The Lithuanian boys were being slowly pushed up Water Street along the memorial park. The crowd was growing by the minute, and as it grew, the noise was that of a full-scale riot so often depicted in the movies."

When the combatants reached Kimber Street, in front of Dr. Boord's home, the fighting broke off momentarily. The Lithuanians were nearing their home grounds and felt a little more secure. As they paused for a breather Tony Griggs, his face a mass of blood and sweat, shouted into the faces of his opponents. "OK, you Irish bastards, we'll be back and we'll even up the odds, we're not finished yet."

The four brawlers headed up Water Street, looking for their comrades-in-arms. They would be back with reinforcements! You could rest assured that they would do everything in their power to tip the scales in their favor. Mickey continued, "I knew the fellas who were fighting, they were tough and mean, and I knew in my heart that it was going to be one long rough night. We continued our walk up Water Street and I can assure you, what I saw I didn't like. All the fellas were comin' out of the bars as word spread about the fightin', and everyone was gathering in front of Victor Ellenousky's bar."

The four men who had been in the first skirmish were whipping the crowd into an angry frenzy. They were determined to bring all their inner hatred of the Irish to a head. The humiliations, degrading remarks, and social slights would be paid in full. The Irish would never forget this dreadful and meaningful night!

Al Edwards and his friends retreated from the first encounter and made their way to the Holy Family Men's Club, which was a gathering place for the young men of the parish. They knew the Water Street contingent would be back in full force with hatred and vengeance in their hearts and fists. Word had spread among the Irish community, as it had in the Lithuanian area. The bars emptied as the young men made their way to the club, where their leaders were making plans for the coming confrontation.

The Irish had their big guns in place, including Fumbler Martin, a professional boxer and one of the best welterweight fighters in the coal region at that time. Eddie Norris, Greg's brother, was an outstanding football player and an excellent fighter. Jim Cavanaugh stood six feet three inches tall and weighed in at 250 pounds, he could handle himself in any fight. And Andy Sura, probably the best street fighter that ever walked the streets of New Phillie.

The Lithuanians also had their heavy hitters. Kid Labarb was a professional fighter, as was Lefty Laurinitus, a true heavyweight at 215 pounds, and Tony Griggs, in the battleship class, tipping the scales at 235.

The Water Street brawlers were ready and eager to start the proceedings. They were determined to make the events of the evening an Irish wake. All was in readiness. They had fortified themselves with illegal booze, beer, whiskey and wine. After all, when you go to an Irish wake you must observe all the Irish traditions!

Meanwhile, Greg Norris was holding forth at the Holy Family Club. He climbed on a chair and lifted a glass of beer high above his head, "The Brollies say it's gonna be an Irish wake, well that's OK with us. We'll make it a real Irish wake. We'll make it a celebration!" Once again he lifted his glass high into the air: "Down with the lousy Brollies." Greg's remarks were an added incentive to bring the Brollies to their knees. The crowd made their way out the door and gathered in front of the church, chanting Greg's favorite slogan, "Down with the lousy Brollies."

Huck Doyle was the lookout for the Irish forces. He stationed himself at the corner of Valley and Water Streets awaiting the arrival of the Lithuanians. At the stroke of midnight they made their appearance. One hundred strong! Huck delivered the message everyone was anxiously awaiting: "They're on their way, the Brollies are comin'."

The Lithuanians turned the corner at Valley Street and headed in the direction of their hated rivals. This was the night the young men had been dreaming about for years. The Irish had gathered at the corner of Kimber Street in front of the rectory and school. The mob scene would take place directly under the street light. If there was going to be a riot, it would be well lighted!

Anna Mae and Kitty Gannon and Annie Wargo were standing at the fringe of the mob, which had overflowed onto Kimber Street a short distance from the front porch of the convent. The noise had awakened the nuns, and three of them, Sisters

Gervaise, Helen Marie, and Kasmirus had opened the front door and had walked onto the porch.

Kitty turned her head and noticed the nuns. "Come on, we'll go over to the Sisters and tell them about the fight."

When they were within six feet of the porch, Sister Gervaise spoke to the girls. "What's going on? What is everyone shouting about?"

"There's going to be a big fight between the Irish and the Lithuanians."

Sister Gervaise motioned to the girls to come into the convent. No words were spoken as the nuns moved through the darkened hallway to the stairway leading to the second floor. They passed through a door which led them to a hallway in the school directly across from the fifth and sixth grade classrooms. These rooms overlooked Valley and Kimber Streets.

Sister Gervaise opened two windows facing Kimber Street and two windows facing Valley Street. As she took her position at the window she nudged Kitty in the ribs. "After all, if there's going to be a good fight, we have the best seats in town!"

Sister Kasmirus ran back to the convent and awakened the three remaining nuns. Sister Kasmirus, whose mother was Irish and her father Lithuanian, was a neutral observer. She often boasted about having the best of both nationalities. "When I was growing up in Scranton, my father prepared all the ethnic foods of the Lithuanians; halupkies, blienies, perogies and haluskies, but never garagekies! My mother, in the best Irish tradition, held up her end of the bargain by making the best ham and cabbage, roast beef and mashed potatoes in town."

When the two opposing groups met in the middle of the street they didn't waste words. They came to fight, and fight they would. Bobby Stutz was standing on Connellys' porch, which was situated about sixty feet from the center of the melee. He describes the action: "I was sixteen years old and not much of a fighter, so I figured if I didn't want to get my head knocked off I better stay clear of the brawl and become an observer. The Irish were strung across the width of Valley Street waiting for the Brollies. Both groups met head-on and the riot was on.

"It was a rough and tumble fight, no holds barred, but it was a fair fight, just bare fists. Each man seemed to pick an opponent his own size and weight. After that it was every man for himself. I never saw anything like it, it was a full-scale riot. Every person on the street was fighting as if his very life depended on the outcome.

"It didn't seem as though any particular group was winning, the only way a winner would be declared would be if one group retreated, and I can assure you that a thing like that would never happen! Both groups were intent on clearing up the matter once and for all.

"Many men were on the ground, bleeding from all parts of their faces and arms, screaming and swearing as the fight progressed. It was a bloody fight with no end in sight. Suddenly, out of nowhere two priests, Father Brogan from Holy Family and Father Lucas from Sacred Heart parish, appeared.

"They walked into the center of the riot, both held up their arms and tried desperately to get the attention of the brawlers."

During that period of time, priests were held in high esteem by the members of their churches, therefore their appearance brought the riot to a temporary halt. Father Lucas shouted to the men, "It's time to stop the fighting and return to your homes. If anyone resumes the fighting, we will have him excommunicated from the church."

Father Brogan stepped forward. "I agree with Father Lucas. Enough is enough. Let the fighting stop once and for all. I want all the men from our parish to report to the Holy Family Club. I'll meet you there in ten minutes."

The riot was over. Within ten minutes the streets were cleared. Calmness and tranquility once again prevailed throughout the community.

It was the first and only time open warfare erupted between the competing nationalities. When the Great Depression overwhelmed the nation in 1929, the ethnic differences were of secondary priority. They would never again reach the apex of hatred and violence that was attained during the summer of 1929.

After the initial trauma of the Depression had worn off, many changes took place in the borough. The unemployment rate was one of the highest in the country; most of the mines were closed and had little or no chance of ever reopening. The alternative for many residents was to go to the large cities or areas where manufacturing offered a better opportunity to secure a job and support a family. Many of the Irish families moved to Philadelphia, while the Lithuanians went in the direction of New Jersey or New England. In any case they wanted a new life, new jobs and a new environment.

After the riot of 1929, there still existed an undercurrent of mistrust and jealousy between the two groups. At the conclusion of World War II, the ethnic violence and petty jealousies finally came to an end. There were intermarriages, the two Catholic schools merged into one, and there was a deeper understanding between the two cultures.

World War II united the country as never before. The people no longer identified themselves as Lithuanians, Irish, English or Welsh. They were Americans!

15 Summertime

Summer was the greatest season of the year for the young. School ended on May 12. From that day until the day after Labor Day it seemed as though someone had opened the doors of heaven and invited me and my friends in for a short stay.

I remember the day school was dismissed for one summer. I had just completed the fourth grade and everyone was anxiously awaiting the dismissal bell signaling the beginning of our summer vacation. It seemed like an eternity until the bell sounded.

We filed out the door by twos, down the four steps to the pavement and it was over. The summer had begun! It was ten o'clock in the morning, the sun was peeking through beautiful puffy white clouds, and it was going to be a great day for swimming.

I ran up Clay Street as though I was competing in the one hundred meter dash in the Olympics. I made a left turn at McGoverns and within seconds I was running up the steps leading to a second-floor concrete landing and the side door into our kitchen. At that point, I slowed my pace to a quick walk, entered the dining room and proceeded to the third floor and into my room. It took me a few minutes to change clothes, grab my swimming suit and a towel and I was off to Alex Creek, our swimming hole.

Alex Creek was a small stream which wound its way down from the mountain towering over the southern end of town. The men in the community had built a breast across the stream to form our swimming pool for the summer. Its appearance wasn't that of an Olympic pool but it provided youngsters a safe and refreshing place to swim. It was three feet deep at its deepest point, twenty feet wide and thirty feet long, an ideal swimming hole for kids from three to ten years.

I remember racing past the railroad station, and when I was within one hundred yards of the swimming hole I thought, "This must be the greatest day of my life. Nothing will ever be better than this. It's the last day of school, I have the entire summer off, and I'm ready to jump into Alex Creek. This has to be heaven!" We swam in Alex Creek until we were in the fifth grade, at which time the breast of the dam broke, never to be repaired.

The summer meant great freedom, doing whatever pleased us, playing baseball, swimming, roaming the street, taking a bath once a week on Saturday night, staying out until nine o'clock every night, and best of all there was no homework.

"Gang" was a favorite word in the vocabulary of young people in the coal region. When a group of youngsters, usually classmates or members of the same age group, played together or spent time participating in other activities, they were known as a "gang." When they reached high school, most members veered in different directions, both socially and athletically, thus bringing an end to the gang era.

Our gang consisted of Mickey Doyle, Jessie Whalen, Tata Foley, Alex Pautenius, Francis Kollessor, Slim and Eddie Berrang and Brother Feeley. Every gang had an enforcer. We had Mickey Doyle! He backed down from no one and was always ready and willing to engage anyone in a fight.

When it came to bravery and guts, Eddie Berrang and Alex Pautenius feared nothing. We defended our territory on Kimber Street and our most hated adversaries were the Lithuanians, better known as Brollies.

We hated them with a passion! We believed them to be dumb, dirty and untrustworthy. Their food was from the old country and we wanted no part of their smelly and greasy eats. Why couldn't they eat meat and potatoes like the rest of us

Americans? We were in numerous stone-throwing encounters with them on Clay Street; however, we must have been terrible marksmen because I never heard of anyone being hit with a rock.

We always knew the summer was in full swing when John and Mary Monahan arrived from Philadelphia to spend the summer with their grandmother, Mrs. McGee, who lived on Water Street. Another Philadelphia contingent also arrived on the scene, Betty, Dave and Bill Scanlon, who spent the summer with their first cousins the O'Neils, who lived in the patch. Mary and Frank O'Neil were second cousins to my mother. Betty Scanlon of Philadelphia and Mary O'Neil were sisters. Each summer, one of the Scanlon children came to New Phillie to spend the summer with the O'Neils. Dave was the first to venture into the coal regions, followed by Betty and finally Bill.

Dave recalls an experience that involved Frank O'Neil, Johnnie Serafin and himself. "We were walking up Valley Street about nine o'clock on a balmy evening in mid-July. As we approached the Feeley residence, Johnnie thought it would be a good idea if we sneaked into the backyard and stole a few apples. At the age of twelve we had little trouble getting over the six-foot fence.

"When we were underneath the tree Frank offered a suggestion: 'I'll climb the tree and throw the apples down to you guys.'

"'OK, Frank, we'll give ya a boost up the tree.'

"Frank had thrown about three apples to Johnnie when a shotgun blast coming from the direction of the Feeley residence knocked him out of the tree. He landed a few feet from where we were standing. When Johnnie saw Frank hit the ground, he vaulted the fence and ran toward Stein's corner."

I was standing with a group of fellows as Johnnie came running up the street. "Doc Kenna just shot Frank O'Neil. Come on, we need some help." Everyone ran toward Feeleys' backyard. By the time we arrived on the scene, Doc Kenna and Dave had lifted Frank's limp body next to Doc's car.

I can't remember seeing a man as excited and nervous as was Doc Kenna. "Where do you want to go, O'Neil, I'll take you to any doctor you want."

Frank was still conscious and lying face down. "Take me to Dr. Boord."

We lifted Frank into the back of the car. Johnnie and Dave jumped in the front seat and I stayed in the back with Frank. Doc Kenna turned the car around and sped out of the driveway. We arrived at Dr. Boord's office within two minutes. It was only three blocks away. We carried him into the doctor's office and laid him on his stomach in the middle of the floor.

Dr. Boord removed Frank's shirt and pants. The sight we saw was unbelievable. He was hit with nearly the full load of shot, his upper legs and backside were a mass of holes the size of the pellets and were covered with blood.

The doctor knelt beside Frank, and after observing him for a few minutes looked up. "We had better get this boy to the hospital. We'll use my car."

Johnnie, Dave and I joined the doctor as we drove to the Good Samaritan Hospital in Pottsville; Doc Kenna remained in New Phillie. Frank survived the ordeal, and after a few months Doc Kenna made peace with the O'Neil family and all was forgiven, but never forgotten.

Bill Scanlon recounts his visits to the O'Neil family. "When I came to visit my cousins, during the thirties, my Aunt Mary worked on the WPA as a piano teacher. The lessons were free and available to anyone who wished to take lessons. She taught her students at the public school, which was a three-minute walk from her home.

"She was the organist at the Holy Family church for thirty-five years. A remarkable woman, she was loved by everyone and I never heard her say a bad word about anyone. She died in 1965.

"Uncle Frank had worked in the mines at Kaska and hadn't had a job since the Depression began in 1929. The second week of my stay was set aside to bring in the winter's supply of coal.

We traveled to the 'shoe fly,' located about a half a mile south of New Phillie, just off Route 209."

(The area had huge culm banks containing millions of tons of refuse which remained after the coal was sized and made ready for shipment to the customers. Coal was in abundance, therefore the coal companies weren't too concerned as to how much coal was wasted and hauled to the culm banks. Over the years, millions upon millions of tons of coal were deposited in the banks. Years later, during the sixties and seventies when coal became too costly to mine, the culm banks were once again "run through" the coal breakers and large quantities of coal were reclaimed.)

"Each morning Uncle Frank, Eddie, Frank and I piled into his Ford car and headed for the coal banks. We placed a large steel screen on the ground in an upright position and shoveled the culm onto the screen. The dirt fell through the screen and the coal and slate dropped to the bottom of the screen.

"After removing the slate, we packed the coal into large burlap bags and loaded them into the trunk of the car. Each day we transported ten bags which were dumped into the coal bins in the cellar of the O'Neil home. We continued our treks to the coal banks until all the bins were filled.

"During the summer of 1939, Frank, better known as 'Bucko,' was one of the stars on the Blythe Township football team. During the 1939 football season Blythe captured the state title by beating Clearfield High School 12 to 0. Bucko was one of the leaders of the team. He played linebacker on defense and tackle on offense. He was the typical good 'coal cracker' football player; tough, mean and aggressive. He was one hell of a football player!

"During that particular summer, Bucko and his buddies played in a baseball league composed of teams from the nearby towns. After each game, win or lose, Bucko went to a bar to celebrate. Each year the favorite bar changed, for what reason I don't know. It was either John Callery's, Van Alexander's, Mono Pretti's or Patrick Kelly's.

"Frank was eighteen years old and I was fifteen, but I was big for my age. When we walked into the bar everyone made a great fuss over Bucko. 'Ya played a great game, Bucko, step up to the bar and have a drink, and how about yer friend?'

"'Yeah, he's my cousin, he kin handle a beer.'

"Bucko gave the bartender the wink and all was OK. I was smart enough to keep my mouth shut and drink the beer. Before we made our exit, I had at least five beers and Bucko might have had a few extras.

"Sunday mornings were special. Frank, Skip Schneider and I made a practice of attending the nine o'clock mass. At the conclusion of the service we proceeded to Mono Pretti's bar, located one block from the O'Neil home, where we socialized for about a half hour. During that time we consumed about five beers, after which we went home and had a hearty coal cracker breakfast. Yes, Sunday was a special day!"

Skip Schneider was one of Bucko's best friends. He was the young man who joined the army in 1942 weighing 115 pounds. When he arrived home on furlough one year later weighing 230 and rapped on his mother's door at 2 a.m. she didn't recognize him and was ready to throw him off the front porch, thinking him to be a drunken soldier.

"Mom, don't ya recognize me? I'm your son Thomas." Skip is now retired and has a part-time job as a starter at one of the local golf courses. He still weighs 230 pounds.

Bill Scanlon says, "During my vacations at O'Neils we always ate good. An abundance of stews, mashed potatoes, homemade bread and cakes. Aunt Mary baked bread every second day, and since she was working, Uncle Frank and the boys did all the household chores.

"Eddie and Frank were always well dressed; comfortable clothes, shoes and jackets. My father was a corporate lawyer; however, he had a heart attack in 1935. In those days such things as unemployment compensation were not available as they are in today's economic structure. The only thing that could possibly save you from economic ruin was to fall back on your savings, if you were fortunate enough to have accumulated any.

"Another avenue of survival was to go on relief, receiving such necessities of life as bread, flour, cheese and butter from the government. My mother and dad were too proud to go on relief. We lived in a beautiful home on 65th Street which my dad had to sell. He rented a comfortable home on Wynnewood Avenue, where we remained until his retirement.

"One year later my father had recovered sufficiently to obtain a job with the Transit System of Philadelphia. The work load wasn't as trying as that of a corporate lawyer, enabling him to continue working until he retired in 1960.

"During the winter, the O'Neils would visit us in Philadelphia. When they walked in, Eddie and Frank were dressed in the best of jackets, pants and shoes. They always brought new jackets, shoes, pants, underwear and socks for me and my brothers.

"My mother dressed the girls, that was her domain. It was all right for the boys to wear hand-me-downs, but not the girls. They were well dressed at all times. Among the children, no questions were ever asked as to where the clothing came from. 'Don't ask questions, just drink the beer and shut your mouth!'

"I often wondered how people who were working on the WPA could ever afford to secure such clothing and help our family. The answer: they knew someone, who knew someone, who knew someone. It's strange, many people believed it was the Scanlons who were helping the O'Neils during the Depression. However, it was the other way around. Those things you never forget!"

Any boy who lived in New Phillie swam in Cats, which was located about one quarter of a mile east of town along the railroad tracks. Every afternoon at 1:30 we made our way to Cats. When we reached the railroad tracks at the movie theater, as though it was written into the script, we inevitably met a group of Lithuanians about our age coming from Cats.

Someone in our gang, usually Slim Berrang, asked them how the water was. "Here come the Brollies, Slim, ask them how's the water."

As they came abreast of our group everyone was quiet. Neither side wanted any conversation, friendly gesture or greeting, which might denote a sign of weakness.

"How's the water taday?" Whoever their spokesman happened to be always gave the same answer.

"It's werm as piss!"

It was an inside joke and we always looked forward to the meeting. We could hardly wait until they got out of earshot before we broke into laughter. Tata Foley always had a comment, "Werm as piss, them Brollies really break me up. Ain't they ever gonna learn how ta talk."

Alex responded, "Them dumb bastards will never learn!"

At Cats no one was allowed to wear a bathing suit, it was strictly B.A.B., "bare ass beach." The Irish undressed and entered the swimming area on the southern side, the Lithuanians used the northern side. We swam at Cats for nearly six years and never set foot on the north side. It was an unwritten law and neither group ever transgressed the other's territory.

Cats was some swimming hole. It measured about sixty feet from one side to the other. The bottom was composed of light brown and yellowish clay and the water was never clear. But to us, it was like swimming in a modern Olympic pool. It was cold and refreshing, which made the hot summer afternoons a bit more pleasant.

16 *Pies and the Bakery Truck*

One evening, a group of us were sitting on Feeleys' porch as a light drizzle was falling. It was one of those extremely dark and miserable nights, with the temperature in the low seventies. It wasn't a pleasant night to be out, but at least we were under roof and not exposed to the rain.

The Berrang brothers, Tata, Alex, Mickey Doyle and I were sitting around talking about nothing in particular when Slim's voice piped above the others.

"Boy, am I hungry. Where kin we get somethin' ta eat?"

Alex made an observation, "Ya know, I've been watchin' the baker's truck fer the last few weeks. The driver has the truck loaded with bread, pies and cakes fer the next day's delivery, and he parks it in Kelly's garage every night. Maybe, if we're lucky, we kin swipe a few pies. What do ya think?"

It didn't take us long to make up our minds; within seconds we were running toward Kelly's garage a block and a half away. We cut across the public square and approached the garage from the back, along the creek. It was a perfect night to steal something, especially a few pies. It was raining and was pitch dark, and a very important point to remember: we knew the territory!

It was a four-car garage with two large folding doors, which could be pulled apart at the top, making it possible to enter the garage from that point. There was never any doubt as to who would go after the pies. It was either Alex or Eddie. Alex was chosen because he was small and could fit through the top of the doors more easily than could Eddie.

Alex climbed on Slim's shoulders and I climbed on Eddie's shoulders, I pulled the doors apart and Alex slipped into the garage. The truck was open and within seconds he handed us four large pies. He then made his way out the side door and we were off and running toward the railroad station.

We made our way underneath the platform where the freight was unloaded and enjoyed our ill-gotten goods. The pies were delicious. We pulled this caper twice and then decided we had better quit while we were ahead.

Alex was the philosopher, thinker and observer of the group. A few weeks later we were once again holding forth on Feeleys' porch. Alex made a suggestion: "Ya know, every night there's a bakery truck that comes down the public hill at nine o'clock, and he goes like a bat outta hell as he heads fer home. I think it would be fun ta see his face if we stoned his truck."

"I bet he'd shit a brick," retorted Tata. "Let's go up and see how fast he comes down the hill."

Within a short time we gathered at the top of Quality Hill, next to Prettis' porch. It was in this area that we did our sleigh riding during the winter months. The hill was steep and you had to round a slight curve before entering the steep part of the incline.

Standing between our house and the top of the hill was the home of Chris and Momma Schultz. There were no street lights in the area, therefore it was the ideal spot to execute our plan.

Alex explained the details, which we decided to put into effect the following night. "After we stone the truck, we'll go through Prettis' yard, down the alley and into Canfields' yard. We'll be there in ten seconds, nobody in the world can stop a truck that fast and find us."

Alex's observation and details were correct. At exactly nine o'clock the dark-painted bakery truck rounded the corner at a high rate of speed. Slim yelled, "Look at that son of a bitch go. Won't he be surprised tamorra night!"

By 8:45 the next night we were in position and ready for the arrival of the unsuspecting truck driver. We each had two medium-sized rocks, which was more than enough ammunition for the exercise as we had no more than two or three seconds to throw them.

Alex gave his final bit of advice: "Fer Christ sake, don't hit the truck driver, or we'll really be in trouble. Remember, don't hit the driver!"

Francis Kollessor, our chosen lookout, came running into the group. "He'll be here in a few seconds."

As it rounded the corner and approached the target area everyone zeroed in on the fast-moving truck. Most of the rocks found their marks, resulting in a sound like a sudden burst of artillery fire. The truck driver must have thought he was in the middle of a gang war in Chicago. We gleefully watched as he struggled to maintain control of the vehicle. He brought it to a screeching halt in front of Reagan's barber shop. The furious driver bolted out of the truck and started to run toward Prettis' house.

We had planned our retreat well. By the time he was out of the truck, we moved to our designated safety zone alongside the fence in our backyard. The loud noise and screeching brakes had aroused the neighbors, including my mother and father, Mr. and Mrs. Schultz, Lottie Pretti and Dr. Flanagan.

We could hear the truck driver talking to Lottie Pretti. "If I ever get my hands on those kids who threw the rocks, I'll have them jailed. They could have killed me."

Lottie tried to console the angry young man. "I agree with you, these kids of taday have no respect for anything. I don't know what's happening to the world. They'll all land in jail some day, mark my word. It was probably those Lithuanian kids; they're a terrible bunch."

Within a few minutes the driver was on his way, vowing to bring to justice those unruly and disruptive hoodlums.

At our next think tank session on Feeleys' porch, Alex made his final report on the truck caper. "The bakery truck driver has taken a new and safer route to his home base. The gossip in town has reported the Lithuanian kids did it. Them Brollie kids are a bad lot."

We were in unanimous agreement. "The Brollies did it!"

The years 1932 and 1933 brought us many exciting and pleasurable days. We weren't dwelling on the fact that when we graduated from the eighth grade our youthful and carefree days were coming to an end. When we entered high school, the days of the gang and our close association with our buddies would become a memory.

During the thirties the young men of the town traveled to Pottsville to attend the dances at Charlton Hall. The admission price was eleven cents, and they enjoyed dancing to the music of a ten-piece orchestra. The crowd usually numbered about four hundred. Everyone dressed in his Sunday best, as though he wanted to make a good impression on every girl in attendance.

The Irish gathered at Pete Worster's and Gummy's pool rooms on Valley Street, where they tossed dice and played cards before making the trip to Pottsville. The Lithuanian contingent gathered at Josh's pool room on Clay Street, where they enjoyed the same recreational activities.

At this particular time of our lives, we weren't interested in girls, we were just intent upon disrupting the lives of our hated foes. One Saturday night, with three inches of snow on the ground and more falling, we decided we would pay a visit to the crap game at Josh's.

Tata, Slim, Eddie, Alex and I entered the backyard and crept within ten yards of the back door, which was located in the center of the card room. There were as many as twenty young men crowded around the table, all dressed in their finest attire.

We each had two large well-rounded snowballs ready to throw into the room. Slowly, Alex crawled toward the door, like a cat approaching an unsuspecting prey. He threw open the door and we hurled the snowballs into the midst of the card game.

What followed was utter chaos. The young men never knew what hit them. Who would ever dream that they would be hit by a barrage of snowballs while playing cards?

By the time they had recovered from the shock, we were well on our way down the back alley, and within minutes we were in Berrangs' backyard and safety. We knew every inch of the alleys and yards, so the darkness, instead of being a hindrance, was our greatest ally.

17 The Railroad Cars

We were sitting on a grassy knoll outside the Holy Family cemetery, which overlooked the town from the south. It was a typical summer evening in July and the time was about seven o'clock. The sun was beginning to set in the west and a soft summer breeze softly blew across the knoll.

From our vantage point, we could observe six large freight cars sitting on a railroad siding. The cars would be loaded the next morning with coal from the strip-mining pits. The coal from the strippings was hauled by trucks to a large chute and dumped into the cars.

Later that evening, the cars which were already loaded with coal and parked on the tracks near the railroad station would be moved to the coal breakers. There the coal would be sized and washed before being shipped to the docks in Philadelphia for shipment overseas.

Slim, Eddie, Mickey, Jessie, Tata, Alex and I were lying on the grass, engaged in small talk and passing time. We noticed my brother Butts, Pickles Pretti, Chipper Connelly, Mooney Finley and Huck Doyle were gathered in a group at the end of the cars. They appeared to be having a discussion concerning the wheels. Huck and Butts had a large dark piece of steel about four feet high which they were placing behind a rear wheel.

All of a sudden the empty cars began to move, slowly, ever so slowly until they reached the stretch of tracks which was downgrade, at approximately a five-degree pitch. The cars gathered speed until there were six runaway cars, out of control and on their way to the bottom of the grade. Sitting in front of the railroad station were six cars loaded with coal.

As the empty cars sped down the incline heading for the inevitable crash, we began to yell and scream. Butts and his pals couldn't do a thing to stop the runaway cars, and they began running toward us on the middle of the knoll.

The empty cars gathered speed. Then came the crash. When the cars collided, the noise could be heard all over the lower section of town. How the empty cars stayed on the tracks without overturning, I'll never know. Many curious people from Valley Street came streaming across the bridge leading to the railroad station to see what had happened.

The stationmaster came running, trying to determine how the runaway cars were started on their way. "The cars could not possibly have started by themselves. There is a large steel plate in front of the first car which won't permit the cars to move. Someone had to tamper with the cars! You can be sure we'll find the culprits."

When the cars collided we were on our way through the cemetery and back to Kimber Street. No one would ever be able to verify that we were anywhere near the scene. Butts and his pals made their way to Gummy's pool hall to set up their alibis.

About a week later, on a Saturday morning, Butts and I had just gotten out of bed. The time was 8:30. We heard a knock on the side door.

Butts bolted to the window to see who was knocking and began to yell, "Jesus Christ, it's Duffy."

Quickly I joined him at the window. "Who's Duffy?"

"You dumb bastard, he's the coal and iron cop, and he works for the railroad. He must be here about the coal cars!"

Duffy was a huge man in his late fifties, six feet tall and built like a moving van. He worked most of his life for the Reading Railroad, riding the trains and walking the tracks. His most distinctive physical trait was his pronounced bowed legs. He could be identified from two hundred yards' distance because of his legs.

My father and Duffy were good friends. They had known each other since they were young men and often traveled to the pigeon matches together. They talked for about twenty minutes before Duffy made his departure.

When Butts and I entered the kitchen, we were greeted by my father. "Mr. Duffy knows all about the railroad cars and has the names of all the boys who took part. You were seen running through the cemetery after the crash. I want you both to get in touch with your friends and have them meet me in my office at six o'clock tonight. If anyone misses the meeting, Mr. Duffy says he will put them in jail. Do you understand?"

Butts answered in a subdued voice, "Yes, Pop, we'll all be there."

On Sunday night we were sitting on the curb in front of McGoverns. Lottie Pretti walked by and stopped to observe the group. "I understand you're all jailbirds. What sentence did you receive?"

Alex was the spokesman: "We were fined two dollars each and we can't walk on the railroad tracks fer a year. That means we can't go swimming at Cats."

"My, my, my. Isn't that too bad! Maybe you'll try and be good boys in the future. Good night, boys."

Alex answered for the group, "Good night, Mrs. Pretti."

After she had gotten out of hearing range Tata spoke: "What the hell's she so high and mighty about? Her son Pickles was the one who started the damned cars rollin'. She has a hell of a nerve ta talk ta us like that."

We stayed off the tracks for two weeks, after which we made a decision. Eddie Berrang was the spokesman. "If that son of a bitch Duffy thinks he's gonna keep us off the tracks and swimmin' in Cats, he's nuts. Tamorra, we're goin' ta Cats!"

Everyone gave their approval except Jessie Whalen. "I can't go. My father told me if I walked on the tracks, he'd kill me, so I'm not goin'." Jessie took the death threat seriously, he didn't swim in Cats or walk on the tracks for a year.

18 School Days at Holy Family

I entered Holy Family Elementary School in September 1925 and graduated from the eighth grade in May of 1933. We were taught by the Sisters of Mercy, whose headquarters and mother house was in Dallas, Pennsylvania.

From the moment we enrolled, we were consumed by the influence of the school, the nuns and the church. Those were the days when the Catholic Church rules were strict and absolute: no meat on Fridays, confession once a week, missing mass was a mortal sin. There was dedication to the saints, and the rosary was recited in most Catholic homes. The priests were a step closer to heaven than the rest of the flock. They were respected and idolized. The nuns were on a pedestal and their words of wisdom and insight were spoken as though they came from the Virgin Mary herself.

Our lives and activities revolved around the church and school, which included grades one through eight. At the time of graduation, the students had the option of attending St. Stephen's High School in Port Carbon or Blythe Township High School, which was located a few hundred yards northwest of New Philadelphia. Most students chose Blythe, which had great facilities and an excellent faculty. As an added incentive, the school produced outstanding football teams.

When we reached fifth grade, most of the young men became altar boys. Our service as altar boys continued until we graduated from high school. Our days at Holy Family were carefree, happy, and the education was excellent.

The nuns ruled the classroom with an iron hand! If anyone broke the rules or misbehaved in class he paid the penalty, which at times was severe. Anyone who attended a Catholic school remembers the reaction of the nuns if the boys misbehaved. The boys were lined up in the front of the room, then held out their hands and received a whack with a ruler or the long blackboard pointer across the open palm. Ouch, I can still feel the pain! They ruled our lives in a most rigid and disciplined manner, but at the same time showed much love, understanding and guidance.

During our year in fourth grade, my friend Tata was almost excommunicated from the church because of a remark he made when answering a religious question. The catechism lesson began each morning at nine o'clock. Sister Benedict was conducting class as usual, asking each student a question and giving a dissertation after each response. She stood a few feet in front of Tata and posed a question, "David, who made the world?"

Tata stood up and answered in a firm voice, "Mrs. Liptock." Before he could blink an eye, Sister Benedict hit him with a right cross, reminiscent of Jack Dempsey, knocking him to the floor.

"Young man, I'm reporting you to Father Ward for that remark and I'll see that you're expelled from school. Wait until Sister Gervaise hears about this."

Tata survived the ordeal because Sister Gervaise was in a forgiving mood. He wasn't expelled or excommunicated but was reprimanded and denied recess for one week.

We were playing in the playground one morning when Alex came running toward us. He was very excited as he gathered us in a circle. Jessie Whalen touched him on the shoulder: "What's wrong, Alex, why are ya so excited?"

Alex lowered his head and pointed to the left side of the playground. "See that guy over there talkin' ta Huck Doyle? That's Geeser McGee! He's the guy who hit Sister Gervaise and broke her glasses. He was expelled, but he came back ta school taday."

We couldn't believe what we were hearing. No one ever hits a nun. That's a mortal sin!

Mickey Doyle spoke as if in a daze. "When ya hit a Sister, you'll go straight ta hell. Geeser will burn in hell, ya kin be sure of that."

"Yeah, he'll go straight ta hell," replied Jessie.

Geeser graduated from the eighth grade and entered Blythe. He would always have the unsavory distinction of being the only student who ever struck a nun.

During the years of fourth and fifth grades, the most exciting and thrilling day on the school calendar was Holy Thursday. As youngsters we looked forward to this holy day. It was the day on which the student body, as well as most of the parish members, participated in the church procession. Very few people worked on Holy Thursday or Good Friday, so the church was filled to capacity.

The country was in the early stages of the Great Depression; therefore, the church took on a new and more meaningful image. It was a place of refuge and hope for the future. Attendance at mass and special services, such as Holy Thursday and Good Friday, was overflowing.

The student body assembled in their classrooms at 8 a.m. The girls were dressed in white and carried a bouquet of freshly picked flowers. The boys wore dark pants and white shirts. The eighth grade girls chose one of their classmates to be queen of the procession. Her reward for being chosen queen was the honor of crowning the Blessed Mother at the conclusion of the procession.

It was a tradition that Patrick Kelly, Michael John Kelly, Owen Crosby and my father carried the canopy, under which the pastor and his assistants walked as they carried the Blessed Sacrament throughout the church.

It was a solemn occasion, and one of the highlights of the Easter season. The services were concluded by ten o'clock and the rest of the day was devoted to enjoyment and relaxation.

During the seventh and eighth grades we were closely associated with the church as altar boys. Special services such as funerals and weddings were handled by the elite corps of altar boys. The group included Happy Berrang, Eddie O'Neil, Alex Pautenius, Francis Kollessor and myself.

Funerals were our top priority. We reported directly to the church and arrived back at school at 10:30 a.m. Because of our participation in church services, we knew every nook and cranny of the church. It placed us in a favorable position to do things that weren't always "kosher."

Holy Family Orchestra, 1931. Front row, left to right: Frank "Bucko" O'Neil, Patrick Canfield, Robert "Butts" Canfield, Edwin Selesky, Pat Catulla, Anna Mae Churnis. Second row: Pat O'Neil, Jerome McNeilis, Andy Ferrance, Adolph Bonenberger, Vernon Melavage, John Kelly, Peggy Reagan. Third row: Betty Leonard, John Konnya, Joe Rompolo, Bill McNeilis, Agnes Reagan. Sister Helen Marie, conductor.

19 Pigeon Business and the Church

Alex Pautenius accompanied me to a pigeon match with my father one Sunday afternoon in early June. We were both impressed and especially enjoyed the excitement of watching the men make bets along the sidelines and the trappers place the birds in the trap.

Eddie Canfield, my first cousin, had brought about ten birds to the match and was engaged as a trapper for one of the shooters. Alex and I watched him very carefully as he prepared one of the birds prior to putting it in the trap.

"Hey Eddie, kin Alex and me come up ta yer house and see your pigeons sometime next week?"

Eddie was a man of very few words, especially when he was working the traps. "Sure, come up on Tuesday about ten o'clock."

Alex and I were thrilled. "Alex, maybe we kin buy a few birds and get into the pigeon business."

"That sounds great! Wait till we tell Slim and Eddie. Maybe my father will let us keep the pigeons in our barn. I'll bet he will!"

Early Monday morning, Alex and I met Slim and Eddie in front of the church. Alex could hardly wait to break the news about our new venture.

"We're gonna get in the pigeon business. Eddie Canfield, from Silver Creek, might sell us some birds. We're supposed ta see him tamorra at ten o'clock. Do you guys wanta come?"

"Sure, why not? Eddie and me like pigeons, don't we Eddie?"

"We sure do, we often watch them at Pete Marchetti's pens."

"OK, it's all set. We'll meet here at nine o'clock tamorra and walk up ta Eddie's place."

We started our trek to Silver Creek, which was situated one mile north of New Phillie. The most direct route was to travel up Water Street, walk through Valley Furnace and into Silver Creek. To local residents it was known as the Creek.

We weren't too keen at the thought of walking the length of Water Street. Those Brollies might be up early and maybe it wouldn't be too safe to be found in that section of town. Why take a chance of getting our heads broken? After thinking it over, we decided to take a detour.

We walked up to the high school, down over the hill, and entered Valley Furnace, better known as the Furnace, thus by-passing Water Street.

Silver Creek was a small mining town with about twenty-five houses. It hadn't changed its appearance in over fifty years. The Derrs lived in the first house and the Bernitskys lived in the last home at the edge of town. Everyone had a dog, therefore it was essential and wise that we walk in the middle of the road as we proceeded through the "business" district.

The Canfields lived in the center of town. I remembered the house, because I had attended my Uncle Ned's funeral a year earlier. Eddie had four hundred pigeons housed in the pens behind the house.

He retrieved two birds from the pens. "Here, take a look at the birds. Be careful ya don't hold them too tight, ya might hurt their feet or wings."

Alex and Slim took the birds and stroked their heads and backs in a gentle manner.

Slim looked at Eddie. "How much will ya charge us if we buy five birds?"

"That'll cost ya fifteen cents apiece. But don't forget, ya have ta buy them some feed and that costs money."

"Yeah, we know," Slim retorted. "We'll take five."

When the transaction was completed, we walked back to New Phillie as entrepreneurs. We were now in the pigeon business. We made our way to Alex's house and placed the birds in the barn. It was decided we each had to pay fifteen cents a week for the upkeep of the pigeons. Alex took upon himself the responsibility of feeding and watering the birds each day.

That evening we were seated on Feeleys' porch when Slim made a keen observation. "Do ya ever notice all the pigeons that perch on the church steeple? They crawl through the openings at night and sleep inside the bell tower."

Alex jumped to his feet. "You're right, Slim. All we have ta do is hide in the steeple and stay up there until Eddie Deem locks the church. Trapping them birds will be easy and it's a good way ta get more birds fer our flock. Why don't we give it a try tamorra night?" All were in agreement, tomorrow night we would become night stalkers and hawkers!

Eddie Deem was the sexton of the church. He was twenty-six years old and a good friend of my brother John. They were in the same class throughout their school careers. He was a good-looking and soft-spoken man, and never seemed to get angry or upset about any of our actions around the church. As altar boys we liked him. He was never nasty and always treated us well as we went about our duties.

Jobs were hard to come by, and anyone who had a source of income was considered lucky. Like so many young men of his age, he was looking forward to better days when he could secure a better position. We never underestimated our adversaries. Eddie was wise, sharp and probably smart, but not as smart as the members of our pigeon association.

The bells were rung each evening at six and seven o'clock, after which the church was locked for the night. We entered the church at 6:30 and made our way to the choir loft. We then climbed a thirty-foot ladder which led to the steeple and loft where the bell was located.

When we reached the top of the ladder, we had to slide aside a heavy two-foot-square, tightly fitted trap door. We moved it about one foot, giving us just enough room to make our entrance into the loft. The loft was approximately ten feet square and ten feet high. The four sides came together as an apex on the roof on which a large cross sat atop the church tower.

About five minutes before the bell rang we prostrated ourselves on the floor and remained as quiet as the proverbial church mouse. We didn't move a muscle! Maybe because of the excitement of being in the tower and the thought of being brought up on charges of breaking and entering, my breathing seemed to be extremely heavy and loud.

Precisely at seven o'clock, the bell would be struck seven times at intervals of five seconds. I will never forget the first time I heard the bell sound. I was lying about one foot away from the bell, which was mounted on a sturdy wooden structure of heavy oak. It was strong enough to hold three such bells.

As the first note was struck, I thought I would die. "Holy Christ, I never heard such a loud noise in all my life; we must be crazy to be up here." I placed my hands over my ears and painfully endured the next six tolls of the great bell.

At the conclusion of the concert of the bells, we didn't move a muscle. It would take Eddie about five minutes to check the doors and lock the windows before making his exit.

About five minutes later, the trap door began moving back and Eddie made his appearance in the loft. He didn't say a word until he righted himself. He put his hands on his hips and pointed his finger at the night raiders.

"OK, climb down the ladder and get outta the church." Once again he pointed his finger toward the choir loft. No one said a word as we made our way down the ladder, ran out into the street and ran to the safety of Feeleys' porch.

We were dumbstruck, bewildered and embarrassed. Slim was the first to break the silence. "How the hell did he know we were up there? We didn't make any noise and I'm sure he didn't see us enter the church."

"He was lucky, that's what he was, just damned lucky," responded Eddie. "We'll give it another try tamorra night, and see if he'll be lucky again."

We made three more attempts at trying to outsmart the streetwise sexton, but to no avail. All forays to the loft had the same finale. Alex made the final evaluation of our futile endeavors. "He's just too damned smart fer us. That bastard knows somethin' that we don't know!"

On our last invasion of the loft Eddie issued a final warning. "If I catch you guys up here one more time, I'll have to report you to Father Ward."

Being reported to the pastor, Father Ward, was like being reported to Al Capone for making a move on the mob. We would be blacklisted for the rest of our lives, dismissed as altar boys and condemned to spend much time in purgatory. Alex played out the scene like James Cagney in one of his gangster movies. "Please, Eddie, don't report us ta Father Ward. You'll never see us up here again. Ya have our word!"

Eddie seemed impressed with the sincerity of Alex's plea. "OK, but remember, if I catch you guys up here again it's up in front of Father Ward."

We were crushed because Eddie was stymying our efforts to increase our pigeon flock. There had to be a way to get into the loft undetected.

If anyone was capable of solving our problem it was Alex. He had all the qualities of a person who should belong to Al Capone's mob in Chicago. Whenever we discussed methods of dealing with the Brollies or any of our other adventures, it was Alex who came up with the solutions. When he was in deep thought and ready to submit an idea, he turned his head slightly to the left, closed his left eye and spoke softly and mean, as if he were on a movie set.

A few nights later we met on Feeleys' porch and as expected Alex brought forth his solution to our problem. "I don't think that son of a bitch kin outsmart us ferever. We're gonna try somethin' new on that bastard. Why don't we hide in the confession boxes and after he closes the church, we'll go up ta the tower and ketch the pigeons."

Eddie was the first to respond. "It sounds like a good idea if we kin pull it off, but if it fails we would probably be on Deemie's shit list forever."

I lifted my head as if I had seen a troubling vision. "Yeah, but how about Father Ward?"

Slim snapped, "Ah Sample, you worry too much. Balls on Father Ward, let's get the pigeons!" Slim's remark set the tone for the evening. Ol' Eddie Deem was in for a big surprise.

We arrived at the church at 6:30 p.m. Slim and I settled ourselves in one confessional, Eddie and Alex in the other. At precisely one minute before seven, Deemie started up the steps and waited for the magic number on his timepiece. After the bells had been rung, he descended the steps and performed the methodical task of shutting the windows and locking the doors.

After a wait of five minutes, we made our way to the tower and awaited the arrival of our most coveted ally, darkness. When darkness had engulfed the tower we began our task of capturing the pigeons. It was a simple matter. We climbed to the top of the enclosure where the top of the roof began to pitch toward the apex. At that point, there was an area about a foot wide where the pigeons were nestled in a comfortable position. All we had to do was reach in and pick up the birds. Our first endeavor accounted for eight birds.

We couldn't carry too many birds because we had to climb down the thirty-foot ladder, and the last one to leave had to pull the trap door into its proper position. We had to be careful not to fall off the ladder or leave any traces of our illegal entry. We placed the birds in our shirts and carefully made our way down the ladder.

After three successful trips into the loft, we decided to terminate our quest for pigeons and quit while we were ahead. On this last trip to the church we were making our exit through the door in the sacristy which led to the garages in back of the church. As we reached the door to make our final exit, Eddie Berrang was leading the way. He turned around and faced us and held his right hand high in the air.

"Just a minute, I'll show ya something."

He went over to the cupboard, reached in and pulled out a bottle of wine. "Let's have a swig."

We each took a big gulp, after which Eddie returned the bottle to the cupboard. "That's a good way ta finish the job. Some day we'll all burn in hell, but fer now, ta hell with Father Ward and Deemie. Let's get the hell outta here!"

Everything was going as planned. We had twenty-nine birds and within a short time we could go to the matches and make some money. We met each morning at Berrangs, then proceeded to the barn to observe our beautiful pigeons. On one particular day we never made it to the barn. Alex met us in front of his house.

"Don't go to the barn, because the pigeons are gone. My father let them out taday. He said they were costin' him money, and they were noisy and dirty. He gave me the word. No more pigeons!"

Our great business venture was over because Mr. Pautenius was a practical man. The pigeons would have cost us money, which we didn't have. They certainly wouldn't have brought us a profit. Another thing, if we continued in our wicked ways we might go back to the church, drink more of the priests' wine, and we would be well on our way to hell and damnation.

As Alex sadly said, "My mother always says, 'Everything always works out for the best.' Maybe she's right!"

20 Music Lessons

On a beautiful day late in April, we were playing in front of the church after being dismissed from school. One of the boys who joined us in a game of tag was John Troutman, who was in fifth grade. As he was getting ready to join us, he placed a black case near the entrance to the church.

"What's in the case, John?"

"It's a cornet. Do ya wanta see it? I'm takin' music lessons from Sister Helen Marie. Ya can't start lessons until you're in the fifth grade, so if ya wanta start you'll have ta wait till next year."

John opened the case and lifted the silver-plated cornet, adjusted the mouthpiece and handed it to me.

"What a beautiful horn! Look at the little buttons on the valves. I think it's great."

I was fascinated with the instrument. When I arrived home for supper I ran into the kitchen as my mother was preparing the meal. "Mom, do ya think I can take cornet lessons off Sister Helen Marie next year? I just saw Johnnie Troutman's horn and it was beautiful."

"I didn't know you were interested in music. I never heard you talk about taking lessons. Your brothers all took lessons. I'll ask your father and see what he has to say."

My father bought me a trumpet at Malarky's music store in Pottsville for thirty dollars. It was silver-plated and it was the most beautiful horn in the entire world. I started my music lessons in September. Each student was given one lesson a week and was allowed to practice one half-hour a day during school. For me it was the happiest part of the day.

I studied with Sister Helen Marie until I graduated from the eighth grade, after which I continued my lessons under the tutelage of Elam Jenkins of Pottsville. He was an excellent teacher, but because of his abrupt manner and strict practice rules, he had few students. The lessons were scheduled for a half-hour. However, my lesson always lasted an hour. At times the lessons seemed like an eternity. He was a tough taskmaster, but also a great teacher.

One of the advantages of taking a lesson on Saturday morning was the treat that awaited me after the lesson. I went to the movies at the Capitol theater, Pottsville's best and most beautiful. The latest pictures were screened at the Capitol and I saw most of them. Shirley Temple, Deanna Durbin, Clark Gable and Sonya Henne were a few of the stars who were big box office attractions at that time, and they were my favorites.

While attending West Chester State Teacher's College, I studied for three years with Harold Rehrig of the Philadelphia Orchestra. During my final two years, I had the privilege of playing first trumpet in both the symphonic band and orchestra.

After my induction into the army, I was sent to Camp Wheeler, Georgia, where I took basic training in the infantry. We were informed that after twelve weeks of training we would be shipped to Africa as infantry replacements. Two weeks before the twelve-week cycle was completed, I was transferred to Wilmington, Delaware, to join the 692nd Army Air Force band. The band was under the direction of Walter Hendl, who had been the assistant conductor of the New York Philharmonic before his induction into the air force.

In 1944 the band landed in Europe as part of the 9th Air Force. At the conclusion of the war we were part of the occupation forces in Germany. Once our jazz band was playing a radio broadcast at the Red Cross in Heidelberg, and I noticed a young infantry soldier looking in my direction. He gave me a wave and indicated he wanted to see me.

After the broadcast, I approached the infantryman. His chest was adorned with numerous medals. He held out his hand. "Didn't you take basic training with me at Camp Wheeler?"

"I sure did! Your name is Robert Taylor and you're from Tennessee. I'll never forget you or your name. You had the bunk next to mine, Company C, 12th Battalion. Isn't that right?"

"You're right. You're the little coal cracker from Pennsylvania."

After a few minutes of reminiscing about our days at Wheeler, I asked him a question that had been on my mind for a few years. "What happened to you fellas after I left Wheeler?"

"Well, you remember that chicken shit lieutenant who used ta tell us we were goin' ta Africa? Well, he was right. We landed in Africa and we got shot ta hell. Only ten percent of the company came out alive. I'm lucky ta be here and you were lucky that you left when ya did."

Yes, I was lucky, all because I could play a horn. Little did I dream, the day I admired John Troutman's cornet in front of the church, that a series of events would unfold which probably saved my life fifteen years later.

My brother John was the oldest of the siblings. He was my senior by ten years, low-key, bright, and was the apple of my father's eye. He graduated from Bucknell University and then went to Georgetown University to earn a medical degree. He completed his internship at the Pottsville Hospital, and during the last years of his medical career he was head of orthopedic surgery at this hospital. He retired in 1983.

Brother Tom, the most handsome of the four boys, should have been born rich. He loved life and was the eternal optimist. At family gatherings, he was the life of the party. It was a family understanding that whenever Tom started to whistle, it was time to leave. His personality and behavior took a downward turn from that point on.

Tom had six children and it broke his heart when he couldn't enlist in the armed forces during World War II. He would have made the perfect army officer in non-combat areas, little work and plenty of time to relax and enjoy himself. He received average grades in school, simply because he didn't apply himself, completing only the required work and no more.

After graduating from Blythe, he enrolled at Mount Saint Mary's College, Emmitsburg, Maryland.

A small contingent of students from New Philadelphia accompanied him to the Mount. Eddie Flanagan and Gerald Callery, who both became doctors, and Eddie Norris who received an athletic scholarship to play football. Tom received a partial scholarship and joined Eddie on the team.

The football coach at St. Mary's was a man by the name of Malloy, who believed there were three great football coaches in the United States: Knute Rockne, Pop Warner and himself. I saw his team play and I can assure you, he was no Knute Rockne. He was more of a dreamer like Alf Landon, who thought he could beat FDR in the 1936 presidential election.

Because of a misunderstanding, it took Tom five years to complete his college career at the Mount. One evening, he and four of his colleagues went on a drinking spree in Emmitsburg. Everything was going smoothly until Tom decided he would direct traffic in the center of town. According to reports, his desire to help the municipality improve its traffic patterns was misunderstood.

"Traffic was moving in an orderly fashion, and my classmates were cheering my every move. I did, however, urge one motorist to speed up the pace. All I said was, 'Come on, buddy, move your ass, you're holding up traffic.' My statement upset the gentleman and he reported me to the police."

When the police arrived, they insisted he relinquish his position as traffic controller and they escorted him and his chums back to school. Tom and his classmates were suspended for the remainder of the school year, but were allowed to apply for reinstatement the following September. Thomas worked the remaining months in my father's construction company. He returned to school in September and graduated with no additional blemishes on his record.

Everyone in our family took music lessons when in grade school. John played violin, Tom piano, Butts piano and drums, Mary Frances the piano and I played piano and trumpet. I was the only one to continue in music; everyone else laid aside their music aspirations after completing the eighth grade.

As much as I enjoyed school and music, my brother Bob, better known as Butts, hated school and music with a passion. He played the drums and piano, and, sorry to say, he wasn't very successful. He never seemed to adjust to one of the cardinal rules of music: "In order to progress, one has to practice." He played in the school orchestra and marched in the Memorial Day parade. That was the extent of his musical career.

Butts and I were scheduled to take our music lessons on Thursday after school, he at 2:30 and I at 3:00. Sister Helen Marie, an excellent teacher and a strict disciplinarian, expected each student to practice each day and make every effort to progress and not miss any lessons. Those rules and regulations didn't fit into Butts' plans.

The scenario seemed to be the same each week. I usually warmed up before I took my lesson. Sister would approach me as I practiced in the hall.

"Where is Robert? He's late for his lesson. Do you know where he is?"

"No, Sister, I have no idea where he is. Maybe he's out in the playground?"

"No, I just checked the area. Do you suppose he's at Gummy's pool room? Why don't you run up and see if he's there. If he is, tell him to come for his lesson."

Gummy's was Butts and his pals' favorite hangout where they played cards, pool, and shot craps. It was located halfway up the block on Valley Street. It took me thirty seconds to reach the entrance. I opened the door and, as expected, there were Butts, Pickles Pretti, Matts Poploskie and Huck Doyle playing cards.

"Hey Butts, Sister Helen Marie wants you for your piano lesson." All eyes turned in my direction amid laughter and a few cuss words.

Butts' voice overrode the others. "Get the hell outta here, you son of a bitch! If you tell Sister you saw me, I'll kick your ass till it's black and blue. Now get the hell outta here."

He stood up and in one sweeping motion pulled off his shoe and hurled it in my direction. It passed to the right of my head and hit the wooden door with a resounding thud. I yanked open the door and made a hasty exit. As I was leaving I heard Pickles give Butts the needle in a high falsetto voice.

"Now, Robert, I think you should leave immediately and go take your piano lesson. Sister Helen Marie is waiting for you."

"Ah, shut the hell up, Pickles, and deal the cards!"

In the future, when Sister sent me to Gummy's to check on Butts, I never entered the pool room. I always returned with the same answer: "Sister, he's not at Gummy's."

My rationale: "Balls on Butts, let him make his own excuses."

21 Butts and His Friends; Winter Sports

My friend Dulla Doyle and I were playing in front of our house. My father had an office on the ground floor, which included a coal furnace, bathroom, and a storage area in the rear. In the front of the building was a five-ton coal bin built under the steps of the front porch. The steps descended from the porch to the pavement and were located on the left side of the house.

Three large concrete pillars, eighteen inches square, supported the porch, which was six feet wide and ran the length of the front of the house. A four-foot-high concrete wall extended from the coal bin to a three-foot opening near the last pillar. The wall continued at a ninety-degree angle toward the house. Inside the pillars a four-inch pipe supported the porch, and there was a six-inch open area between the pillar and the porch.

Dulla reached his hand into the opening and pulled out some small white envelopes.

"Patty, look at what I found, I think they might be from the church." I joined Dulla and began putting them in piles as he continued to retrieve the envelopes. When he finished, we counted over five hundred. I ran into the house and returned with two large brown paper bags, into which we stuffed our newly found discovery.

Dulla scratched his head and voiced his concern. "I think these are the envelopes from the church that Pickles and Butts are supposed to deliver to the people every month. I'll bet those bastards hid them here and never delivered them."

"I think you're right, Dulla. What will we do?"

"I don't know, but I'll bet your mother will give Butts hell if she finds out."

"Come on, we'll show them to my mom. Butts and Pickles never treat us nice. Those no good bastards treat us like we were Brollies."

"Yeah, when they treat ya like a Brollie that ain't too good." Dulla was a half-breed; his mother was Lithuanian and his father was Irish. He traveled with the Irish but his older brother Tommy joined the Brollie clan.

We entered the kitchen where my mother was baking bread. She was wearing a babushka around her head, which she always wore when baking or cooking.

"Mom, look what Dulla and me found out front!"

My mother turned around, placed her hands on her hips, and stared at the two bags on the floor. "What do you have?"

I retrieved a few envelopes and handed them to her. She examined them carefully.

"Patrick, set the bags in front of the cupboard and I'll get you and Joseph a glass of milk and some cookies."

"Mom, don't tell Butts that Dulla and me found the envelopes. He might get mad."

"I won't tell Robert or Cyril, but I think it would be better if you boys said nothing to anyone about what you found."

"OK, Mom, we won't say a word." We never heard of any repercussions from the incident. However, we never found any more envelopes.

Butts hated school, and his report card was a reflection of his feelings and attitude toward his studies. With a few exceptions, most students enrolled at Blythe Township High School after graduation from Holy Family. Usually two or three students from each graduating class continued their studies at St. Stephen's High School in Port Carbon. Blythe had a high academic rating and was classified as a class B school district, because of the size of its enrollment. In its class, Blythe football teams were rated superior.

For Butts this was the ideal setting to continue his studies. He loved all sports, especially baseball and football, and he was a die-hard follower of the New York Yankees and Notre Dame. To the surprise of everyone, including Butts himself, he entered St. Stephen's in September. He was heartbroken but never complained about the choice of schools. My mother must have done a super selling job.

The real story as to why Butts went to St. Stephen's came out many years later when my mother divulged the secret. My father had been superintendent of the New Philadelphia schools in the twenties before he entered the construction business. He was also one of the pillars of the church and community. My mother received a message that Sister Gervaise, the principal, would like to see her at the convent. After a cordial greeting and a few words of small talk about the family, Sister Gervaise motioned to my mother to have a seat.

"Mrs. Canfield, in spite of Robert's poor marks this past year, I've observed him very closely. I believe with proper guidance and a change of environment, Robert might enter the priesthood."

My mother was surprised at the nun's statement. "I had no idea Robert was so inclined. He doesn't seem the type of a boy who would enter the priesthood."

"Mrs. Canfield, believe me when I tell you, I firmly believe that some day Robert may be a priest. My statement is more of a request. I would hope that Robert could attend St. Stephen's High School in Port Carbon; I believe a change of scenery would be a blessing."

"Robert has his heart set on going to Blythe. However, my husband and I will discuss the matter. Thank you, Sister, for inviting me for this little chat. I'll get back to you in a few days."

Butts received the bad news in late August, just in time to ruin his Labor Day weekend. Mickey Doyle, Alex Pautenius and I were given a slight insight as to his feelings on the matter when we approached him on Valley Street. Mickey shot the first bullet into his side.

"Hey, Butts, how come yer not goin' ta Blythe? We heard yer goin' ta that sissy school St. Stephen's."

"Shut yer damned mouth and go ta hell, ya little shithead."

We cleared a wide path so he wouldn't whack us, as he made his way to Gummy's. Alex finished the conversation. "Yeah, Butts is a great guy, he's gonna fit right in with those sissies!"

In retrospect, Sister Gervaise must have been sipping the altar wine when she got the idea Butts was going to be a priest!

When we were in seventh and eighth grades we could never understand how Butts and his friends could find so much fun and excitement with girls. Slim and I were attending a shooting match with my father at the Minersville ballpark. We had a chance meeting with Speck Stutz and Spud Spudis, who were waiting around until the next shooter was ready to continue the match.

"What are you kids doin' at the match?"

"We're here with my father. We can hardly wait until the match is over, so we kin eat supper and then go up to the Sacred Heart Hall and see a doubleheader movie."

Speck and Spud broke out in a fit of laughter.

Speck nudged Spud. "Did you hear that, they're goin' to a doubleheader movie. What a thrillin' night they have to look forward to."

"What's so funny about that?" asked Slim. "Where are you guys goin' that's better than seeing two movies?"

Spud could hardly wait to tell us about their evening plans. "We're goin' to the dance at Lakewood. All those beautiful girls from Cumbola and Port Carbon will be there. How about it, Speck?"

"Yeah, I kin hardly wait. We'll wheel those babes around the dance floor, and we might even sneak a few hugs and kisses. Come on, Spud, let's go over and make a few bets."

As they moved away I looked at Slim. "What the hell's the big deal about girls? Kin ya imagine dancin' with girls? Holy Christ, them guys must be nuts."

"Yeah, them bastards must be losin' their marbles. Kin you see them runnin' around with them girls from Cumbola? They're a bunch of dogs! Come on, Sample, let's go get a soda and ferget about them creeps."

Butts and his gang, Mooney Finley, Huck Doyle, Matts Poploskie, Pickles Pretti, Cyril Toomey and Speck Stutz never acknowledged us in any way. They wouldn't give us the time of day. To them, we were little kids who were always in the way.

Winter or summer, we always ran and played in the streets until nine o'clock. The fire company siren going off at that time was our cue to head for home. All youngsters the age of sixteen and under had to be off the streets at nine o'clock.

The snows came in late November or early December. There was very little auto traffic and the tires weren't nearly as safe or durable as they are today. There were no such things as winter tires or all-weather tires. When the snows came, to travel the slippery streets all cars had to have chains. There was little auto traffic on the side streets and once the snow covered the roads it usually stayed until the spring thaw, around March or early April.

There were two places to sleighride, the Sacred Heart Hill and the Public Hill. The Sacred Heart Hill on Clay Street was four blocks long, starting at Laurinitus' house and going down to Valley Street. It was some ride! The first block was very steep and it was here that sleds gathered speed. The next two blocks were gradually sloped until you came to Kimber Street, which was flat. One block away was Valley Street and the end of the ride.

If you wanted a short fast ride, Public Hill, which started at the public school and ended one block away at Clay Street, was the place to go. It was a steep hill. Our house was located at the bottom of the incline. Once the snows came and covered the hill, we could sleighride the entire winter.

Butts and his cronies were at the age when they thought girls were so cute and a barrel of laughs. About three times a week, at eight o'clock, they arrived on the scene with three large "flexie flyer" sleds and five or six girls. They tied the sleds together and began sleigh riding on Public Hill.

Lowie McQuail, Virginia Flanigan, Helen Connelly, Mary O'Neil and Marie Connelly were regulars at the sledding party. They were all so happy, it was a continuing chorus of laughing, squealing, and every so often a loud, shrill scream. We younger boys were fascinated but at the same time upset by their behavior.

"What the hell's so funny? They're always laughin' and screamin'," observed Tata.

Slim echoed his feelings. "Yeah, those jerks can't be that happy. How the hell can they have that much fun with a bunch of girls?"

Alex read our minds. "The only reason they take them sleigh ridin' is to get a good feel. Look at the way Mooney Finley has his hands on Virginia Flanigan's boobs."

I agreed with my buddy. "Yeah, that's it, Alex. Them bastards just want a free feel, I hope they freeze their balls off."

When the siren sounded we vacated the hill. Butts and his cronies continued their night of laughter and joy and, perhaps, a few more "feels."

During the winter months we went sleigh riding almost every night. We ate at five o'clock, and it was dark by five-thirty. During the week, because of school, we had to be home by eight o'clock. On the weekends we were on the hills all day, taking time out only for meals. Most of the Irish kids had sleighs, many of which were "lightning guiders." These were the cheap models. Some kids were lucky enough to have a "flexible flyer," which was the top of the line, the best on the hill.

Many of the Lithuanian families were not in a financial position to buy their children sleds. Therefore the kids had to be innovative if they wanted to enjoy the winter sports. Instead of riding sleighs, they made homemade skis.

These weren't like skis which you saw in the movies or in sport magazines. They were made of old curtain rods, which were about eighteen inches long and one inch wide. In order to perform on the snow-covered hills they filed the curtain rods until they were razor sharp.

When the kids came down the hill using the curtain rods as skis, they moved at fantastic speeds, at times faster than many of the sleds. They became expert skiers. We often stood at the bottom of the hill and observed our archenemies perform magic on their homemade skis.

Alex Pautenius became very upset with their demonstration of skill. "Those Brollies, they kin really ski. I wish I could do that. Every time I try it, I fall on my ass."

We would rather die than let them know how envious we were of their expertise on the curtain rods.

22 Memorial Day and Lithuanian Day

Every town had a parade on Memorial Day, which honored the deceased soldiers of World War I. In New Phillie the parade started promptly at 8:30 and was led by the Sacred Heart band and the children from the Sacred Heart school.

The Holy Family students assembled at the school at 8:00 a.m. The girls carried fresh flowers which were placed on the deceased soldiers' graves, and the boys carried small American flags which were also placed on the graves.

As the band passed by the Holy Family school, the students fell in line and joined the parade. After winding its way through the crowded streets to the applause of the borough residents, the band played its final march at the town square. A brief ceremony honoring the dead was then conducted by town officials.

At the conclusion of the ceremony, the Holy Family students proceeded to their cemetery and the Sacred Heart students to theirs. In each cemetery a short service was conducted by the parish priests. The Memorial Day activities were concluded by eleven o'clock.

Before proceeding to the school for the parade, we took great delight in observing the veterans of World War I, who were assembling and preparing for the parade. Approximately twenty veterans would assemble on Kimber Street in front of Connellys' house. Most were wearing parts of their World War I uniforms. All wore hats; some had army jackets or shirts on which they displayed their war medals. Each carried a rifle of some type.

We invariably searched out our hero, Sam Schoener, who displayed more medals than any of his comrades. He seemed to enjoy our youthful enthusiasm and pride. We didn't comprehend the merits, origin or significance of the medals, but the one that caught our eye was the sharpshooter's medal.

Alex, as usual, was the observant one. He looked Sam up and down, inspecting his attire and military presence and giving him an appraising look like that of an army sergeant.

Turning to our group he spoke to us in a whisper. "Sam don't look much like a soldier, but he has a sharpshooter's medal. I wonder if he ever killed any Germans?"

Mickey Doyle picked up the conversation. "I'll bet he killed a few Germans. Sometimes Sam looks like he could be a mean soldier."

Francis Kollessor prodded Mickey. "Why don't ya ask him if he ever killed any Germans?"

Mickey wasn't afraid of anything. "Sure, I'll ask him. Hey Sam, did you ever kill any Germans in the war?"

Sam looked down at his young admirers, paused for a few moments, then gently took his gun from along his right side and placed it in front of himself as though he was straddling the rifle.

"Hell, yes, I killed a few of those German bastards! How do ya think we won the war?"

We jumped up and down clapping our hands and cheering to express our approval of Sam's statement. What better way to start the celebration of Memorial Day than having our hero Sam tell us how he killed the Germans and helped win the war?

As we started on our way to school, Mickey put the icing on the cake. "Didn't I tell ya Sam was a mean soldier!"

This was a day of celebration for Sam and his buddies. No work, a day of drinking, eating and raising a little hell. A day when the citizens of the town paid homage to the veterans for their sacrifices while serving their country in time of war.

After the parade, they spent the rest of the day and far into the wee hours of the following morning at the American Legion. It was here they would recall and embellish the stories as to how they wooed the beautiful French girls and how they won the war.

The Legion opened at 6 a.m. and the veterans had a few "miner's specials" to start them on their merry way. They were reminded not to drink too much before the parade. Sergeant Sheik Stapleton cautioned the men, "Remember, it's a long parade and we must make a good impression on the townspeople. Don't drink too much. We'll have plenty of time ta drink later."

Watching the veterans fire the three volleys after the playing of taps was something to behold. By the time they reached the cemetery to participate in the brief ceremonies, some of the men hadn't taken the sergeant's words seriously. They were about three sheets to the wind and the majority of them didn't know whether they were shooting over the graves of their comrades or the battleship *Maine*.

They were given strict orders by Sergeant Stapleton. "Take yer time when ya load them guns, and fer Christ's sake shoot high. We don't want ta kill anybody!"

Another holiday was special to the Lithuanians of the county. The Lithuanians were not as well off as the Irish and were not as modern in their attire or social customs. Their clothing, in many respects, was a throwback to the old country. The children wore hand-me-downs and most of their clothing was made by their mothers. Very seldom was it bought in stores.

The young boys wore gum boots. The old women wore babushkas, a scarf or bandana wrapped around their heads and tied under their chins. The clothing for the men, women and children was mostly dark in color.

The Irish diet was bland, consisting of meat and potatoes, bread, ham and cabbage. The Lithuanians ate ethnic foods which were foreign to the Irish, English and Welsh. Their menu consisted of halupkies, blienies, perogies, haluskies, bundukies, black bread and thick soups.

We couldn't understand how they could eat such food. As Tata Foley was heard to say, "How the hell can those Brollies eat such food, they must be outta their minds."

Yet the same Tata Foley said to me forty years later, "You know, Pat, those Lithuanians weren't as dumb as we thought they were. Remember how we used to make fun of their food? Now when I come back to the coal region it's the favorite food of my wife and me. Maybe we weren't as smart as we thought we were!"

August 15 was Lithuanian Day in Schuylkill County. It was a day cherished by all citizens young or old who had Lithuanian blood flowing through their veins.

Mickey Puzauskie describes the happenings at a typical celebration on that day. "Since 1920, Lithuanian Day was celebrated as the greatest day on the calender. People who had their roots in the county came back to their birthplace to join in the fun. Residents from as far away as Philadelphia, New York City and states along the eastern seaboard made the yearly trek.

"The event was held at Lakewood and Lakeside parks, which were successful amusement parks during that period of time. They were located six miles from New Phillie and people who planned to attend started preparations weeks in advance.

"The ethnic foods were prepared and transported to the parks early on the morning of the 15th. Most families sent men to the park the night before to secure tables, cook the soups and prepare and ice the beer. A crowd of forty thousand people would show up for the festivities, so it was important to stake out a claim to a specific area and secure enough tables to accommodate all members of the family.

"Cars and buses began transporting people to the parks as early as 4 a.m., continuing until everyone who wanted to attend was accommodated. The morning began with a 6 a.m. mass, which was said in Lithuanian, at the Lithuanian Catholic church, after which there were very few Lithuanians remaining in town. Each table was supplied with bottles of boilo, a Lithuanian drink made of moonshine and honey. To obtain and enjoy its full fragrance and aroma it was best served hot. It was also advisable to remain seated while partaking of this ethnic drink.

"It was our greatest celebration. Everyone enjoyed the day to its fullest. The theme for the day seemed to be eat, drink and forget the worries of the world. Tomorrow was another day, at which time the worries could commence all over again.

"The party continued far into the night. Some men stayed over until the next morning to clean up the area before returning to town. An added incentive to join the cleanup crew was the opportunity to continue the celebration the next morning.

"Lithuanian Day continued to be observed until 1941. After the war it was all but forgotten. The parks were dismantled and August 15 was just a memory. The old-timers often recall those glorious and wonderful days which will never return."

23 *The South Anthracite League*

Baseball played an important part in our lives during the late twenties and up until World War II. My earliest recollections of the national pastime were from 1928. Memorial Day was the official opening day of summer, and was the day the South Anthracite Baseball League opened its season.

On Sundays and holidays everyone in town ate dinner at noon and ate supper at five o'clock. This was a carryover from the working schedule of the miners. At one o'clock on opening day, the Sacred Heart band lined up at the town square ready to proceed to the baseball field, located at the western end of town, just beyond the section known as "the patch."

I looked forward to marching in the parade alongside of Bill Wassell, the manager, and my father, who was involved in politics and an avid supporter of the New Phillie Tigers. My dad and I carried small American flags. We were part of a contingent of approximately one hundred fans, including the mayor and town council, who marched behind the band.

It was traditional that the Tigers opened each season against the St. Clair Pirates, usually one of the best teams in the league. Pitching for the Tigers was Paul Stone, a fastball right-hander who in 1934 signed a contract to pitch for the Brooklyn Dodgers. Playing for St. Clair at shortstop was Eddie Delker, who later played thirteen years in the major leagues for the St. Louis Cardinals and the Phillies. Catching was Joe "Socks" Holden. He signed with the Phillies in 1934 and spent thirteen years in the Phillies and Detroit Tigers organizations.

I saw many games as my father's traveling companion. At age nine, the New Phillie Tigers were as glamorous and famous to me as the New York Yankees. I could name every man and the position he played. In 1936 Walter Farquer, sport editor of the *Pottsville Republican*, Schuylkill County's leading newspaper, compiled a list of the outstanding players in the S.A. League from the 1920s through 1936.

Pitchers: Dutch Kline, Lefty Kurdock, Paul Stone, P.J. Quirk, Harry Deitz, Lee Hinkle, Fred Steele, Paul Sell, Jackie Williams, Joe Haverdy.

Catchers: Joe (Socks) Holden, Doggie Julian, Jim Troy, Russ Hand, Pete Ulmer.

First base: George Dimmerling, Bill Ratsin.

Shortstop: Harry Cooper, Harry Korper.

Second base: Frank Baran, Eddie Delker.

Third base: Andy Mattock, Charles Ulmer.

Outfielders: Emmett Kimmel, Barney Miles, Mike Conroy, Stanley Dobis, Eddie Singley.

Best hitter: Knocker Weldon.

The greatest days of the South Anthracite League were between 1928 and 1941. Thirty-nine players from Schuylkill County went on to play in the major leagues during those years. At that time the league was made up of teams from south of the Frackville Mountain and from the central and western sections of the county: New Phillie, Cumbola, St. Clair, Tower City, Minersville, Pine Grove, Donaldson, Pottsville, Middleport, Schuylkill Haven, Tremont, Buck Run and Cressona. When World War II erupted, the league was dissolved and within a short time faded into the county's history.

During the early twenties and mid-thirties, the outstanding team in Schuylkill County was the Cressona Tigers, under the management of Sam Huff. He gathered together the best players of the county and his team took on all comers from various sections of the state, including major league teams. The team was spearheaded by Gump Labengood, an aspiring second baseman who had recently signed to play for the New York

Yankees. Labengood, playing his last game for Cressona, broke his leg sliding into second base. He shattered not only his leg but his dream of playing in the big leagues.

The blue laws were in effect in the state of Pennsylvania, which meant that baseball could not be played in Philadelphia on Sundays. Teams which finished their games on Saturday afternoon and were scheduled to play in Philadelphia on Monday bypassed Philadelphia and came directly to Schuylkill County, where they played local teams on Sunday. This practice enabled the major leaguers to sharpen their baseball skills at the expense of the locals, and at the same time it was an ideal way for management to pick up some easy money, as the games were a guaranteed sellout. It also afforded the residents of the county an opportunity to observe the major leaguers in action.

Socks Holden recalls the attitudes and atmosphere as the great stars made their yearly trips to the coal region. "At first, the major leaguers treated those games as a lark. It was a day to have fun, play the yokels and have a few drinks and laughs. However, the big leaguers were in for a few surprises. The Cressona Tigers were ready and waiting. One year they beat quite a few major league teams: the New York Yankees, New York Giants, the Phillies and the Chicago Cubs."

It became an embarrassment to the front offices to have their teams beaten by the locals. The word went out: "Don't take the yokels for granted. Have no mercy. Beat them into the ground." From that time hence it was strictly business, and a matter of pride. The spectators, however, were given an added bonus; they were treated to the real brand of major league baseball. The major leaguers also played games at Mahanoy City, Shenandoah, Tamaqua, St. Clair and Pottsville.

Knocker Weldon, of the New Philadelphia Tigers, was considered the best hitter in the South Anthracite League. He worked for my father in the construction business. I had many a ride and conversation with Knocker as he drove the large Mack trucks on the construction sites. It also afforded me the opportunity to observe him at close range.

He was six feet one inch tall and weighed about 190 pounds. He was a mild-mannered man and very seldom raised his voice in anger. He had little education and reminded me of Wallace Berry, the famous movie actor of the thirties and forties. He was a fair outfielder. But how he could hit a baseball! Why he never made the major leagues was a question that was on the minds of many people throughout the county. One day I put the question to my father. "Pop, how come Knocker's not playing in the big leagues? Everybody says he kin really hit the ball, so how come he's not playin' fer the Yankees?"

My father, an ardent baseball fan, sat me down and explained Knocker's situation. "Many baseball scouts have looked at Knocker and they all agree that he's a great hitter and could possibly hit major league pitching. But he's much too slow to play the outfield in the majors. If he was as fast as Joe Holden or Eddie Delker he'd be in the big leagues right now, but unfortunately that's not in the cards for Knocker. He's just too slow!"

If Knocker had an Achilles heel, it was women. While hunting for small game in the fall of the year, in the Lewistown Valley four miles south of New Phillie, he struck up a conversation with a young girl. In due time he was accused of raping the girl, he was apprehended, tried and sentenced to a year in jail.

The rules governing the South Anthracite League were not rigidly enforced or forged in steel. They could be manipulated and altered, as long as no one objected too strenuously and the alterations did not affect the outcome of the league championship.

Kieran Monahan and John Holden were two of the leading citizens of St. Clair and were followers of their entry in the SAL. They were close friends of my father and a friendly rivalry existed when the New Phillie and St. Clair teams played. A small wager was placed on the outcome of the games.

In 1930 neither team was in contention for the league championship. Therefore, if the rules were overlooked, or stretched a bit, no one was upset. My dad and I attended a game in St. Clair. We joined Mr. Monahan and Mr. John Holden in the bleachers. I looked out to left field and to my surprise, playing left field was Knocker.

"Look, Pop, there's Knocker out in left field. I thought he was in jail." My observation brought forth a hearty laugh from Monahan and Holden.

My father didn't seem to be upset about my inquiry. "Knocker's still in jail, but they gave him a day off." Throughout the ball game my father took a good ribbing from the fans.

"Hey Pat, what time do you have ta have Knocker back in his cell?"

"How many days does he get off in a week?"

The verbal barrage didn't affect my father; he always had Knocker back in jail by 6 p.m.

24 Blythe High School and the Prom

We were slowly but surely coming to the end of our carefree and happy preteen days. The summer of 1934 would ring down the curtain on the close and intimate relationship we enjoyed as members of our beloved "gang." In September we would enter Blythe High School and our lives would be changed forever.

I remember the first day I entered Blythe. As Alex and I approached the school we were both excited and apprehensive.

"Alex, I wonder how it's gonna be? I'm a little scared, how about you?"

"Yeah, I'm a little scared. But what the hell, it's just another day at school. I know it can't be as tough as Holy Family. Those Sisters were somethin'."

"Yeah, I know what ya mean! Let's see what this Blythe bullshit is all about."

We entered the school and were directed to the auditorium to be welcomed by Mr. Gibbons, the principal.

"You students are in a new school. Maybe it will be a bit different from the school from which you came, but in a few days you'll become adjusted and everything will fall into place. Each of you has been issued a schedule and homeroom numbers. When you report to your homeroom you will be given further instructions as to your classes and equipment. Your homeroom teacher will answer any questions you may have."

We reported to our homeroom. Our teacher was Miss Mary Reilly, the most beautiful woman I had ever seen. I fell in love from the moment I set eyes on her. I couldn't believe that any woman could be so beautiful and yet so pleasant. I enjoyed her every move and was infatuated with Miss Reilly throughout my high school career.

On the second day, Alex and I entered the chemistry class. Our teacher was Chickie Paul, a most interesting man but no disciplinarian. We enjoyed his class from the first day. The class was so large that Alex and I had to sit behind Chickie as he taught and demonstrated the experiments to the class.

"Alex, can you believe this school? At Holy Family we walked in single file, and no talking at any time. If you did talk you'd take a hit alongside the head. Here everyone is so relaxed, they talk and laugh in the halls. It's so different! All at once we're meetin' new people. Did you notice all the good-looking girls?"

"Are you kiddin'? My God, my eyes have been poppin' ever since I got here. I never saw so many good-lookin' babes in all my life. I hear they dance in the gym during lunch hour, I can't believe it. It looks like we'll have ta learn how ta dance!"

We entered Chickie Paul's class on the third day and took our assigned seats behind his desk. I nudged my buddy. "Alex, take a look at the girl in the middle row, the blondie. She's a good-lookin' kid, I wonder what's her name?"

"I don't know, but we'll find out when class is over."

As we made our way out of class, Alex asked one of our classmates, "That blonde girl over there, what's her name?"

"That's Mary Rice, she's from Middleport."

Alex relayed the message to me.

"Alex, she's a good-lookin' girl. God, she has such a pretty face. I've only been in this school three days and already I've fallen in love with two girls. How long has this been going on? Maybe Speck Stutz had something when he said, 'Going out dancing with girls is a lot more fun than going to a double feature movie with your buddies.'"

For the first time in our lives we were separated from our classmates from Holy Family. It was a strange but exciting change. Blythe was composed of students from Cumbola, Silver Creek, Valley Furnace, Kaska, Middleport, Tumbling Run and New Philadelphia. Mary D, Tuscarora, and Brockton were located in Schuylkill Township, which was outside the school district. Tuition for students from these schools was paid by their school district.

Moving from one class to another and having a new teacher in each class was different and exciting for us. It wasn't long before we adapted to the many changes and began to develop new outlooks and make new acquaintances.

We carried our lunch in a brown paper bag. We had the choice of eating in the cafeteria or eating outside in the woods surrounding the school. At first, Jessie, Alex, Mickey Doyle and I would dash outside, run to the hills and enjoy our lunch as we sat among the beautiful elm and oak trees.

It wasn't long before we changed our routine. It seemed to be more interesting and entertaining to eat with our new classmates, which included girls. We eventually ventured into the gym to observe the dancing and enjoy the popular records of the day, by such artists as Shep Fields, Benny Goodman, the Dorsey brothers and other top-name bands.

My first cousin Joan Carrigan, from Cumbola, was in the commercial class; Alex and I were in the academic. We began eating lunch together and she introduced us to her girlfriends Rita Boyle, Anna Scripko, Jetta Kemple and Anna Kadany.

Alex was fascinated by the dancing. "Hey Patty, do you think Joan would teach us to dance? I'll bet it would be a lot of fun. Why don't you ask her?"

"I'm with you, Alex. Maybe Eddie O'Neil would like to learn too. In any case, I'll ask her."

The next day at lunch I approached my cousin. "Joan, do you think you girls could teach us to dance? Eddie, Alex and me?"

Joan liked the idea. "Sure, we'll meet you here tomorrow after lunch."

The next day we began our dancing lessons. I danced with Joan, Eddie with Anna Scripko, and Alex with Anna Kadany. Our dance lessons began in November and by January we were fixtures at the noonday dances. Most of the girls were eager to dance, so we had no problem getting dancing partners.

The prom was scheduled for May. It would be a great accomplishment and a thrill if we could go to the prom, the social event of the year. On our way home from school I suggested the idea to Eddie and Alex. "Do you think the girls would go to the dance with us? I'll bet we could have a great time."

Eddie thought it was a great idea, but there were glaring flaws. "First of all, we don't have a car, and you can't go to the prom unless you have a car."

"You're right, Eddie, but I still think I'll ask Joan about us going to the dance."

I could hardly wait for the morning classes to finish so we could have lunch with the girls and probe the possibility of attending the prom. The girls were thrilled at the suggestion, but they had to face up to the fact that we had no car.

The next day Joan came up with a solution. "I talked to my brother Michael last night. He's a senior and his girl is sick, therefore he's going to the prom without a date. He said he'd be glad to drive the girls to school if you boys would meet us there."

Everything sounded super. We had the opportunity to attend our first formal dance and it sounded as though we were in for a great time. Eddie offered an excellent suggestion. "If we're going to the dance, we must go first class. We'll get dressed in our Sunday best and we'll have to buy the girls a corsage. We must do it right!"

"You're right, Eddie. Here we are, only in the school eight months and already we're goin' ta the prom. There's only one way ta go. Go first class!"

The affair was top drawer. At the conclusion of the dance, Michael drove the girls home. Eddie walked to his home in the patch, Alex and I walked home by way of Kimber Street. As we parted company, Alex put his hand on my shoulder.

"Patty, you were right. When ya go any place, go first class. And we certainly went first class tanight. Holy Family was never like this. If Sister Gervaise could only see us now!"

25 Miss Murray's Spanish Class; Pickles and the Senior Play

Blythe was an excellent school. The curriculum included many subjects and activities which were not available in the parochial schools, such as art, library science and physical education. We had a beautiful auditorium where school plays, band concerts, movies and outside programs were presented for the enjoyment of the student body. Considering the economic conditions, it was a well-equipped and well-maintained school.

There were only three things on our minds during our high school years; girls and sports vied for first place and studies came in a poor third. During my four years of high school, I never took a book home to study. I usually had two study periods a day, which gave me ample time to prepare my homework.

I made excellent grades in all subjects except languages and art. Miss Heffner, my art teacher, once told me, "Patrick, you are one of the worst art students I've ever had! Your appreciation of art and basic ability are nil."

In our art class was a boy by the name of Cooper who did outstanding work. He was Miss Heffner's favorite student. Whenever she reached a point of high frustration because of the efforts of students such as myself, she would remind us of Cooper's great artistic talents.

"Why can't you boys do work like Cooper? After graduation, I can picture you boys sitting on the big bread box in front of the A&P hoping to get a job. And mark my words. Cooper will be the only one fortunate enough to have a job."

Over the years I often wondered, "What ever happened to Cooper?"

Foreign languages and English were my worst subjects. I knew that someday I would have to face up to my shortcomings and rectify the situation. I developed the attitude of Scarlett O'Hara, "I'll think about it tomorrow." When I entered college I bit the bullet, and after a year of private tutoring my English grades became acceptable.

I took first-year French with Miss Moore, who was a close friend of my Aunt Julia, who was the school nurse. As I was leaving the room on the last class of the year, Miss Moore called me to her desk. As I approached, she rose from her seat.

"Patrick, you're a wonderful and pleasant boy, who never gave me a minute's trouble; therefore, I'm going to give you a final mark of C." She paused a moment. "But please, Patrick, don't come back next year!" I was overjoyed by her benevolence and understanding. The only words I uttered were "Miss Moore, you're wonderful, I love ya."

German, French and Spanish were the languages which were offered the following year. After much discussion with my classmates as to the easiest one to pursue, my cousin Joan gave me the best advice. "Take Spanish. Not only is it easy but Miss Murray is a doll. If you keep your mouth shut and don't cause any trouble, she'll give you a passing grade."

As Gabriel Heater used to say on his radio broadcasts during World War II, "There's good news tonight." How lucky can a guy get? Miss Murray, here I come!

The first day I arrived in her class, I knew I had made the proper choice. The class had only fifteen students and they were from all grade levels because it was an elective subject.

Miss Murray introduced herself and laid down the ground rules for her class. "We have two groups in this class. Each of you must make a choice as to which group you would like to join. The first group will be made up of students who expect to go to college and want to get a good foundation in basic Spanish. Those students will sit to my left. Those who wish to perform the minimum amount of work in order to receive a passing grade will sit to my right. I will work with you the first fifteen minutes of the class, after which I will give you an assignment which you can finish in class. Therefore you will have no homework.

"There are two things I ask of you. If you must talk, do so in a soft voice so as not to bother the other section of the class. Secondly, I expect all of you to behave like ladies and gentlemen. If those rules are agreeable, I will give you five minutes to make up your minds. At that time, we will begin our class."

My prayers had been answered. It was a better deal than I received from Miss Moore. Some people are just born lucky!

Our class was scheduled for the last period in the day. Therefore some students who were involved in basketball or football would skip class and go to the gym, giving them more time to devote to their sports activities. No one ever checked their early arrival at the gym and Miss Murray abided by her promise, "Don't give me any trouble and I'll give you a passing grade."

On one occasion, my cousin Frank O'Neil, a future football star, arrived for class. It was his first appearance in three weeks. Miss Murray noted his presence as he took his seat: "Boys and girls, I would like you to take note that Frank O'Neil is with us today." Everyone rose and gave Frank a standing ovation.

He acknowledged the appreciative gesture and raised both his hands high in the air, in the style of Presidents Eisenhower and Nixon. "Thank you, classmates. I appreciate your warm reception, and it's nice seeing you again Miss Murray. Please continue!" Once again Frank received the applause of the class. He continued his irregular attendance for the remainder of the school year. He kept his side of the bargain and was rewarded with a passing grade.

My high school days, from the fall of 1934 through the spring of 1938, were completed during the depths of the Great Depression. However, the dark economic climate never affected our attitudes or activities. We were aware of the high unemployment and the scarcity of money, but we had much to do to keep us busy. Sports and music flourished throughout school systems and in spite of the depressing economy our high school days were filled with excitement and happiness.

Every six weeks we were entertained by the county WPA orchestra, made up of unemployed musicians from throughout the county. Their programs were well received and greatly appreciated. One member of the orchestra, John Michaels from the Shenandoah area, wrote the song "Once in a While" which became one of the standards and all-time great songs of the big band era. He sold the song to Tommy Dorsey, who recorded it and made millions of dollars from records and sheet music. Michaels sold the song to Dorsey for seventy-five dollars!

Every Friday afternoon the student body was treated to a full-length motion picture, which was a wonderful way to ease into the weekend.

Cyril "Pickles" Pretti was president of the Student Council in his senior year. A popular student and excellent football player, he was also the class clown and cut-up. He and Paul Kuhn were the two leads in the senior class play, under the direction of Hilda Moore, head of the Language Department. Thursday and Friday performances were presented without a flaw and the show was a rousing success. A party for the members of the cast was planned at Paul Kuhn's home at the closing of the play on Saturday night.

I was playing in the orchestra, which afforded me one of the best seats in the house. Near the end of the third act, Paul made his entrance and began his dialogue. He turned to address his co-star, but to his surprise Pickles was not on the stage.

Miss Moore was sitting stage left behind the curtain line holding her prompting book. She looked up and noticed the absence of Pickles. "Where's Cyril? Where's Cyril? He's supposed to be on stage!"

Mary Feeley, her student assistant, shook her head. "I don't know, Miss Moore."

Mary relates the story as it unfolded. "I thought Miss Moore was having a heart attack, and her face turned ash white. She lifted her head, brought her hands to her ears and closed her eyes as if she was seeking guidance from above. Her forehead was wet with perspiration as she gritted her teeth and groped for words. She looked at me and said in a controlled soft voice, 'Find Cyril and bring him to the stage.'

"I ran into the hall where a number of cast members had assembled. 'Where's Pickles? He's supposed to be on stage.'

"No one had seen him for some time. I ran down the hall, checking all the classrooms near the auditorium area, but Pickles was nowhere to be found. Mary Brennan, who was helping me in the search, yelled, 'Let's go up to the third floor. Maybe he's in one of the classrooms.'

"'OK, let's go, but we've got to hurry.'

"When we reached the third floor, I checked the typing room as Mary checked Mr. Yesville's homeroom. Miss Moore's homeroom had six large six-by-four-foot tables, instead of the usual movable desks. I switched on the light and there was Pickles, asleep on a table."

It seemed that along with other members of the cast he had been sipping wine during the performance. By the third act the wine began to have an effect on the budding thespian. He became drowsy and listless and decided to lie on the table and rest his eyes for a few moments.

"I ran over to the table and shook him out of his sleep. 'Pickles, get up, you're supposed to be on stage.'

"'Holy Christ, I just closed my eyes for a minute. How long have I been off?'

"'About three or four minutes.'

"'Holy God, Miss Moore will kill me.'

"He made his way to the stage and completed his performance. In spite of his absence from the scene, the play was a huge success. The party went on as planned and it too was a rousing success!"

There were repercussions. Pickles was suspended from school for three days and dismissed as president of the Student Council. Hilda Moore was devastated. At the conclusion of the performance she was in a state of exhaustion and on the verge of a nervous breakdown.

After an absence of two weeks she recovered her composure and regained her strength sufficiently to return to the classroom. She was looking forward to her return; the two-week self-imposed respite was the tonic she needed to once again face the challenges of her classes.

Always an early arriver, she drove her car into an empty parking lot. The first person she saw was none other than Pickles. When she brought the car to a stop, he opened her door with a greeting.

"Welcome back, Miss Moore, I came to carry your books and apologize for my terrible behavior."

When he closed the door, she handed him her briefcase and said in a soft voice, "I should never forgive you for your behavior, but I do. Your performance on stage was excellent and the show was a success."

Pickles put his arm around her as they proceeded to the entrance. "I thought you needed a few weeks off. In fact, I think you look well-rested and more charming than ever."

"Oh, Cyril, stop your flattery before I start crying."

Pickles' questionable behavior was also noted at the nightly card game at Gummy's pool hall. My brother Butts couldn't wait to stick the needle in his old friend. "Cyril, I understand your behavior at the senior play wasn't appreciated by the faculty, especially Miss Moore."

Pickles wasn't amused. "Shut the hell up, Butts, and deal the cards."

26 Boxing and Other Recreations

When you live in an area where the unemployment rate is extremely high you become aware of the changes taking place, especially changes in the buying habits and social behavior of young people. In the pool halls cigarettes were bought for a penny apiece; seldom did anyone buy a full pack, which cost fifteen cents. The pots in the card games became smaller, and there was less money on the crap tables and dart games.

Prior to World War II, the most important sources of news and information of any kind were the radio and newspapers. Sports and political figures were glamorized and immortalized by radio commentators and sports writers. Movies provided the masses with an emotional outlet which helped them survive the Depression and the pains of poverty and hunger. Attendance at the movies, for as little as ten cents, provided the population a few hours of relief from the boredom and worries of their daily routine. It afforded them an opportunity to spend a short period of time in the fantasy world of Hollywood. On a county level, local newspapers provided readers with local and national news. They also gave extensive coverage to sporting events, movies, and the latest news, gossip and fashion tidbits from Hollywood.

All forms of the arts, free of charge, were available under the auspices of the WPA: painting (oil, watercolor, acrylics), cooking, sewing, dancing, and music (lessons on piano and instrumental). There were night classes where foreign-born citizens could learn to speak English. On all levels, national, state and local, government was endeavoring to do everything possible to soften the harsh realities of the Depression.

Outwardly, the young people seemed to be oblivious to the hard times. Everyone, young or old, was suffering and trying to make the best of the bad economic conditions. Youths were intent on enjoying themselves, just as the generations before them had. They relinquished the privilege of fretting and worrying to their elders.

Softball and basketball leagues were formed throughout the county. The winners of the town leagues would advance to the southern county tournament. The winner here was declared the county champion.

New Philadelphia had a league composed of six teams. The two best teams were Josh's, composed of Lithuanians, and Pete Worster's which was the Irish contingent. Each year these teams battled for the championship. Josh's team featured a pitcher by the name of Denny Daukshus, Josh's brother. Denny had one of the fastest arms in the county. Worster's countered with Bill Dooley, a slowballer with a spinning curve which the hitters found difficult to hit. Most playoff games were won by Worster's, who then advanced to the southern county championship tourney.

My brother Butts was the catcher. Pete and Jackie Feeley, Pickles and Beppo Pretti and Jack Ziegler headed the heavy hitters list. However, their ace in the hole was Bill Dooley. Most hitters in the leagues were accustomed to hitting fastball pitchers. When they opposed Dooley he drove them into a frenzy as they tried to hit his slow curveball. By the time they had made an adjustment to his pitching style, it was too late.

Charlie Dimmerling, who later served as a County Commissioner, pitched for the Pottsville team. He was the most outstanding softball pitcher in the county, and averaged twenty-two strikeouts in a nine-inning game. Over a five-year span, Pottsville and Worster's were the finalists in the county playoffs each year. The games were low-scoring and were usually determined by one or two runs. It was a one-game playoff. Because of the extensive news coverage, the games attracted a crowd of over five thousand people. In five years of championship play, Worster's won three and Pottsville two.

The sport fans in the coal region had four priorities: family, church, sports and work. At times those were interchangeable. They loved Notre Dame and the Yankees. In later years when Joe Paterno made his appearance on the football scene and upgraded the football fortunes of Penn State, the Nittany Lions had as many followers as the Fighting Irish.

To be in a local bar during a game between Penn State and Notre Dame was an experience. You had to make a choice as to which side of the bar you wanted to be seated on. The lines were clearly drawn: Penn State or Notre Dame. No in-betweens!

Boxing played an intricate part in the lives of the sports enthusiasts throughout the nation. Fans in Schuylkill County were no exception. During the era of Jim Braddock, Joe Louis, Max Schmeling, Billy Conn and Tony Canzenari, the enthusiasm on the night of a championship fight was at fever pitch. Everyone was a fight expert. Each person had the fight figured and everyone had to listen to the various evaluations and analyses of the coming brawl.

Radio and movies were the sources of relaxation and current events; television was certainly not in anyone's imagination during the trying times of the thirties. Because of the great popularity of boxing, the championship fights were held on Friday nights at ten o'clock, a time designed to draw an audience from all four time zones. To accommodate the huge crowds, the bouts were held in large stadiums, such as Yankee Stadium or the Polo Grounds in New York City. Because of the three-hour time difference between the east and west coasts, the bouts were rarely held on the west coast.

The "million-dollar gate" came into being during the reign of Jack Dempsey as heavyweight champion. If the news media predicted a championship fight would have a million-dollar gate, it added an additional hype and incentive to listen to the fight on radio. It was the main topic of conversation among fight fans for weeks prior to the main event.

Skip Schneider recalls the attitudes and anticipation of the people on those hot summer nights. "Joe Louis was the most popular fighter since the days of Dempsey. The streets were jammed with people waitin' for the magic hour of ten. Families invited their neighbors and friends in to hear the fight. Drinks were always served, but food rarely offered. It was too hard to come by.

"Pool halls were bulging at the seams. Extra radios were set up to accommodate the overflow crowd. The intensity and concentration of the patrons on the comments of the commentator was something I'll never forget.

"People were packed around the radio and hung on every word as the commentator described the fight. In case of a knockdown there was bedlam! After the winner was announced, or a knockout occurred, almost everyone rushed outside to the sidewalk where they discussed, recalled, analyzed and recounted nearly every movement and maneuver of each fighter.

"Within two days, the fights were shown in the local movies to a sellout crowd. I can never forget how we looked forward to watching the Joe Louis fights in the theater. At that time most fight fans considered him to be the greatest champion of all time."

In 1951, when he was well past his prime, Louis fought Rocky Marciano, the reigning champion, and was knocked out in the seventh round. My wife and I were watching the fight. When Louis was counted out, she placed her head in her hands and cried. "I always loved Joe Louis, I hate to see him close out his career like this."

A few smart fighters like Gene Tunney and Rocky Marciano retired while they were reigning champions and at the zenith of their careers. Not many defeated champions were ever able to make a comeback. In the vernacular of the fight game, "If you stick around long enough and prolong your career beyond your prime, someone's going to knock your brains out." Muhammad Ali, Larry Holmes, Sugar Ray Leonard and Willie Pep, all great champions, learned that lesson the hard way.

Professional and amateur boxing bouts had a large following throughout the coal region. My brother Tom fought as an amateur under the name of "Killer Kilbane." His record was eight wins and two losses. Skeeter Gannon was his manager and acted as his second in the ring. He sums up Tom's career: "Tom was a good boxer. He had a good right hand and was a good hitter. His career was on the rise, and he won eight straight fights. I could picture me and Tom someday ta be on easy street. Yes, we were on our way to fame and fortune!

"Everything was going according to plan until he fought a black kid, named Joel Stanley, from Harrisburg. Stanley beat Tom in two close fights. After the second loss, I advised Tom to reconsider his career as a fighter. Stanley wasn't that good, and if Tom lost to a mediocre opponent maybe it was time to hang up the gloves. He took my advice and retired to his role of spectator."

Money was tight. Men on WPA crews received a weekly paycheck of fifteen dollars. A boss of a working crew was paid seventeen dollars and fifty cents. Professional fighters, on the county level, earned thirty-five dollars if they won and twenty dollars for a loss.

Top fighters during the thirties and forties were Matt Rice and Lefty Laurinitus, heavyweights; Fumbler Martin and Pat Igo, welterweights; Gene Pinter, a middleweight; and Joe "The Cat" Flannery, a flyweight. Whenever any of those fighters appeared on a fight card a capacity crowd was assured. Bouts were held in Charlton Hall in Pottsville, Walter's Hall in New Philadelphia, Maher's Hall in Shenandoah, Dream City Park in Port Carbon, and Lakewood Park in Mahanoy City.

Fumbler Martin was one of the outstanding fighters in the history of the county. He was a fighter who didn't relish the strain and monotony of training, a man who enjoyed drinking and living the good life. He was nearing the end of his career in the late thirties and wasn't too eager to participate in any future fights.

Joey Kripitz, from Pottsville, was making a name for himself as an up and coming welterweight. He had compiled a record of seventeen straight victories and his manager believed he was ready to move up in class.

The headlines on the sport page of the *Pottsville Republican* read, "Kripitz Wants Fumbler Martin!" What better way to attract immediate attention than to defeat the aging but still dangerous Fumbler? When Al Edwards, his manager, approached Fumbler about the Kripitz statement in the paper, Fumbler was unimpressed.

"I don't wanna fight that kid. My fightin' days are over. I don't feel like trainin'."

"Just tell me one thing, Fumbler. Do ya think ya can take this kid if ya get in shape?"

"I just told ya, Al, I don't wanna fight the kid."

"OK, but what if I get ya a good purse. Would that change your mind?"

"It all depends on what kind of money you're talkin' about."

"I'm gonna see Bill Walsh the promoter and see if he'll come up with some cash. At least I kin ask him. I'll get back ta ya later."

Al returned the next day and reported on his meeting with Walsh. "Bill will give ya one hundred and fifty dollars if ya fight Kripitz. What do ya say?"

"Fer that kind of money I'll take the fight."

"That's great! But I'll tell ya something. Kripitz is young and hungry, and he packs a pretty good punch. It's not gonna be a cakewalk!"

"I know, Al, I'll be ready. But remember, this is my last fight!"

The eight-round bout was scheduled to take place at Charlton Hall, three weeks later. Fumbler did a little training but it wouldn't make any difference. He wasn't about to change his training habits at this late date.

Al describes the events the evening of the fight. "We arrived at the hall at eight o'clock and the place was packed. His fans were gonna give him a rousing farewell. Kripitz also had his followers. After all, they thought he was the new kid on the block and it would be a feather in his cap if he could beat Fumbler.

"About 9:30 I taped Fumbler's hands and offered him a bit of advice. 'Fumbler, the only way you can win this fight is to take this kid out in the first round. Yer not in shape and if the fight goes more than one round, he'll kill ya. There's no way you kin go eight rounds. Do you understand?'

"Fumbler seemed unconcerned. 'Yeah, I understand.'

"He was sitting on the rubbing table awaiting the call to make his final entrance. I was rubbing his back trying ta keep him relaxed. He turned his head to the left and looked up. 'Al, give me the pint of whiskey you brought with ya.'

"I took the bottle out of my coat and handed it ta him. It was half full. He lifted the bottle to his mouth and emptied it. He looked at me and pounded his gloves together. 'Now I'm ready. Let's go!'

"We walked to the ring amid the cheers of the crowd. It was his final bout and they were gonna send him out in style. Just before the bell sounded, I cradled Fumbler's face in my hands and our eyes met for a brief moment. 'This is your last fight, Fumbler, how do ya feel?'

"'I'll be all right.'

"When the bell sounded, Fumbler bolted out of his corner and charged across the ring almost as if he was runnin'. Kripitz rose from the stool with his hands at his side. He was just about ready ta lift his hands into a fightin' stance when Fumbler hit him with a crushing right-hand blow to the side of his face. Kripitz's knees buckled and he hit the canvas with a resounding thud. He was counted out in fourteen seconds. The crowd went wild. Fumbler was carried around the ring holding both hands high in the air. A sure sign of victory!"

It was Fumbler's last fight and he retired to his home in Valley Furnace. He never married and lived with his sister, making a comfortable living as a piano player and entertainer. He died in 1975.

27 Jack Ziegler; Dan Coyle and the Amateur Fights

In 1936, Hughie Feeley, the former postmaster of New Philadelphia, was the boss on a twenty-man WPA project digging rock out of the mountainside and delivering it by truck to another WPA crew working on the state highway between New Philadelphia and Cumbola.

After receiving the rock, the crew cut each piece by hand into sizes approximately eight inches in depth, twelve inches long and six inches in width. A ditch eight inches in depth and three feet wide was dug along the edge of the road, after which the rocks were set in place as a dentist would insert an inlay or fill a cavity. This procedure was called "rip-rap."

The main purpose of the project was to eliminate the soft shoulders along the highway and protect motorists if their vehicles left the road for any reason. Rip-rap has withstood the ravages of time; most of the stone shoulders are still in use after more than a half a century.

Although it was exacting work, the men were proud of their accomplishments and were in no hurry to finish a project of any kind. When a project was finished, the crew was laid off and had to go on relief until another job was available. Often this meant months of idleness. The workers preferred to stay on a project where they had the feeling of satisfaction from doing something constructive. The alternative was a life of boredom; standing on street corners, sitting on park benches, or drinking in bars.

The bosses seldom, if ever, pushed the men; everyone was laid back and relaxed. The secret of getting along on a project

was to never give the top man any flack, and occasionally contribute something to the work effort.

Tuesday was fight night at Dream City. One Tuesday afternoon Jack Ziegler was resting in the bush, his body stretched
out, hands behind his head and his eyes closed. Hughie thought
Jack was taking advantage of his good nature and not contribut-
ing his share to the work load. He walked to the edge of the tree
line. Hughie had a high-pitched voice and it had the tenderness
and warmth of a squealing chicken.

"Hey Ziegler, get your big ass down here and do a little
work. Who the hell do ya think ya are, one of the DuPonts?" Jack
jumped to his feet, joined the crew and began the task of jarring
the rocks loose.

Matts Poploskie approached Hughie and whispered in his
ear. "Hughie, I'd take it easy on Jack, he's fightin' tonight and we
all have a few bucks bet on him ta win."

"What are you talkin' about, Matts? What do ya mean he's
gonna fight tanight?"

"Ain't you been readin' the papers? Jack has five first-round
knockouts. He's the hottest professional fighter in the county.
We're all goin' ta the fights tonight, so why don't ya come along?
Maybe ya kin win a few bucks."

"Yeah, maybe I will."

"Hey Ziegler, come here." Jack approached his boss expecting another reprimand. Hughie, a bantamweight, looked up at
Jack. "Matts tells me yer gonna fight tonight. How do ya think
you'll make out?"

"I don't know, I feel pretty good, I'll give it a good shot."

Hughie paused for a few moments. "OK, Jack, go up in the
bush and take it easy the rest of the day. Don't worry about a
thing, just be ready fer the fight tanight."

Dream City Hall had a capacity of one thousand people.
The fights were popular and capacity crowds turned out for the
Tuesday bouts. Ziegler had been receiving good press notices;
therefore many people from his hometown who weren't fight
fans joined Jack's entourage.

The fans from New Phillie were betting heavily that their hero would improve his record to six knockouts. The gamblers in Pottsville, the Sophy brothers and Sol Cutler, were laying three to one odds that Jack wouldn't win by a first-round K.O. Everyone on the project took the opposite view. They gathered as much money as possible and placed the bet on Jack.

Jack, a southpaw, was a light heavyweight, with a devastating left hand as his main weapon. He was not a polished boxer. He was a hitter! That night he finished off his opponent in less than two minutes of the first round. Big Jack was on his way, displaying the qualities of a champion.

He returned to work as the conquering hero. His work load was reduced as Hughie took a personal interest in his newly found hero.

Hughie whispered to Matts, "Why kill Santa Claus? We'll take care of the kid; we might have a future champion in the makin'."

Two weeks later Jack was ready for his next encounter. When he arrived at the project, Hughie set the tone for the day. "If any of you guys have an extra sandwich, give it ta Jack. Don't forget, he's fightin' tanight. Jack, you go up in the bush and rest. Remember, nobody disturbs the big fella." Matts collected fifty dollars and placed the bet with the Sophy brothers.

Jack ran his streak to ten straight first-round knockouts. The WPA crew was rolling in dough and Hughie was ecstatic. He could picture himself as Jack's manager, strolling arm in arm with the big fella, amid the cheers and applause of his admirers, as they walked toward the ring in Madison Square Garden.

The press interviewed Hughie regarding Jack's training habits and physical condition. Hughie could lie with the best of them. "Jack runs to and from work. That adds up to six miles a day. He punches the bag and spars about six rounds each night. He's in tiptop shape, and he's headin' fer the big time." Hughie could lie to the press, but his working companions knew better. Jack never trained.

My dad took Alex and me to the next fight, a sellout. The noise and tension were beyond description as the patrons awaited Jack's arrival in the ring. He was greeted with a thunderous ovation as he made his way through the ropes.

His opponent was a black kid from Philadelphia with a record of eight wins and five defeats, just a run-of-the-mill club fighter. When the bell sounded Jack went to work; his first punch, a looping left, decked his opponent. By the end of the round, Jack had his opponent on the canvas five times. It was just a matter of time before the bout would be over.

The second round was a continuation of the same. Jack dropped his opponent to the canvas four times. How the Phillie kid ever came out for the third round was beyond belief; however, he made his way to the center of the ring and made the traditional gesture of touching gloves with his opponent.

Jack's training habits finally came home to roost. He had never gone beyond the first round in his career, and the beginning of the third round was a new and devastating experience. After one minute of fighting, he was completely exhausted, and the kid from Philadelphia knocked him out after two minutes of the third round. Hughie's dream of being the manager of another "white hope," and a trip to New York and the big time, was dashed forever.

When Jack arrived for work the following morning, he was greeted by his former admirer and confidant. "Ziegler, you no good son of a bitch, get your ass up on the rock pile and from now on yer gonna work like the rest of the men. No more layin' in the bush and no more free sandwiches!"

During the depressing times of the thirties it was difficult for anyone to make extra money, especially young single men. There were no jobs available, not even menial work. Therefore, they pursued any avenue of activity which might generate extra income.

Father Walsh of St. Ambrose's Parish in Schuylkill Haven conducted Thursday night bouts every second week. Dan Coyle, a professional boxer, received a call from the good Father. "Dan, do you think you can bring four young lads to box on Thursday night? We get excellent crowds and they expect good fights. It's always good for business if they see some new faces. If you bring the boys, they must put on a good show. I hope you under-stand."

"Sure, Father, I'll bring four fellas and I guarantee you that they'll give the customers their money's worth."

Dan gathered his four proteges, Mooney Finley, Pickles Pretti, Matts Poploskie and my brother Butts. Father Walsh and Dan had an agreement: three dollars to the winner, two for the loser, two for Dan and a dollar for gas.

On the way to the arena, which was eight miles from New Philadelphia, Dan briefed his fighters. "I don't think it'll look very good if the fans know you're all from the same hometown, so I'll have ta change yer names and where yer from. Butts, you're gonna fight Mooney and fer Christ sake make it look good. Pickles, you're well known throughout the county, so we'll have ta say yer from New Phillie. Matts, yer from Kulpmont, Butts yer from Scranton, and Mooney yer from Harrisburg."

Pickles won a three-round decision and Matts won by a knockout in the second round. Things were going well for the boys from New Phillie! It was now time for Butts, alias Bobbie Conroy from Scranton, to battle Mooney, alias Johnnie Stutz from Harrisburg. Dan was intent on making a good showing. If the boys looked good, there was a possibility of being invited back to fill out some future boxing card.

Butts and Mooney agreed they would take it easy, but at the same time give the spectators a good show. Moments before the bell rang, Dan gave Butts his final instructions.

"Listen, Butts, Mooney's expectin' the fight ta be a waltz. Go in there and knock him out!"

"But Dan, Mooney and me agreed we'll take it easy."

"Listen, you dumb bastard. If you don't knock him out in the first round, I'll break this stool over yer head. Now get the hell in there and knock his brains out!"

When the bell rang, Mooney slowly approached the center of the ring to touch gloves, which was the customary thing for fighters to do. He extended his hands expecting Butts to complete the traditional gesture. Instead, Butts landed a roundhouse right to Mooney's chin sending him to the canvas and into no-no land. The knockout took exactly fourteen seconds.

When Mooney and Butts met in the dressing room, Butts was admonished by his friend. "Jesus Christ, Butts, what's wrong with you? I thought we were gonna take it easy."

Butts was prepared for the question. "Dan said he would break the stool over my head if I didn't knock ya out." He looked in Dan's direction for confirmation of his statement.

"Gee, Butts, I was only kiddin'. I never thought you would take me serious. That was a hell of a thing ya did ta Mooney!"

Butts turned to Dan in disbelief. "Dan, how kin you say a thing like that? You no good bastard, I'll never trust you again!"

Dan broke out in a fit of laughter as Pickles and Matts joined in the fun. He put his arms around Mooney and Butts. "Father Walsh said they were the best fights he's had in over two months. We're invited back fer the next fight card."

Everyone agreed that they would return and take part in the next scheduled bouts. Mooney was a bit apprehensive. "I'll come back, but I'll never trust you two no good bastards again. So help me God!"

28 *The Rat Races*

During our junior and senior years of high school our prime concern was girls and dancing. We attended dances at every opportunity; Wednesday at Dream City, Thursday at Lakewood, Saturday at Charlton Hall and Sunday at Holy Family Hall, which was located across the street from my home.

Saturday night was special; everyone dressed in his best attire. Most everyone assembled at Pete Worster's, Gummy's or Josh's pool halls, where they played cards and shot craps before proceeding to the dance at Charlton Hall in Pottsville. The dance was known as the "rat races." Admission was eleven cents and the patrons danced to the music of an eleven-piece band.

Tickets were never issued. The entrance was manned by two gentleman, John Trabash and Bernie Connors, whose reputation for memory was known throughout the region. Once observed paying the admission price, patrons could come in and out of the dance as many times as they desired. They were never issued a pass for reentry. Trabash and Connors never forgot a face and no one ever entered the hall without paying.

Each town's patrons assembled in the same area of the dance hall each night. The New Phillie, Middleport and Cumbola crowd congregated in front of the bandstand. St. Clair, Minersville, Pottsville, Schuylkill and Port Carbon each staked out their territory in different parts of the hall.

Butts held first priority on the car on Saturday night. Reluctantly, and with a little persuasion from my father, he agreed to take me to the dance. We made our exit from town at 8:30 with the usual occupants: Matts, Pickles, Mooney, Huck and myself.

Butts followed his regular Saturday night routine. His entire life was one continuous schedule from the moment he arose in the morning until he placed his head on the pillow at night.

He dropped me off at the dance at nine o'clock and then proceeded to Harry Hughes' bar with his buddies. It was here they convened their Saturday night seminar on the art of beer drinking and the analysis and settlement of all questions relating to sports and politics. At the conclusion of the meeting they sauntered down to the dance hall located one block away.

The group did very little dancing. They spent the evening in front of the bandstand viewing and commenting on the action. Pickles was another story. He was an excellent dancer and gave us many laughs and light moments with his antics on the dance floor.

One of the highlights of the evening was the dancing exhibition he performed, in front of the bandstand, for his appreciative hometown audience. When he was ready to perform, he always chose the same girl as his partner. She wore a tight-fitting red dress, black stockings and bright red high heel shoes. Her hourglass figure, when viewed from the rear, could easily be mistaken for that of a Hollywood starlet. However, a frontal view revealed a different image. The beauty of her face was marred because of the lack of symmetry in her cosmetic make-up. Her curled-up eyelashes and eyebrows were heavily laden with black mascara, and she wore flaming red lipstick and bright red rouge. She epitomized the image of a tough and salty broad!

Matts announced the impending arrival of the dancing marvel. "Here comes Pickles! Get ready fer the show!" All eyes focused on the dancing couple as they approached the viewing area. Dancing to a slow melodic tune, they were the personification of the perfect lovers, dancing cheek to cheek and so much in love! Their eyes closed to block out all the earthly senses, except the dolce musical strains of Norman Dropkin and his orchestra.

He gently turned her, in a smooth clockwise direction, slowly moving his right hand down her sleek body and placing it in the middle of her right buttock. He then rotated his hand in a slow and effortless motion for the remainder of the dance. She was well aware of the sexual insinuation of the maneuver but her facial expression never changed. She had the look of a young girl in a mystic or prophetic trance. At the conclusion of the dance, Pickles and his partner faded into the crowd and we didn't see them again for awhile.

In spite of their shenanigans (or perhaps because of them) they were the best dancing couple in the hall. On numerous occasions, as they danced to a fast jitterbug tune, the patrons would form a circle to better enjoy the performance.

On one particular Saturday night, the usual crowd was gathered in front of the bandstand. Charlie Art's orchestra, one of Charlton Hall's favorites, was playing. Brother Feeley, Chipper Connelly and my old boyhood buddy Tata Foley were part of the group listening to the orchestra and observing the dancing couples.

"Tata, how come you're at the dance tanight? You're usually singing at Alexander's on Saturdays."

"You're right, I was scheduled ta sing but I have a slight sore throat so I thought I'd take the night off."

"I don't get ta see ya much anymore since you moved to Pottsville, I hear you're runnin' around with a fast crowd and they do quite a bit of drinkin'. Is that right?"

"Yeah, you're right. I guess I drink a little too much, but I'll tell ya this, I meet up with a lot of weird people. The other night I was at a party. I was drinkin' pretty good and havin' a hell of a good time. I was sitting next ta this gorgeous girl. She looked like she was a few years older than me, so I turned and looked into her pretty face. 'Are you married?'

"'Yes, I'm married and I have two kids. It's a relief to be away from them for a few hours so I can have a little peace and quiet.'

"'Do you mind if I ask you a question that's been on my mind for some time?'

"'No, I don't mind. What's your question?'

"'Does it really hurt when you have a baby?'

"She turned her head and took a long drag on her cigarette. 'Did you ever try ta shit a ham?'"

Tata's story brought a chorus of loud laughs.

29 Stasia

While attending a Sunday night dance at Holy Family Hall, I met the love of my young life, a girl named Stasia Gogotz. She was of Russian heritage, and, as has been spoken by lovers all over the world, "She was as beautiful and refreshing as the breath of spring."

I was standing near the entrance of the hall with two of my friends when this attractive, vivacious girl approached me.

She pointed her finger toward my face.

"You have a sore on your lip, I'll bet it hurts."

"Yes it does, but it'll be healed in a few days."

That was our introduction.

As the orchestra began to play a slow tune, she turned and walked toward her girlfriends. I followed her and asked, "Would you like to dance?"

"Yes, I'd like that." It was the beginning of the romance of my youthful and carefree years.

Neither of us drank alcoholic beverages. When we dated, we went to the movies and usually ended up at the Black Diamond restaurant on Route 61. It was located between Pottsville and Schuylkill Haven and was the meeting place of many teenagers. We ate ice cream, sipped cokes and danced.

In spite of our attitude toward drinking, we attended some wild parties where an enormous amount of booze was guzzled. The doggie roasts on top of Peach Mountain, located a few miles north of St. Clair, were weekly affairs during the summer. There were some great parties and wonderful memories.

On one such outing, about twenty people were in attendance. The cars were parked in a semicircle with their headlights
turned on. We built a good-sized fire to roast the hot dogs, and
as the fire grew in intensity a half barrel of beer was being
readied for the festivities. When the fire reached the point of
giving off bright glowing embers, the car lights were turned off
and the party was on. There were no formal arrangements at
such outings. Some couples sat around the fire cooking the dogs
and drinking beer, while others stood in groups conversing and
enjoying the cool summer breezes.

As the evening progressed, more beer was consumed and
the party intensity was turned a few notches higher. It wasn't
long before the highlight of the evening took place, the chug-a-
lug. Each person took a turn lifting the beer stein high in the air
and then proceeding to consume the foaming lager as the crowd
chanted the famous line, "chug a lug." Before long, many of the
partygoers were feeling no pain and the celebration and "chug a
lug" chants became louder. The merriment and laughter didn't
disturb any neighbors because we were on top of Peach Mountain and miles away from any community.

Stasia and I were sitting on the grass. I asked to be excused
for the purpose of relieving myself. As I walked between the
parked cars, I tripped over something on the ground and as I fell
forward I heard a loud, shrill scream. Some of the revelers came
running toward the area from which the scream emanated.

"What's goin' on? Who's doin' the screamin'?"

I stood up, trying to figure out what had happened. The
person on the ground was moaning, apparently in extreme pain.
I yelled back toward the fire, "Bring a flashlight so we can find
out what's goin' on."

The flashlight arrived and within seconds the area was illu-
minated. Lying between the cars, a hand pressed against her
profusely bleeding face, was a young girl. I had accidentally
walked on her face as I passed between the parked cars. She was
helped to her feet, her face a mass of blood. To make matters
worse she was in a drunken stupor. Her speech was garbled,

making conversation almost impossible. Two cars' headlights were turned on as four men placed her on the ground and endeavored to evaluate the extent of her injury. Stasia recognized her as a girl from St. Clair.

After a quick examination, Tim Holden offered a suggestion. "Her face looks pretty bad. It's only ten o'clock; maybe we can take her to a doctor in Frackville." Everyone seemed to agree that the girl should be taken to a doctor as quickly as possible. We placed her in my car and within minutes Tim Holden, his girlfriend, Stasia and I were making our exit from Peach Mountain.

When we arrived in Frackville, we stopped and asked directions to the nearest doctor's office. There was one just a few blocks away, a large white house that was well lighted. On the outside, encircling the house and neatly manicured front lawn, was a three-foot black wrought iron fence. We made our way along the concrete pavement, up two steps and onto the large porch.

Our fallen angel was being supported by myself and Tim Holden. We were ready to present her to the doctor for examination. I rang the bell, and stepped back so the physician could have an unobstructed view of the patient.

The doctor, dressed in a lounging robe, opened the door. He was a man in his middle fifties, wearing glasses and sporting a mustache. He moved his head slowly from side to side, making no attempt to conceal his disgust. "What do you people want? Do you realize what time it is?"

I spoke for the group. "Doctor, we'd like you to take a look at this girl's face. We think she needs medical attention."

His voice rose in volume to almost a shout. "I'll tell you what she needs. She needs to be taken home and put to bed. She's drunk! You're all drunk! If you're not off this porch in one minute I'll call the police. Now get the hell off my porch!"

He slammed the door and turned off the porch lights. Tim Holden fired the first volley of insults. "You no good son of a bitch of a quack, I hope you'll rot in hell." Everyone joined in the verbal abuse as we returned to the car.

Stasia offered some sound advice. "We better get out of town before the cops pick us up."

We arrived back at the party at eleven o'clock. We placed our injured companion on a blanket, placed an ice pack on her face and rejoined the party. At its conclusion, Tim Holden, Stasia and I assumed the responsibility of escorting the young lady to her home. Stasia knew where it was, on the main street in the center of St. Clair.

We arrived in front of her home at about 1:30 a.m. hoping to deliver the injured girl inside as quickly as possible and leave without being detected. To succeed in this endeavor, we would need the help and guidance of the angels themselves.

The house was set back about fifty feet from the street and the area wasn't too well lighted. Fortunately for us, there was no one on the street who could possibly identify us. But sneaking the inebriated girl into the house undetected was not going to be easy.

I sought a little information before we entered the house. "Stasia, what are her parents like?"

"Her father is tough. He keeps a tight rein on her, so don't dilly-dally when you get to the door."

"Are you crazy? Don't dilly-dally! Fer Christ sake, we might get our heads knocked off when we open the door."

Tim whispered his final instructions. "Pat, when we set this girl inside the door we better be ready ta run."

"OK, Tim, I'm with you, but fer God's sake, let's be quiet."

The porch in front of the house was enclosed with jalousie windows. It was ground level, which was to our advantage; at least we didn't have to climb any steps. I could just imagine the old man coming to the door and flattening both of us.

I was carrying the girl on the right side, therefore I was in the best position to open the door. All the while the girl never made a sound. She was out like a light! The thought occurred to me that after we placed her inside the room, our job as Good Samaritans was finished, and we could run like hell and hope for the best.

I turned the door knob slowly and opened the door as far as possible. The room was pitch black. We maneuvered the girl about two feet inside the entrance, stood her in an erect position and darted out of the house. In retrospect, we should have placed her on the floor and then made our exit.

We weren't more than five feet down the walkway when we heard a resounding crash. It sounded as though she had knocked over a table or a lamp. In any case, the noise was loud enough to awaken everyone in the household. It took us about ten seconds to reach the car and make our escape.

Three days later I had a date with Stasia. "What happened to your friend?"

"The next day her father threw her out of the house. She's now living with an uncle. Her father is trying to find out who the bums were that got his little girl drunk."

"Does he have any idea who the bums happen to be?"

"No, but someone said he was checking cars. He's looking for a big brown Chrysler. By the way Patty, your car is a Chrysler, isn't it?"

"Yeah, maybe if I'm comin' ta St. Clair in the near future I better thumb a ride. What do you think?"

"Patty, if you value your life, you better thumb a ride."

After I entered college in September of 1939, Stasia and I slowly drifted apart. Stasia eventually married a businessman from Iceland and had three children. Her husband died in 1983. The last time I heard from her she was still living in Iceland.

In November of 1942, Sheridan Mackey and Chipper Connelly, both close friends of Stasia and me, had dinner with her in New York City, a few days before they sailed for the European theater of war as lieutenants in the U.S. infantry. Both were killed in France in 1943.

In 1944, two nights before I sailed for Europe, I also had dinner with Stasia. It was a comfortable and reassuring feeling to be with someone from back home prior to sailing overseas. We took great delight in reminiscing and recounting our happy and carefree days in Schuylkill County.

30 Blythe Township Politics and the High School

Starting in the twenties and continuing for three decades, politics was very intense throughout Schuylkill County and especially in Blythe Township. Both political parties functioned under the Andrew Jackson philosophy of "To the victors belong the spoils."

The Republicans had been in power for more than thirty years. Their control was absolute: they controlled every office and job in the township. It was unthinkable for a Democrat to apply for a job or ask for a political favor. But in 1932 the Democrats did sweep into office on the coattails of Franklin Delano Roosevelt in his resounding defeat of President Herbert Hoover. FDR's popularity throughout the country had a positive effect for the Democratic candidates in many local elections. Such was the case in Blythe Township.

After the victory celebrations had subsided, the political executions began. The Republican job holders were fired, and for the first time in three decades, the Democrats were in control of the school board.

Some important changes took place at the high school. It was 1935, the depths of the Depression, and jobs were hard to find. Teaching positions, considered to be top-of-the-line, preferential jobs, were part of the pork barrel system controlled by the school board. Many of the teachers came from out of the school district. In most cases they were of high caliber and did their utmost to remain above politics. Even the most ardent and vocal Jackson-style Democrats realized it would be foolish to disrupt the learning process by hiring less qualified teachers. However, it was no secret that many of the teaching positions were secured through political connections.

Politics played an especially important part in the selection of the superintendent of schools. Eddie Spelyng, a talented and dedicated administrator, was the superintendent in 1935. He was a soft-spoken and low-key individual who came across to many of his detractors as arrogant and aloof. A newly elected member of the school board was quoted as saying: "There's going to be some changes at the high school and you can be sure of one thing, Eddie Spelyng must go. I'm tired of looking at that smug and aloof bastard."

T.R. Gibbons, the high school principal, was well respected throughout the community and had accumulated few if any political enemies. As a result, he retained his position.

After the elections in May, the Republican teachers in the high school were secretly notified to bring their textbooks to the boiler room after school on a specified date. No questions asked, just bring the books to the designated area. The books were tossed into two large coal-burning furnaces and burned.

One teacher recalls the incident. "Very little was ever said about the burning of the textbooks. Such questions as 'Who gave the orders and for what reason?' were never answered. When the subject of the books was brought to the attention of the administration, the question was ignored. All acted as though the incident had never taken place."

Many of the teachers believed it was done to embarrass the new school board so they would have to purchase new textbooks. This would raise the level of the new school budget and not set too well with the voters. An inside joke among some of the teachers was, "Did Adolf Hitler learn the trick of burning the books from the Blythe administrators or vice versa?"

Spelyng was notified by certified mail that he would not be retained as superintendent and would be replaced by Jimmy Nash, who at the time was superintendent of the Mahanoy City School District. Once again politics and personal friendships had come into play. Dr. Carroll, of Cumbola, was president of the Blythe school board. He was a close friend, both politically and socially, of Dr. Nash of Pottsville, who was the brother of Jimmy Nash.

Nash was forty years old, six feet five inches tall and tipped the scales at 250 pounds. He had been an outstanding four-letter athlete in high school and college. He and Spelyng were complete opposites. He was loud, boisterous and outgoing, the perfect example of an extrovert. He had a fiery temper and ran the school like a top sergeant in the Marines.

He had a Jekyll and Hyde personality. When he stepped out of his role as superintendent and the pressure was off, he was relaxed, soft-spoken, witty and a most gracious individual. Few members of the student body were ever afforded the opportunity to observe Nash under those peaceful and serene circumstances. When carrying out his school duties, he had the eyes of an eagle, the heart and ferocity of a lion, and an extremely short fuse. When he became upset or angry, he was one mean individual! Give him a wide berth and plenty of room to operate.

His right foot made a flapping sound when he walked, the result of a basketball injury during his college career. When walking through the corridors, he could be heard forty feet away. At various times, as groups of students approached a corner in the halls and heard the sound of his flapping foot, they hurriedly made a hundred and eighty degree turn and headed in the opposite direction.

While I was studying in the library one afternoon, I had the opportunity to observe Nash in action. The eight sturdy rectangular tables, each of which could seat eight students, were occupied by approximately twenty-five students in all. Jerry Faye, a tenth grader and a classmate of mine, was sitting with three girls at one of the tables. They were engaged in conversation, but not necessarily pertaining to their studies. The girls, amused by Jerry's conversation and antics, were giggling.

He arose from his seat to illustrate a point. As he proceeded with the demonstration, the girls interrupted the silence of the library with loud laughter. At that moment Nash appeared at the library door and observed the antics.

He walked across the room, turned Jerry around and in one sweeping motion knocked him over the table. He hit him with the palm of his hand, not with a closed fist. The girls brought their hands to their faces and sat silently shuddering in disbelief at Nash's behavior.

Nash walked around the table and stood over Jerry. "Young man, get to your feet and go to my office."

Later that day I talked to Jerry. "What happened when you went to the office?"

Jerry scratched his head as he responded, "Ya know, that Nash is as crazy as a bedbug. When I entered his office, he turned ta me and said, 'Jerry, I didn't mean to hit you so hard, but I had to make an example of you. Go to the bathroom and clean yourself up, then go back to class.'

"As I left his office, he handed me four candy bars. I tell ya Patrick, he's as nutty as a fruitcake!"

Jimmy Devine lived in Palo Alto, a small community of about one thousand people, located between Pottsville and Port Carbon. The borough had no high school, therefore the students had the choice of going to Pottsville, Port Carbon or Blythe high schools. Whichever school they chose, their tuition was paid by the borough.

Jimmy opted for Blythe, which was three miles away. The bus fare was fifteen cents each way. He didn't have the fare, so he hitchhiked a ride to school. Most of the time he arrived before the opening bell. He decided to go to Blythe because he wanted to play football and basketball under the tutelage of Jack Shields, one of the outstanding coaches in the county. Jimmy was six feet six inches tall and had great potential in both sports. He would be an asset to any athletic squad in the region, and Shields was ecstatic because of Jim's decision to attend Blythe.

Being a potential football and basketball star, he had an excellent rapport with Nash. He tells the following story which adds to the mystique and behavioral patterns of the superintendent.

"Nash was a great drinker, but he was a streaker. By that I mean at times he wouldn't take a drink for weeks on end, but when he started to drink, let me tell ya, he was some drinker!

"On various occasions he and I were drinking partners. Each morning I thumbed a ride on Mulhall's corner. Most of the time I was picked up by various teachers or by Nash. At least once a month, he would pass me and point his finger in the direction of Hughie Cantwell's bar, located across the street. I'd cross the street and together we'd enter the establishment and take a seat at the bar.

"Hughie always gave us a cordial greeting. 'Good morning gentlemen, what'll it be?'

"Nash was first to respond. 'I'll have a bourbon. How about you, James?'

"'I'll have a beer.' Hughie set the bottle of liquor in front of Nash, who then poured his own drinks. Hughie always kept my glass full of beer. The fact that I was sixteen years old never seemed to bother Nash or Hughie.

"Our conversation was mostly about sports and the comments were confined to the three of us. We began drinking about 7:45 a.m. and made our exit about 10:00 a.m., neither of us feeling any pain when we arrived to begin our day at school!

"As we entered the school on one occasion, we were greeted by T.R. Gibbons, the principal.

"'Good morning, Mr. Nash. Good morning, James.'

"Nash kept walking. 'Mr. Gibbons, will you join James and me in my office?'

"We followed Nash into the office. He went to his desk and sat down, opened the large drawer to his right and produced a bottle of bourbon and three water-sized glasses."

"'Would you like a drink, Mr. Gibbons?'

"'No thanks, Mr. Nash.'

"'How about you, James, would you like a drink?'

"'No, Mr. Nash.'

"'Well, I hope you don't mind if I have one.'

"He poured himself a half glass of bourbon and downed it in a matter of seconds. 'OK, James, you better get back to class. Mr. Gibbons, I'd like a few words with you.'

"I thanked Nash for the ride and went to class."

In my senior year, I knew some of my classmates were drinking. It usually happened on the weekends or after sporting and social functions held at school. However, Jimmy Devine sheds some new light on the subject of socializing on school time.

"We did a lot of drinking during our senior year. It was a school rule that no one was allowed to leave the premises at noon except students from New Phillie who walked home to eat lunch. Happy Berrang, Alex Pautenius, and Francis Kollessor lived in town and were permitted to leave school at noon. Alex invited me to have lunch at least three times a week.

"It took us five minutes to walk to his house. However, we didn't eat there. We ate our lunch at his father's bar, which was located next door. His dad worked on the WPA and his mother worked as a cleaning lady for some of the more affluent residents in town.

"The bar was locked, but Alex had an extra key. We sat at the bar, ate our lunch, shot darts and were served beer by the hospitable Alex. We usually had about five beers before we made our departure. We were never questioned or reprimanded by any teacher or member of the administration."

I asked Jim, "How come I was never aware of the noontime escapades?"

"Ah, you were always chasing girls or playing in the band!"

Three family names dominated the sport pages in Schuylkill County during the thirties and the early forties. They were the Dimmerlings, Shields and Rompolos. All members of the families participated and starred in the three major sports.

The Dimmerlings were represented by Bill, Charlie and Paul, in addition to their cousin George. The Shields clan included Louis (Gas), Jack, Mickey, Dan, Joe and Charlie, plus Catherine, Doris and Vivian who all starred in track and basketball. The Rompolo family contributions to the sport pages were Duke, Rudy, Frank, Joe, Happy and Agnes. Agnes was an outstanding performer in track and basketball.

In addition to the Shields girls' exploits in track, one of the legends of Blythe track was Bessie Coyle, from Kaska, who was undefeated in the hundred-yard dash during the 1931 and 1932 seasons.

Blythe was a member of the North Schuylkill basketball league. During my high school career two teams dominated the league, Frackville and Mahanoy City. Charlie Dunkleberger was the mentor who guided the basketball fortunes of Frackville, and he compiled a most enviable record. His teams hadn't lost a league game in six years. The winning streak was broken with the emergence of Mahanoy City as a basketball power in 1935.

Dunkleberger, besides being an outstanding coach, was fortunate to have two superior athletes on his teams. Eddie Shillo led the league in scoring for three years, followed by Ron Northey who also led the league in scoring for three years. Shillo completed his education at Lebanon Valley College while Northey went directly to baseball's National League. In a career of twelve years in the majors, he played for the Philadelphia Phillies, Chicago Cubs, and the Chicago White Sox of the American League.

Mahanoy City, coached by Bill Goefert, began their dominance of the league during the 1935–36 season. Following the same format as Frackville, they were brought into prominence by the play of George Senesky and Jack Goefert, son of the coach. Both became scoring leaders of the league.

Senesky was six feet one inch tall and had great leadership qualities in addition to being a gifted shooter and superb ball handler. He was a coach's dream. During the 1937–38 season, he was leading the league in scoring and the fans throughout the county were eager to catch a glimpse of the new scoring phenomenon. Whenever and wherever Mahanoy City played a capacity crowd was assured.

I was on the Blythe team in my senior year, twelfth man on a twelve-man squad. Jack Shields called the team together to map plans to stop the Mahanoy City juggernaut, which meant holding Senesky to a low-scoring game. "I don't know whether we have the talent on this team to stop Mahanoy City. If we can keep Senesky under control, we have an outside chance of winning the game."

He selected Dulla Doyle as the person he believed had the ability and smarts to contain Senesky. "Here's the plan. We're going to simulate every move Senesky makes. I've observed him on numerous occasions and he follows a certain pattern of play. You're all aware that he's a left-handed shooter. Therefore, when he gets the ball, he fakes to his left, takes two quick dribbles to his right and shoots.

"Dulla, your job is to crowd him and keep your hands in his face. Remember, he's quick and if he gets a step on you, he'll score. Do you think you can do that?"

Dulla, oozing with confidence and thrilled at having the opportunity to stop the great Senesky, stepped forward. "Coach,

I'll do a job on Senesky that he won't forget fer a long time. He'll think my hands are part of his face."

Coach Shield was elated with Dulla's attitude and confidence. "That's great, Dulla, I know you can do the job."

The anticipated moves of Senesky were rehearsed over and over for four days. The Mahanoy City scoring machine was in for one big surprise!

Dulla was apprehensive as he waited for the game to begin. It was going to be a thrill to match wits and athletic ability with his renowned opponent. Shortly, Shields would find out if all the hard work and preparation were going to pay off.

Before taking the floor, Shields gave Dulla his final instructions: "Remember, don't give him an inch!"

Dulla nodded his head. "I'm all set, Coach."

The game began to unfold as predicted. Senesky took the ball, faked to his left, took two fast dribbles to his right and shot. Within eight minutes he handled the ball eight times and scored sixteen points. Mahanoy City won in a walk, as Senesky scored thirty-one points.

After the game, Coach Shields asked the obvious question. "What happened to the plan, Dulla?"

"I really don't know. When Senesky shook my hand at the beginning of the game, he said, 'Don't guard me too close, kid, and I'll make ya look good.'

"I was all set ta climb all over him, but when he said that ta me, he shook me up. I gave him too much breathin' room. I think that no good son of a bitch conned me!"

After graduation, Senesky enrolled at St. Joseph's College, at that time one of the basketball powers in the East. During his junior and senior years, he was selected to the All-American basketball team. He played in the National Basketball Association for ten years.

When he retired as an active player, he became coach of the Philadelphia Warriors and maintained the position for five years. After his association with the NBA ended, he became a sales representative of a large Philadelphia manufacturing firm, before retiring to Florida.

Jack Shields had graduated from West Chester State Teacher's College as a physical education major. He played second base on the varsity baseball team for three years. His coach, Glen Killinger, an All-American football player at Penn State during the twenties, took him aside in his senior year. "Shields, if you could hit you'd be in the major leagues. Take my advice, go back to the coal region and get a job teaching school. Don't plan on a baseball career."

Jack took his mentor's advice and secured a position as athletic director at Blythe in 1932. He coached baseball, football and basketball. His baseball and basketball teams were average but his football teams were superb.

Blythe, because of the size of its enrollment, was classified as a Class B school. The graduating classes hovered between ninety and one hundred and five students. Between the years 1932 and 1940, Shields never had a losing season in football.

Although he never played football in college, he was an exceptionally fine coach. His grasp and concept of the game was uncanny. He was a perfectionist in every aspect of the game, and he worked endlessly until his teams functioned like a Swiss timepiece.

He had a great rapport with his players. During the summer he would assemble his backfield and center at least three times a week. They piled into his Ford convertible and went swimming at Kunkle's Dam. The swimming dam was located five miles from New Phillie in the Penn Dutch farmland area.

Along the way, he pulled his car off the road and went into the farmers' fields where they practiced the basic plays for the coming season. On the way home, they repeated the procedure. When the football season opened in September, they were like a well-oiled piece of machinery.

In those days, there was very little auto traffic along the farmland roads. Stopping in a farmer's field to run some football plays never attracted any attention or created any controversy from the public or the farmers. Besides, Jack knew all the farmers because he taught most of their children in his physical education classes.

His life was dedicated to his athletic teams and their success. During the football season he lived and breathed the sport. His high school hygiene classes were skull practice sessions for the members of the team. He gathered them around his desk where he diagrammed, explained and demonstrated new plays and techniques. For students who were not members of the team it was a rest and conversation period. No one complained. Why kill a good deal?

Jack Shields and Jimmy Nash were good friends and possessed the same philosophies of sports on a high school level, how they should be played and the price to be paid for success.

The state of the nation, the economy, educational values and the future of the youthful athletes had a direct bearing on the attitudes and moral values thrust upon the athletic coaches and athletic directors in Pennsylvania and throughout the nation. What did the future hold for high school athletes upon graduation? With no money or any prospects of obtaining any, their chances of attending college were minimal. One of the opportunities available was the possibility of obtaining an athletic scholarship. Other than that, the only avenue open to the graduates was to join the armed forces, which at that time were not held in high esteem by the American public.

Doctoring the records of high school athletes was rampant in Pennsylvania during the thirties and forties. The Pennsylvania Interscholastic Athletic Association (PIAA) rules state: "No student over the age of eighteen years shall compete in high school athletics." Many athletic directors throughout the state did not adhere to the rule. The prevailing attitude seemed to be, "Everyone is doing it; therefore, if we're going to survive, we'll have to make some adjustments." If the rule was to be broken and the records altered, it took two to tango. The administration and the athletic department often must have collaborated in making the changes.

Allentown High School won three state championships in basketball during the thirties but were stripped of the titles after being convicted of tampering with the academic records of members of the team. President Nixon and Allentown had something in common. "Everyone was doing it; however, they got caught and had to pay the price."

In 1934 Schuylkill Township, which included the towns of Tuscarora, Middleport, Mary D and Reevesdale, decided to transfer their high school students to Blythe. In the past, their students had attended Tamaqua High School. The transfer of students was a bonanza for Jack Shields and his athletic teams. He searched out the athletically inclined students and convinced many of them to try out for the teams. The 1935 football team compiled a record of seven wins and two defeats. His hard work and enthusiastic recruiting were about to pay off. At the conclusion of the season, he had a meeting with his assistant coach Frank Rompolo.

"If everything goes as well as I think it will, next year's team should be sensational. I have a feeling that we're ready to roll."

"I hope you're right, Jack. It's a great feeling when you have a team that's loaded with talent."

"Well, I'll tell you this. We're loaded!"

Over the Thanksgiving holiday, Jack gathered four of his senior players for a conference.

"Boys, let me give you a little fatherly advice. If you graduate in June, the opportunities of securing a job or continuing on to higher education are mighty slim. You will either join the unemployment ranks or join the armed forces. Each of you is sixteen years old. If you quit school now, you can re-enter in September and have the opportunity to play another year of sports, and you won't be breaking any PIAA rules.

"I'll tell you another thing. Next year we'll have one hell of a team. If we go undefeated, and there's a good chance we will, I'll get each of you a scholarship to a college somewhere in the South. I can't tell you the name of the school, but I assure you it's a top-rated college. Think it over and let me know your answer when you return from the Thanksgiving holiday."

Three of the boys, Jerry McNeilis, Judgie Shelesky and Pete Koslosky, took Jack's advice and returned to school in September. He couldn't have chosen three better players. The T formation was unknown at that time. All schools were using the old "Notre Dame shift," and his three red-shirted seniors were the ideal players to fit into his dream backfield.

McNeilis was a good solid quarterback, Shelesky and Koslosky were halfbacks. Shelesky was one of the fastest runners in the county. He ran the hundred yard dash in 9.8 seconds; the state record was 9.6. Give him an opening on the outside and he was off to the races. No one could lay a hand on him. Pete Koslosky was a born leader. When on the field, he was in complete charge. He called the plays and was the driving force which inspired his teammates to perform beyond their natural abilities.

The line averaged 195 pounds, which was unheard of at that time. It was anchored by Doc Walters, Happy Rompolo and Johnnie (Younnie) Puzauskie. After graduation all three went on to play for major colleges. Doc Walters eventually became a practicing physician in Pottsville.

Shields' prediction came true. His team was not only sensational, it was a juggernaut. They completed the season undefeated and were known as the "Wonder Team." The team compiled a record of eight wins and no losses, scoring a total of two hundred and sixty points against only seven for their opponents. To give an idea of their ability, they played the East Stroudsburg Teacher's College freshmen team and beat them by the score of 40 to 0.

True to his word, Jack obtained scholarships to the University of Florida for the three returning lettermen. Koslosky transferred to Lebanon Valley College after completing his freshman year and received a B.S. in education. McNeilis transferred to Temple University and eventually became a mortician. Shelesky transferred to East Stroudsburg Teacher's College and graduated as a physical education major.

Michael Carrigan was the quarterback on Blythe's 1934 team, which compiled a record of seven wins and two defeats. Pete Koslosky was a sophomore that year and a third-string halfback. Both were natives of Cumbola and were friends on and off the field. After graduating, Michael was appointed as a typing supervisor for the county, setting up remedial programs for typing students. He later received a B.S. degree in art education and retired in 1975 after thirty years in the public school system of New Jersey.

He and Pete spent many hours discussing sports, especially the fortunes of the Blythe football team of 1936, the Wonder Team. "Pete was extremely knowledgeable about the game. On numerous occasions throughout the season, he would describe to me, in an emotional and enthusiastic manner, the plays he would call in certain situations if they presented themselves on the playing field. He was a real student of the game!

"He was proud of his Lithuanian heritage. He reminded me at every opportunity how proud he was to be born a Hunkie. On one of his visits to our home we made our way to the living room, and as we took our seats he handed me a piece of paper with a list of names.

"'Here, Michael, take a glance at this paper. This is the way our lineup should appear in the newspaper when we win our next game.'

"I looked at the names and began to laugh. 'Pete, you're some guy. Whoever gave you the idea of coming up with this list?'

"'Well, the coach is Irish; however, I believe all the members of the team should be Lithuanian. What do you think of the idea?'

"'Pete, only you could come up with such a list. You outdid yourself the way you changed the names.'

"'Give me the paper and I'll read them for you. McNeilis is Macnavage, Walters is Walakouskie, Rompolo is Rompulskie and Kelman becomes Kelmonouskie. Do you think Coach Shields will let me put this lineup to the newspapers?'

"'I doubt it. He might be Irish, but I don't think he's dumb enough to submit that lineup to the press!'"

After graduating from Lebanon Valley College, Pete Koslosky obtained a teaching position in a nearby community. At that time he changed his name to Kane!

Shields' 1937 and 1938 teams compiled records of seven wins and two defeats. In 1939 he put together another great aggregation which won the Pennsylvania Eastern Conference title with a record of nine wins and one defeat. On December 2, Blythe defeated Clearfield High School 12–0 in the Central Pennsylvania Inter-Scholastic Football Conference championship game at the Clearfield County fairground before an estimated crowd of ten thousand. It was a great accomplishment since Blythe, which had a student population of four hundred and fifty students, beat a team from a community with over fifteen thousand residents.

As with his Wonder Team of 1936, Shields produced a bumper crop of future college stars. Dunch Franko enrolled at Albright College. Eddie Berrang attended Villanova and played in the NFL for ten years with the Washington Redskins and the Detroit Lions. George Pavalko was an all-state guard in his junior and senior years in high school. He attended Villanova, where he played three years as a starter. Frank O'Neil attended West Chester Teacher's College. Fritz Laurinitus played for Lawrence College in Lawrence, Kansas, and played professionally for Brooklyn.

Shields resigned his position at Blythe in 1940. He became the head football coach at St. Joe's Prep in the tough Philadelphia high school parochial league. In his first year as head coach his team won the city championship. He resigned after his second year and accepted a job with the Philadelphia city administration as coordinator of recreational activities in the city.

When his coaching career had come to a close, he retired and made his home in Florida. He died in 1987. On his last visit to Pennsylvania, he visited me at my camp. Our reminiscing took us back to his activities and successful years at Blythe. "Yes, they were happy and fruitful years, probably the happiest days of my life. I have many beautiful and satisfying memories. They were tough times and we had to overcome many obstacles, but we did what we had to do. Yes, they were great years!"

It is the opinion of many sport fans throughout the coal region that the greatest high school football team to play the game during the thirties was the 1938 undefeated Hazleton High School team. The team was spearheaded by the famous "coal dust twins" Joe Andrejco and George Cheverko.

Hazleton won the Big 15 Conference when they defeated the Pottsville Crimson Tide 25 to 0 before eighteen thousand fans, the largest crowd ever to watch a scholastic sports event in northeastern Pennsylvania. Andrejco and Cheverko, because of their athletic prowess, were household names throughout the state. They were selected on the all-state teams in basketball and football in their junior and senior years. The football team's quarterback was Michael Vickson and the line was anchored by Joe Yachanick. All four were recruited by Fordham University, which at that time was one of the football powers in the East. They played in the 1942 Sugar Bowl game in Florida in which Fordham defeated Missouri 2–0.

32 Shenandoah, the Toughest Town in the East

During the Depression, Shenandoah was the toughest town in Schuylkill County, if not in the state of Pennsylvania. Young people between the ages of sixteen and twenty from surrounding towns seldom, if ever, made forays into that borough to look for girls or drink in bars.

Bobby Stein, Sheridan Mackey and I were listening to Tommy Dorsey records in the Stein living room. Mackey's voice projected over the sound of Tommy's trombone.

"Why don't we take a ride up to Shenandoah and see if we can pick up some girls? It's only 7:15, and if we hurry, we'll be there before it gets dark."

"Somebody was tellin' me that Shenandoah is a rough place. The guys in that town are supposed ta be tough and mean and always ready fer a fight."

"Ah Canfield, you really don't believe all that bullshit. It's just talk. Come on Bobby, do you think you can get your dad's car?"

"I don't know, but it sounds like a good idea. Right now he's having office hours, and I don't think he'll be overjoyed if I interrupt him. Maybe it would be better if I asked my mother."

Within a few minutes, Bob reentered the room holding the car keys high above his head. "Let's go, they say there's some good-lookin' babes in that town. Maybe we'll be lucky!"

Mackey had the last word. "We'll soon find out!"

Within a half hour, Bobby wheeled his dad's Franklin into a parking space on one of Shenandoah's side streets. We got out and proceeded in the direction of center city.

We hadn't gone more than twenty-five yards when I observed six tough-looking gorillas heading in our direction. They were our age or a few years older. One fella looked as though he could be a sparring partner for Joe Louis and the others looked like they had just finished a shift at the number six coal mine.

"Mackey, take a look at the group ahead of us. Holy Christ, they look mean as hell."

Mackey tried to bolster our confidence. "Just take it easy and everything will be OK."

Their spokesman, a kid about five-eleven, built like a Mack truck and as mean-looking as Al Capone, broke the ice. "Where the hell are youse guys goin'?"

Mackey wasn't intimidated. "We thought we'd look around and see if we could pick up a few girls."

The Mack truck continued, "There ain't no girls in this town. If ya know what's good fer ya, get back in the car and head fer home. And talkin' about home, where are youse guys from?"

"We're from New Phillie."

The mention of our hometown brought a chorus of laughter and catcalls. Eventually one of the gorillas stepped in front of Mackey. "New Phillie? Are you kiddin'! All the guys in that town are a bunch of sissies. Now get the hell outta here, and if we see youse guys in this town again, we'll beat the shit outta ya. Now move yer asses and get outta town."

As we journeyed home, Mackey was the first to comment on our ill-fated invasion of Shenandoah. "They weren't that tough. They didn't scare me."

Bobby evaluated the trip a bit differently. "I think we were lucky we didn't end up in the hospital. As far as I'm concerned, that's my first and last trip to that damned forsaken hell hole."

The kids in Shenandoah between the ages of six and twelve seemed to enjoy the football season more than the average citizen. If any visiting team was victorious, it was a tradition that the buses carrying the victors were stoned as they departed the stadium area.

When the buses began to move the command was given, "Everybody on the floor, except the bus driver." The driver seemed unconcerned as to the events that were unfolding. He was relaxed and content to concentrate on the driving. If you listened very carefully, you might catch some of the commands and jargon of the leader of the group stoning the departing bus. "Kill them bastards, but don't hit the bus driver."

When the incident of rock throwing was brought to the attention of a resident of the town, he simply smiled and replied, "Ah, the kids ain't that bad. After all, they never throw at the bus driver."

Jerry Faye was playing safety on the Blythe football team during a game at Shenandoah. As the game moved into the third quarter he continually glanced around as though he was looking for something. After the game I asked him why he continually turned his head. "I wasn't worried about their ends catching a pass. I was trying to find out who the hell was throwin' the rocks."

Clarence Hess, a native of Shenandoah, recalls the "Margie trick" which was played on the famous big bands that toured the country during the thirties and forties. During that time Shenandoah was a favorite stop as a one-nighter for the big bands. The dances were held at Maher's Hall, located in the center of town. It was a beautiful setting and reputed to have one of the smoothest dance floors in the region. In addition to the dance hall, there was a bar and the most popular ice cream parlor in town. The Dorsey brothers, Cab Calloway, Wayne King, Sammy Kaye, Paul Whiteman, Kay Kyser and other top bands looked forward to playing at Maher's. Perhaps it was because of the relaxed attitudes and atmosphere which prevailed throughout the coal region.

The members of the bands made their headquarters at the Ferguson Hotel, located two blocks from the dance hall. The bands usually arrived at the hotel about two o'clock in the afternoon. After checking into their rooms, many band members made their way to the hotel bar.

Tommy Dorsey's band was playing on this particular night. His was the most popular band to frequent the hall. He was born in Shenandoah Heights, a mile outside of town. The townspeople were overjoyed to have the famous musicians in their midst. If the opportunity presented itself, those frequenting Maher's bar looked forward to sharing a drink or two with the visitors.

The "Margie trick" operation was slowly put into motion. While they were enjoying their drinks, the main concern of the hosts was to find out the identity of the "lover" in the band. After that fact was established, special treatment and niceties were extended to the specially selected musician.

While they were enjoying the hospitality of the locals, the question was put to a member of the band. "Who's the lover in the band?"

"There he is over at the other table. He plays lead trumpet. His name is Bill, and he loves the women!"

Bill was invited to the table to have a drink. As he was seating himself, Stella made her entrance. She was a beautiful Polish girl who looked like a movie starlet and had the body to match. She took a seat at the bar and ordered a drink. Bill spotted her the moment she made her appearance.

"Who's the chick at the bar?"

"That's Stella. Ain't she a beauty?"

Bill seemed to be in a trance. "Mother of God, look at the build on that babe! Holy Christ. She is a beauty!"

"Would you like to meet her? She's easy ta get along with and if she takes a fancy ta ya, you can have a fun night. Come on, we'll go to the bar and I'll introduce ya." He took the bait. The rest would be easy if he followed the usual behavioral pattern of previous selected "lovers."

As they made small talk and leisurely sipped their drinks, the lover made his initial move. "I finish playing at 1 a.m., and I should be back here at 1:30. Maybe we can have a few drinks."

"That sounds like a good idea. My husband is at a firemen's convention in Philadelphia, so I'm in no hurry to get home. The more I think of your suggestion the more I like it. I can hardly wait till the end of the dance!"

Bill nearly fell off the bar stool. Her statement was mind-boggling. "Her husband's at a convention in Philadelphia. Holy Christ, how lucky can a guy get!"

When he arrived on the bandstand, he took his horn out of the case and began to warm up. One of his fellow musicians sat beside him and nudged him in the ribs. "How did you make out with the chick?"

"How did I make out? Are you kiddin', I couldn't have written a more perfect script. Would you believe this, her old man is at a firemen's convention in Philadelphia and won't be home for a few days. She loves musicians and she thinks I'm cute. What a night I'm gonna have. I hope I have enough energy to finish this gig, so I can enjoy that bundle of joy."

The band played "Good Night Ladies" at 12:55 a.m. Precisely at 1 a.m. the house lights were turned up and the patrons began to make their exit. Bill had his horn in the case within minutes, and walked into the bar at 1:10 a.m.

Stella was seated at her favorite stool eagerly awaiting the arrival of her newly found lover. When he approached, she lifted herself off the stool and gave him a warm embrace and a passionate kiss.

It was a typical Thursday night. After the dance many of the patrons made their way to the hotel bar, hopefully to continue their night of enjoyment. The barroom setting had all the earmarks of a New Year's Eve party, with an abundance of liquor and good fellowship. All that was missing were the noise-makers, balloons and streamers.

After a few drinks, Stella and Bill departed. They walked hand in hand, retreating to the quietness and seclusion of his room, which was located on the first floor. The room overlooked a grassy terrace which extended about fifty feet, at which point there was a twenty-five foot incline, with a pitch of about forty degrees leading to a wooded area consisting of maple and oak trees. In this area about one hundred people, including the members of the band, lay prostrate on the ground awaiting the well-orchestrated performance to begin.

Ten minutes was the allowable time for the lovers to finish the foreplay and begin the serious business of lovemaking. At the height of their passion, there was a loud knock on the door.

Stella responded in a shrill and excited voice. "Who's there?"

"It's me, Stash, let me in. Is there anybody in there with ya? If there is, I'll kill him. Now let me in!"

"Who's Stash?"

"He's my husband!"

"Holy Christ, I'm dead!" He jumped out of bed as Stella switched on the overhead light. The pounding on the door grew louder as Stash's resounding voice echoed through the dimly lighted hallway. Bill pulled on a pair of undershorts as he ran to the window, lifted the shade and struggled to open the window.

"Jesus Christ, somebody nailed the window shut! How the hell will I get outta the room? If your husband catches me I'm as good as dead. Holy shit, what am I gonna do?"

"Your only chance is to go through the window. I don't know how you're gonna do it, but the only way out of the room is through the window. Unless you think you can get past my husband."

"Are you out of your mind?"

"The window is only two feet from the ground, but for Christ's sake get outta the room."

The performance was to begin when the lights were turned on in the room. The next move was up to the lover. He had a few options as to how he was going to make his exit; he could throw a chair through the window and jump, or save a few seconds by diving head-first through the window. In either case, he stood a good chance of castrating himself.

Bill made a quick decision. He dived head-first through the window and landed on the soft turf amid the shattered glass. Terrifying thoughts were running through his mind, "I might ruin my lip or break a few bones, but it's better than getting killed at the hands of an irate husband."

He had a problem. Where was he going to hide now that he had made a safe getaway? Many of the previous victims of the prank landed on the grass in a pair of shorts, that is if they were lucky and had enough time to put on their undergarment. The unfortunate ones landed on the turf in the nude.

Bill ran into the bar and headed for the men's room. As he neared his goal and a possible haven of safety, he was seized by three men. They dragged him to the center of the room where he came face to face with the outraged Stash, a husky Lithuanian miner.

Stash was being held back by four men as he tried to reach the man who was in the room with his wife. "I'll kill that no good son of a bitch. He was in the room with my beautiful Stella. I'll kill him!"

By this time, Bill was on the verge of a nervous breakdown or a heart attack, whichever came first. He was pleading for his life. "I didn't mean any harm, I didn't know she was married! Honest ta God! I didn't know she had a husband. I don't do things like this. Please fellas, tell Stash I didn't mean any harm. After all, I'm a happily married man and I have four kids."

One of the conspirators stepped forward and held up his arms high in the air and requested quiet. Within a matter of seconds they followed his suggestion.

"This man has done a terrible thing. But because he plays for Tommy, we'll forgive him if he'll buy us all a drink. How about it, Stash, is that OK with you?"

"It sure is. Let's all have a drink on the lover boy."

Roars of laughter filled the room. Bill was speechless. "You mean this was all a joke? You set me up—well I'll be a son of a bitch. I thought I was getting ready to die. Well, if I'm buying the drinks, I need a big one. Come on, Stella, get Stash and we'll have a drink together. Now I can understand why Tommy sometimes acts a little strange. You miners are all crazy!"

The "Margie trick" was staged on many occasions without any real harm coming to the unsuspecting musicians. Except for a few scratches and wounded pride, it was an experience they would long remember. That is, if they ever fully recovered from their lover's nightmare.

In 1976, I was the president of the Tourism Promotion Agency of Schuylkill County and chairman of the bicentennial committee. Clarence Hess was the executive secretary of the

TPA and my chief assistant. We were escorting a group of Philadelphians through the county, pointing out historic and important tourist attractions. We arrived in Shenandoah at 12:30 p.m.
in time to have lunch at Paskie's, the town's famous bar and
restaurant.

Being a native son, Clarence explained, "This is the most
popular and best eating place in town. It's noted for its ethnic
foods, specializing in Lithuanian, Polish and Slovak dishes."

As we were waiting to enter, a group of people were making their exit. They were laughing and everyone seemed to be
having a wonderful time. One of the Philadelphians asked one
of the group, "What's the celebration? Is someone getting married?"

"No one's getting married; we're coming from a funeral."

Clarence turned his head and spoke to the visitor from the
city of brotherly love. "Shenandoah is the only place in America
where they take the ice off the body and put it on the beer!"

In the late twenties Shenandoah was a thriving city of thirty
thousand people. Its educational system was one of the best in
the county. No one passed to the next grade level without passing all the requirements set up by the teachers and school board.
That brings up the story of Big Eddie. (I never knew his last
name.)

When Eddie had completed the second grade, his teacher
decided he should repeat and not progress to the third grade. He
stayed in the second grade until he was twenty-one years old
and he became known as Big Eddie. No one seemed to mind, his
parents, classmates or the community. Eddie was somewhat re-
tarded, and it was in the best interest of everyone that he complete his school career in the second grade.

As one of his former classmates recalls, "I remember when I
was in the sixth grade and I would see Eddie playing with his
classmates. I, and my friends, didn't think anything about it and
paid little attention to the situation."

There were also some pluses. He helped the youngsters get
into their winter clothing when they went out for recess. When it

was raining, it was Big Eddie who helped the teacher get the children ready for dismissal. Keeping the room neat, cleaning the erasers and being the teacher's aide were all part of Eddie's daily routine.

When his teacher retired someone asked her, "Did you mind having Eddie in your class all those years?"

"Having Edward in my class was a blessing. I don't know what I would have done without him. He was like my own son. As long as the school board members and his parents didn't complain, I thought it was to his advantage to remain in school. When he left school, I went to one of the local merchants and obtained a job for Eddie. It was a menial job, but he was happy and he performed his tasks well. Yes, Eddie was something special!"

33 Working on the WPA

My happy and carefree days of high school came to an end on June 5, 1938. When I graduated I thought the pleasures of high school would never end. Surrounded by my friends, it seemed that each day was a new adventure. The summer, as usual, was a time of much activity: softball, swimming, dances and a continuation of the good life. September was another matter; it ushered in a new beginning and the reality of the real world.

My father was head of his own construction company, and I was the only member of the family who had never worked for the company. As I was a musician I spent most of my time practicing trumpet and piano. Working in construction didn't appeal to my way of life.

When high school classes began the day after Labor Day and I was no longer a part of the scene, suddenly I realized that a new era in my life was beginning. Most of my friends were either going to college or planned on leaving the area to look for work or to launch a new career. Prospects of advancement or securing a job in the coal region were very limited.

I always enjoyed school but I was undecided as to what career I wanted to pursue. My father wanted me to be an engineer but I was still not sure. I was so busy having a good time that planning a career never entered my mind. However, the day of reckoning was upon me.

Finally my father called me aside. "What do you expect to do now that you're finished high school?"

"I don't know, Pop, I really don't know. Do you have any suggestions?"

"Why not work for the company until you decide what you would like to take up in college? I can use a truck driver on one of the WPA projects. The job's good for at least a year. During that time you can give some thought as to what you want to do. How does that sound?"

"It sounds good ta me, Pop. I'm your new truck driver!"

Within a few days I joined the WPA ranks. I had been driving a car since I was thirteen years old, but my experience as a truck driver was limited. I was told to report to the work area in Valley Furnace where I would receive information about the job.

I entered the office and was greeted by Joe Tobin from Tucker Hill. I had known him since I was a kid. "What the hell are you doin' here, Patty?"

"Joe, I'm your new truck driver."

"Well I'll be a son of a bitch. I can't believe you'd ever end up as a truck driver. Things must be real tough at the construction company when old P.S. will send you on a job."

Joe "The Cat" Flannery was standing to the side of Tobin's desk. "Hey Cat, can ya believe that old Pat sent Patty as the new truck driver?"

"Jesus Christ, this place is gettin' like a kindergarten. The last time I saw him, he was in short pants."

After the laughter had died down Joe handed me a piece of paper. "Report to the rock pile just outside of Silver Creek. It's up on the side of the mountain. Do ya know where it is?"

"Yes, I know the place. Those hills are pretty steep!"

"Hell yes, they're steep. You're taking Feezie's place. He was transferred to another job. Take it easy on those mountains; they're old strippin' roads, so watch yourself. They can be dangerous, especially if you're comin' down with a load of rock."

"OK, Joe, I'll take it nice and slow."

"Don't forget, give that paper to old Tommy Whalen. He's your boss."

Old Tommy Whalen was the father of my old buddy and classmate Jessie. He had been coming to our home for years, and he and Mrs. Whalen were members of my parents' bridge club.

It was beyond my wildest dreams that I would some day be working on the WPA and Tommy Whalen would be my boss.

As I drove out of the parking area, I was apprehensive about my life as a truck driver. However, it wouldn't be long before I would be part of the work force. As my old friend Alex Pautenius used to say, "What the hell, if we survived the Sisters at Holy Family school we can face anything."

I started the trek up the old stripping road toward the working area. The road was narrow and steep, in addition to being muddy and slippery because of a severe rainstorm the previous evening. I was having a difficult time getting any traction and my progress was slow. There's no doubt a more experienced driver would have had less difficulty than I was having.

I had only fifteen yards to go before I would reach the top of the incline and a clearing where I could turn the truck around and back it into the loading area. I had the accelerator pedal to the floor and the wheels were spinning but the truck didn't move an inch. I was stuck!

Finally Tommy Whalen came to the side of the truck. "It's no use. You can't go any farther, I'll get the men to give you a push."

The men were standing along the road observing my ordeal "OK you men, get behind the truck and push." Tommy Whalen's request wasn't well received by the onlookers.

One of the men muttered, "Jesus Christ, Feezie never got stuck! Now this kid gets stuck the first day on the job."

Another was quick to continue the disparaging remarks. "Yeah, I don't think the son of a bitch ever drove a truck before. Why the hell don't P.S. hire a real driver?"

My first day was off to a rousing start!

I had the feeling my driving didn't rate high marks among my working companions. I made four trips to Middleport and delivered the stone without any further mishaps. Even the ride up the mountain incline began to seem less treacherous. However, my first day on the job was no picnic.

On the WPA, I found myself working with men I had known all my life. Many had been successful businessmen while others had had good-paying jobs in industry. At this juncture in their lives any work was a matter of pride and survival. Working on a WPA project at least was less of a stigma than being on relief.

It was a strange feeling to work alongside the fathers of my boyhood buddies. They were proud men and working on a government project was a bitter pill to swallow. The outlook was bleak; it seemed as though no one had the faintest idea how the nation would ever surmount the difficulties which engulfed it.

As the winter approached and I felt more comfortable in my job, I looked forward to the days of working with the men. I seldom, if ever, entered into their conversations unless I was asked a specific question.

Despite the apparent hopelessness of the situation, their sense of humor never diminished. Of course frustration and resentment at times pierced the thin veneer which shielded their inner feelings. But on the whole they tried to maintain a cheerful atmosphere.

There was little doubt that I was inexperienced and naive about many worldly things, and some of the men enjoyed watching my reaction to unexpected situations. On one occasion they were loading rock onto the truck along one of the farm roads in the Pennsylvania Dutch area. A young girl whom I knew, although she was a few years older than I, drove by in her dad's car. I casually remarked, "There goes a pretty girl who's also a nice person."

The fellow standing next to me nudged me in the ribs. "She's the easiest piece of ass in the valley. Just touch her and she spreads her legs."

I was shocked by his remarks. "That's a lie, I don't believe what you're saying and I think you're all wrong about that girl, I never heard anyone say anything bad about her before. I still think you're wrong."

My surprising reaction to his biting remarks, and the way I stepped forward to defend the girl's honor, were all the encouragement they needed to pursue the matter. One of the fellows standing to my left side tapped me on the shoulder. "No, Patty, he's right about that girl. She's an easy piece of ass. All the farm boys in the valley had a piece of her. She's an easy lay, take my word, she's easy."

I couldn't bring myself to believe their remarks. It ruined my day; I couldn't get it out of my mind. Later that evening I met Jack Gannon, my first cousin, who was among those working on the project. "Jack, were those fellas pulling my leg taday when they were talking about the farm girl, or were they tellin' the truth?"

"Don't believe those lying bastards. They were just having a little fun with you. From now on don't pay any attention to them and don't act so surprised at some of their statements. Just act like you know as much as they do."

The coal region was well known for the practical jokes which were played on everyone. No one was immune! I was moved to various job locations throughout the county. The work crews remained at the same locations but the trucks moved to wherever they were needed.

In the middle of July, I began working on a rock pile located between Tuscarora and Mary D. In order to get to the rock source, I had to back the truck about one hundred yards along a culm bank until I reached the bottom of the mountain and the rock.

On this particular day, the temperature had reached 90 degrees. After finishing lunch, I got in the loaded truck and left the area on my way to Middleport to deliver the rock. About a half mile up the road, a terrible odor seeped into the cab. It was so overpowering and obnoxious that I had to pull the truck alongside the road. I jumped out and threw myself on the grass. Within a few seconds I began to vomit. I lay on the grass in a state of exhaustion, as sick as I've ever been in my life.

I delivered the load of rock and returned to the loading area. I must have looked terrible as I stumbled out of the truck. Two men took hold of my arms and laid me on the ground. "What's wrong? You look like you're sick."

"There must be some kind of a dead animal under the hood. There's a terrible odor coming into the cab. I don't know what it is, but it made me sick. I don't think I can make another trip."

Pat Dowling, the boss on the project, leaned down and whispered, "Don't worry about a thing. You stay here under the trees and rest. One of the fellas will make the run to Middleport, you take it easy."

A few days later, the truth came out. While I was eating lunch, the jokesters had spread limburger cheese on the truck's manifold. The heat of the day, plus the hot manifold, generated the terrible odor.

As the years passed, I often wondered if anyone in that crew remembered the incident, or did it really happen?

In 1985, I was attending a firemen's picnic in Tuscarora and enjoying some of the ethnic foods being served. A man walked up to me and introduced himself. He didn't look familiar, but after a few minutes conversation I realized he was a classmate of mine at Blythe. "Do you remember the day on the WPA when we put limburger cheese on the manifold of your truck and you got as sick as a dog?"

"Yes, I remember. But how come you were on the job? You were too young to be working on that project."

"Yes, you're right about the age. I had been out of high school since June and I didn't have a job. My father was on that project and he got sick, so I substituted for him. That was a dirty trick to play on you, but at the time we thought it was funny."

Working on the WPA was an eye-opening experience. It made me realize if I wanted a worthwhile life and the better things in this world, I had better go to college and get an education.

I entered West Chester State Teacher's College in September 1939, the day Hitler invaded Poland. The country was slowly emerging from the Depression. The bright future we so ardently dreamed about was put on the back burner. A new challenge was on the horizon, World War II.

How lucky could our generation be? We survived the Depression only to face the possibility of going to war.

The Pioneer Tunnel, Ashland, Pennsylvania, showing supporting timbers.

Testing for gas in the mines.

Part III

Pigeon Matches in Modern Times

Neither Rain Nor Cold Can Keep Schuylkill County From Trap-and-Handle Shoot With $1000 at Stake

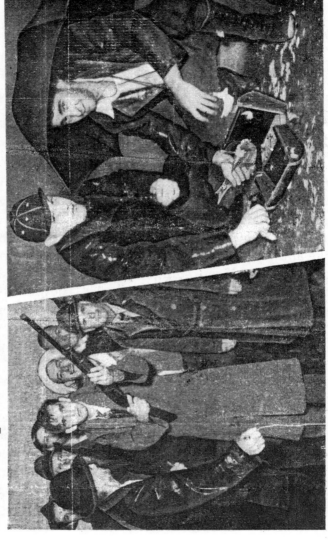

Winner of the match shoot and $1138 at Port Carbon was Reed Middleton (center with gun). At left, watching Middleton intently, is his trainer, Harvey Baney, who is about to pull trap string releasing bird. In picture at right Jiggers Quinton (left) and La Mar Lurwick are planting belled bird in trap. The bird is an archangel crossed with a swallow. Honest!

34 After the War

When World War II ended in 1945 and servicemen began returning to their families, Schuylkill County, like all parts of the
country, welcomed them home with open arms. There was a
festive and joyous mood throughout the land. The soldiers had
made many sacrifices, suffered much, and returned to their
homeland minus many of their comrades. They had served their
country well, and now was the time to celebrate and endeavor to
catch up with the world.

Money was in abundance. They had discharge pay; bonds
they had accumulated during the war were cashed (most servicemen bought monthly government bonds while in the armed
forces). Many took advantage of the 52-20 club, a fund set up by
the government which paid returning servicemen twenty dollars
a week for fifty-two weeks to help ease them back into a peace-
time world and to sustain them until they could secure a job.

Many were looking forward to marriage and starting a new
life. They wanted the whole ball of wax—cars, clothing, homes—
and were eager to begin the task of building a new world for
themselves and their children. Others had entered the armed
services as young men, some in their teens, and had never enjoyed a taste of the good life. Now was the time to make up for
those lost years. The single men were going to fulfill the cherished dreams they had talked about in chow lines and barracks
bull sessions or as they headed into battle. One of the most
familiar phrases heard in the service was, "When I get home,
you know what I'm going to do." What weren't they going to do

when they got home! Someday all those dreams would come true. That someday had finally arrived.

In New Phillie, every day was like a Saturday morning and every night was like New Year's Eve. The bars were bursting at the seams. Old buddies talked, drank and reminisced about the good old days and their escapades in the service. Every now and then, after there had been a bit too much to drink, a fight would erupt. When the skirmish was over, everyone returned to the bar and drank to the health of the winner and the loser.

The big bands were riding high, never dreaming that rock and roll was just around the corner to change the music scene forever. Tommy and Jimmy Dorsey, Vaughan Monroe, Benny Goodman, Harry James, Artie Shaw and Les Brown were still packing them in and breaking all attendance records wherever they appeared.

The underlying theme seemed to be, "Why shouldn't we raise hell and celebrate? We won the war, didn't we? We're the conquering heroes!"

I was at Camp Lucky Strike in Le Havre, France, preparing to board a ship for my return to the U.S.A. About two hours before our departure, we were ordered to report to our chaplain for a final briefing.

I can remember the gist of his remarks as if it were yesterday. "You're returning to your loved ones as conquering heroes, but most of you have been leading a wild and unchristian life. You've been drinking, carousing and sleeping with these European girls. You had little concern for decency and clean living. When you rejoin your families, I pray that you'll come to your senses and begin leading a good and decent life." We left the room in silence, knowing full well the words of the clergyman were fitting and true.

Gradually, a state of normalcy returned to the pigeon scene in Schuylkill County. Shooting clubs, pigeon matches and promoters came to the fore, just as before the war. Most sections of the county had an array of shooters who were ready and willing to exhibit their prowess as marksmen and had the money to back it up.

During the years between 1946 and 1970 there were hundreds of excellent shooters. They weren't of the caliber of Rol Holley, Norman Erbe, Sammy Lehman, Reed Middleton or Jake Lurwick, but they aroused great enthusiasm and produced many exciting times. It is important that these men be remembered. They helped promote and prolong the sport that is unique to the anthracite region of Pennsylvania.

In recent years, one other feature of the sport has changed. Some individuals and animal rights groups have attempted to stop the pigeon matches, especially the Hegins Labor Day Shoot, a one-day extravaganza that attracts hundreds of sportsmen from all over the world. The protesters claim that this particular event, and pigeon matches in general, should be classified as cruelty to animals. These do-gooders never mention the fact that millions of dollars are spent each year in places such as Philadelphia, Pittsburgh and New York in an effort to exterminate the pigeons that infiltrate, contaminate and overwhelm the inner cities.

Pigeons killed at the matches are taken home by the nearby residents, to be eaten as roasted squab or made into soups. Very few pigeons are wasted. During the Depression the pigeons provided food for the poor families of the region, which was one of the most depressed areas of the country. The food issued by the government was meager, and the extra food and nourishment provided by the pigeons was a welcome addition to the sparse menu of the unfortunate.

Most of the retired shooters and the present-day shooters share the same opinion regarding the people who are attempting to stop the shoots. Reed Middleton expresses his feelings. "We don't want to take rights away from anyone, yet these people are attempting to deprive us of our basic right of enjoyment and relaxation. They would benefit the country much better if they concentrated their energies and marches to stop the use of drugs and crime in our country instead of harassing the people of Schuylkill County."

Fats Umbenhauer has participated in pigeon shoots since the forties, and is at the present time an active shooter. "We don't hurt anyone. The matches, especially the Hegins Labor Day Shoot, which attracts thousands of visitors, bring much-needed revenue to this depressed area. All the funds earned by the Labor Day Committee, after expenses are paid, are donated to the Hegins Park Association, the fire company and other worthwhile community projects. Now these people want to put a stop to the shoot. They're trying to take away our rights and I think it's outrageous!"

Willie Murray, still active as a trapper after sixty years in the pigeon business, expresses his opinion. "I often wonder who these people are who protest against us? Do they ever work? Where do they get the time to march and protest, and who supplies the money for these projects? I believe that some newspaper or TV station should investigate and see who they are and where they come from."

35 Return of the Big Matches; Kelly versus Lehman

When the war ended, Sam Russell, Eddie Murray and Joe Piel were among the outstanding shooters at Willie Murray's Golden Rod Club. Many matches were taking place, but these were the shooters who drew the greatest number of patrons. Russell compiled a record of thirty-five wins and fifteen losses over a ten-year period.

One of the biggest matches at the club took place on October 16, 1946. Willie engaged Tony Bell of Tamaqua in a match for fifteen hundred dollars, seventeen birds. Willie edged Bell by killing the last bird for the win.

The Sophys, the Hallahans and the Dutch Hill gang still believed they had a winner in Bell. They arranged a match between Bell and John Starr of Middleport for two thousand dollars, fifteen birds at the Golden Rod Club.

Bell had a style of shooting in which he drove the birds (he permitted the birds to fly a long distance before firing). Because of this, the Starr forces decided to use a new tactic against him. They had the privilege of setting the trap during the second half of the match. At the halfway point, Bell was ahead by one bird. They set the trap at the end of a rise with the assumption that if the birds flew straight they would disappear and Bell wouldn't have a shot.

The tactic didn't work as planned. Instead of flying straight the birds flew to the right, giving Bell a clear shot. He killed the last seven birds and won by one bird.

The gamblers were ecstatic with Bell's victory. They were convinced he was on a roll and in a position to challenge some of the better shooters in the county. Bill Sophy and Bill Heck made a trip to the Golden Rod Club to see Willie Murray.

"Willie, do you think Bell can beat Sammy Lehman?"

"I'll tell ya, Bill, Sammy's one hell of a shooter. He's a tough man ta beat, especially if he shoots at his Ten Pin Club."

"We know all those things, Willie, but if Sammy thinks he kin take Tony in a breeze, he'll take the match lightly and maybe we'll sneak one in and make a killin'. If Sammy's at his club makin' all that money on the booze, maybe he'll have one too many drinks and not concentrate on the match. We might have a chance and we'll kick his big fat Dutch ass. What do ya think of the idea, Willie?"

"Ya might have somethin' there, but don't sound too anxious. That Dutchman's pretty smart. He's not as dumb as he looks."

Sammy and the westenders jumped at the chance to engage Bell. He was a good shooter, but no way could he handle Sammy! Both sides assembled the best trappers in their area. The westenders had the Hartmans, the Barnhardts and the Felty brothers in their corner. Bell had Willie Murray, the Dutch Hill gang (with their famous archangels), and Pete Petrole and his elusive black birds.

The match drew a capacity crowd, and Sammy made quite a haul at the bar. Beer, whiskey and moonshine were the favorite drinks of the day. Boilo, the potent Lithuanian drink made from moonshine and honey, was also available.

Bell had a good day and beat the west end favorite by one bird, 14 and 15 out of 17 birds. Sammy's forces were disappointed but not downhearted.

When asked if he took Bell too lightly he replied, "Hell no. Anyone who kin kill 15 out of 17 birds is shootin' a good match and Tony shot one hell of a match. Let's go up to the bar and have drink, I'm ready fer some cards and maybe a good chicken fight."

After the war, Eddie Kelly's career as a shooter and trapper was on the rise. If he wasn't engaged in a match, he was trapping many of the important matches in the region.

He was attending a small match at the Golden Rod Club when he met Windy Curry of Cumbola, who promptly issued a challenge.

"How'd ya like ta shoot seven birds fer fifty bucks?"

"It's OK with me if ya wanna lose yer money."

Eddie killed six out of seven birds. Windy killed five.

After the match, they were in the clubhouse enjoying a few beers and chewing the fat. "Ya know, Eddie, you were pretty damned lucky taday. We were shootin' at a bunch of barn birds. How would ya like ta shoot a real match, say twenty-five birds fer a thousand bucks a side, trap and handle?"

There was a bit of contempt in Eddie's voice as he bragged. "First of all, I won't have any trouble gettin' some people ta back me with the money. And another thing, I kin beat you any time, any place, drunk or sober! Mister, I kin tell ya now, you got yourself a match."

Eddie had no trouble getting people to back him in the match. The Sophys, Monk Miller, Dave Smith, Jackie McDonald and the Lurwicks were more than willing to jump on Eddie's bandwagon.

Windy also had his followers: Willie Murray, Windy's hometown buddies Rudy and Duke Rompolo, Sammy Lehman, and the Hazleton boys Georgie Breen, Harry Beech, J.J. Maguire and Al Meiss. Willie Murray, Allie Sublosky and the Petrole brothers took care of the trapping.

The match took place on Sunday, September 17, 1946, at the Mahanoy City ballpark. It was a terrible day, overcast, raw and misty, and a continuous chilly drizzle fell throughout the contest. Because of the prevailing weather conditions, many people went outside the park and sat in their cars between shots. Eddie was shooting well, and by the fifteenth bird he held a five-bird lead over Windy.

In 1946, the Boston Braves were overwhelming favorites to win the National League pennant. They were leading the league by five games and their pitching staff was headed by Warren Spahn and Johnnie Sain, two of the outstanding pitchers in baseball.

Rudy and Duke Rompolo, backers of Windy, were not doing well at the match. Their friend was getting trounced and they were a few hundred dollars in the red. They returned to their car after the fifteenth bird, turned the radio on and began listening to the Braves-Phillies game.

Warren Spahn was knocked out of the box in the first inning. The Phillies had an eight-run lead going into the seventh inning. When Rudy and Duke returned to the match, they met Sammy Lehman and Big Bill Heck.

Rudy opened the conversation. "Hey Sammy, how'd ya like ta make a bet on taday's ballgame between the Phillies and the Braves?"

Sammy hesitated a few moments. "It's OK with me, Rudy. Who do ya want?"

"We'll take the Phillies."

"How much do ya wanna bet?"

"Well, we ain't been doin' any good on the match, how about six hundred bucks on the Phillies."

"That sounds OK with me."

As they began to move away, Sammy had the last word. "Win or lose, we'll pay off after the match."

Later that evening, Duke and Rudy met Eddie at Lurwick's bar. Eddie had won the match and was celebrating his victory. Rudy related the story to Eddie. "It's a damned good thing we made the bet with Sammy. You really cleaned us out taday. The bet with Sammy saved our asses."

Joe Zacko owned a sporting goods store in Pottsville and was considered to be an above-average shooter. Phil Laudeman thought he could be a winner.

Eddie Kelly's advice was often sought, but not necessarily followed. "Eddie, I'm backin' Joe Zacko in a match with Harry Hoover later this month, I'd like ta have ya trap fer me."

"I'll trap fer ya, Phil, but Zacko will never beat Hoover in a million years. There's no way he kin beat Hoover." In spite of Eddie's forthright statement, Phil arranged the match. Eddie's prediction proved accurate. Hoover easily defeated Zacko and Phil lost a bundle.

Eddie Kelly, with little education, was one of the most prominent and controversial figures on the pigeon scene in Schuylkill County. During the years between 1941 and 1949, he worked in a bootleg coal hole called the Hurry Up. The coal hole was owned by Dave Smith, a successful businessman and an above-average pigeon shooter.

The land was leased from the Reading Coal Company and was located near Seltzer City, about three miles northeast of Pottsville. Even though the land was leased, the operation was often referred to as a "bootleg hole." The term was a carry-over from the Depression days, when the unemployed miners simply took over the coal land, owned by the Reading Company and the Lehigh Coal and Navigation Company, and mined the coal illegally in order to survive.

The Hurry Up hired sixteen men and had two mules. The gangway, or tunnel, traveled two thousand feet into the side of the mountain. Eddie worked as a laborer and was paid nine dollars a day for an eight-hour shift.

Among his mining buddies he was known as a "mucker." He spent the day in the gangway scooping coal and rock into the coal cars. As the miners progressed farther into the mine in search of coal, they laid track for the coal cars, which were then loaded with rock or coal to be removed from the mine.

There were two cardinal rules under which the miners worked: Always work with a buddy, and make your working conditions as safe as possible. The gangway had to be made safe so the miners could do their work properly; therefore they placed timber along the roof of the tunnel. The timber, made of oak, was supported by large twelve- to eighteen-inch-thick oak support columns. Someone once asked Eddie, "Is the gangway safe?"

He didn't hesitate a moment. "I kin tell ya this, the gangway is as safe as if ya was sittin' in yer own livin' room at home."

In order to move forward in search of coal, drillers made dozens of holes in the face of the tunnel, some as deep as three feet. When the drilling was completed, the chargemen came on the scene. They filled the holes with dynamite and the charge was set off, filling the gangway with coal and rock. After the smoke and dust had cleared, the miners inspected the area. No one reentered the gangway until it was declared safe.

The workers carried a safety lamp whenever and wherever they worked. This was to detect "black damp," a deadly, odorless gas which was a miner's nightmare. If the safety lamp flame became large and bright or the flame went out, it was an indication the deadly gas was present and the miners evacuated the area immediately. Experienced miners were always aware of the lamp as they worked or traveled throughout the mine. Many young and inexperienced workers had been killed because of haste or negligence or because they became so engrossed in their work that they failed to watch the safety lamp.

After the area was declared safe, the muckers loaded the rock into the waiting cars and sent it to the surface. When they came to the coal, the muckers were assisted by the miners in loading the cars. The miners were paid by the carload and made excellent wages. The muckers, such as Eddie, who performed the back-breaking work, were paid a meager daily wage.

In 1946 Sammy Lehman was still considered one of the premier shooters in the county. Dave Smith, at the urging of the Sophy brothers, approached Sammy as to the possibility of a match between himself and Eddie Kelly, at Laudeman's on Sunday, November 1, two weeks in the future.

"You must be kiddin', you know damned well that Eddie's no match fer me. You'd be a fool to arrange such a match."

"You're probably right. Would you be interested in givin' us some odds, say two ta one?"

"They're pretty high odds. Why don't I get back to ya in a few days?"

Sammy contacted Jackie McDonald, owner of the Brandonville Country Club, and asked if he would be interested in backing him in such a match.

"Holy Christ, Sammy, they're pretty big odds. You better be damned sure you can beat that Irish bastard. When he's having a good day he's a pretty good shot."

"Don't worry, I can handle Eddie, I know he's Irish but he can't be that lucky. Sometimes he tightens up a bit when the stakes are high. Maybe it would be a good idea ta make the stakes high enough that Eddie would worry a bit. I know I can handle him!"

"OK, get the agreement signed, and we'll put up as much money as you want."

Jackie gathered his money people, Charlie Simons, Battler Delago, Al Meiss, Dr. Frank Alimenti and Monk Miller. They were well oiled with the green stuff and were ready to take Dave Smith and his crowd to the cleaners. The site of the match was Laudeman's gun club.

All the smart money in the Pottsville area was backing Eddie, especially with two to one odds. If Eddie won, Christmas would come early to the county seat.

The Sophys and the Hallahans couldn't pass up an opportunity like that. They had a side bet of three thousand dollars with Georgie Breen, who was laying odds of five to three on Sammy.

Two thousand people descended on the club, the largest crowd at Laudeman's since the end of the war. The gate of one thousand dollars went to the winner. Thousands of dollars were bet on each bird. The noise and excitement were music to Phil Laudeman's ears. "I've been waiting fer a crowd like this since the beginning of the war. It looks like the good ol' days are back."

This was the type of match which the public had been expecting since the return of the G.I.'s. It looked as though things were getting back to normal. The gamblers were in their glory. Petie Joseph wisecracked to Bill Sophy, "Let the suckers have their fun. Before the night's over, our pockets will jingle."

The glory of the day went to Eddie and his crew. He won the match, killing 19 out of 25 while Sammy killed 18. It was a nail-biter, but Eddie prevailed.

The celebration was on, and the gamblers, winners and losers, joined in the fun. Eddie was king for a day and he enjoyed every minute of it. He was given five hundred dollars from the gate and the gamblers supplied him with all the drinks he could handle, plus two hundred in cash.

"This is the way a man should live; plenty of friends, booze and money. Tamorra I'm a mucker but tanight I'm the king."

As the night progressed the king gloried in his achievements. He began to hallucinate and imagine he could perform as well as Rol Holley, or perhaps even better than the renowned Rol.

He was seated at a table with Dave Smith, Bill Sophy, Jackie McDonald, Phil Laudeman, Sammy Lehman and Georgie Breen. Turning to Sammy, in his best Irish brogue he preened his feathers. "You thought I was lucky taday didn't ya, Sammy? Well, I'll tell ya this. I think I have yer number and I kin beat ya any day in the week. Whatta ya think a that?"

Sammy was a quiet man, and in no way a braggart. He turned and looked in the direction of Dave Smith. "Eddie feels pretty cocky tanight. He beat me taday, but he was pretty damned lucky. How about another match on Thursday over at the Ten Pin Club? Thursday is half-holiday for the professional men and we can draw another good crowd. But this time we'll make the odds even. Would ya like ta tie the match?"

"How about it, Eddie, do ya think ya can pin the Dutchman's ears back?"

"David my boy, ya don't have nothin' ta worry about. It's in the bag."

Eddie's pockets were loaded with the gelt as he traveled back to Seltzer City. Another happy man was Phil Laudeman. As he bid Eddie good night, he placed his hand on his shoulder. "Eddie, you and Sammy should shoot here every Sunday. Thanks to you two, I never made so much money in my life." He pressed a fifty dollar bill into the shooter's hand as they parted. "Thanks, Eddie, fer a great day."

Gamblers and promoters never dwell on the past. During the match on Sunday Dave Smith, Phil Laudeman and their followers reaped the harvest. All the breaks and money went their way. But Thursday's encounter would be a new day; new surroundings, new bets, new pressures and new opportunities.

It didn't matter to the gamblers who was shooting, or where the match was scheduled or the amount of the purse. As Petie had stated, at the end of the day they would control the money. If they didn't win it on the match, the activities which commenced after the match were the key to their monetary success.

In addition to the gamblers, the owners of the private gun clubs made a financial killing on the games of cards and dice. They automatically took ten percent off the top. To enter a chicken in a contest, a fee of fifty dollars was required. Added to the revenue derived from the sale of the drinks it amounted to a tidy sum. Sammy was not only looking forward to a victory, but also to a financial bonanza at the club.

Thursday was a beautiful day, with a temperature of fifty degrees and an abundance of white fluffy clouds dotting the autumn sky. The match was scheduled to begin promptly at three o'clock because darkness would engulf the premises about five-thirty. It was in the best interest of everyone to conclude the event in the allotted time.

By noon five hundred spectators had arrived to witness the shoot-off, and the gamblers were settled in for a long day. Those fans not engaged in shooting pigeons or making bets along the sidelines were in the club drinking, playing cards or shooting craps. All the activities added to the excitement and hype of the occasion. The more the booze flowed, the higher the bets, and from all indications it was going to be a better's paradise.

Sammy was well rested and prepared for the encounter most diligently. At practice he shot at least fifty birds daily and his confidence was sky high. On the other hand, Eddie, working as a mucker, had little time to practice.

On the day of the match, he started work at seven o'clock and finished at two. He arrived at the club at 2:45 still wearing his working clothes. It allowed him just enough time to go into the club and have a "miner's special," a shot and a beer, before the start of the match.

The events which took place in the first encounter and those which were unfolding on this day had some similarities, but not necessarily the same results. A vast amount of money was being wagered on each bird along the sidelines, and the consumption of booze was tremendous. However, that's where the similarities ended. Sammy killed 20 out of 24 and grabbed the victory, while Eddie killed 18.

As Eddie was leaving the shooting area, he was confronted by a disappointed Dave Smith, his boss and principal backer. "You looked tired taday Eddie, ya didn't seem ta have good concentration like you usually have. Why didn't ya sit down and rest when ya were at work?"

Eddie never missed a step or blinked an eye. He looked straight ahead. "I don't sit down on my buddies! Scoopin' in the slope all day ain't easy. If ya wanted me ta win the match, why didn't ya give me the day off?" Dave never replied!

The celebration was as expected. The gamblers and spectators retreated to the club to pursue their games and drinking. Eddie's enthusiasm was much more subdued than after his victory on Sunday, but he was the eternal optimist. "What the hell, so I lost the match and my friends are out a few bucks. I'll win a few more matches before I die, so they'll get their money back. I'm still enjoyin' myself, drinkin' with my friends and forgettin' my worries. The mornin' will get here soon enough and I'll be back muckin' in the mines."

36 The Irish Clan and the Petrole Brothers

Monk Miller was the gambling and bootlegging kingpin north of the mountain, and he was also deeply involved in pigeon matches and chicken fights. Others who played an important part in those activities in that area of the county were a group of men of Irish extraction better known as "the Irish clan."

The group included Jackie McDonald, Cletus Coyne, Charlie Simons and Billie McCue. Added to this group was a tough and lovable Italian by the name of Battler Delago. Collectively, they represented a formidable force of monetary capital and muscle. Each was a successful businessman and a pillar of strength in his community.

Gambling had a different connotation in the coal region. Everyone gambled! The women played bingo and the numbers; the average worker, successful businessmen, and professional men at one time or another participated in gambling, whether it was pigeon matches, pro football, baseball, basketball, horse races or other sporting events. It was a way of life. Therefore, a reference to a person who liked to gamble wasn't necessarily taken as derogatory.

Jackie McDonald was the proprietor of the Brandonville Country Club, located four miles east of Shenandoah. He was a successful and popular politician who served three terms in the state legislature.

Battler Delago operated a gas station in Girardville. In his youth he was a popular welterweight fighter, winning thirty-two fights and losing only eight.

Billie McCue ran a bar, located on the Vulcan Mountain, a few miles west of Ashland. Charlie Simons, married to Jackie McDonald's sister, operated a restaurant and bar in Girardville. Cletus Coyne was the owner of a successful plumbing company in the same municipality. If there was any action north of the mountain these were the men who were in the midst of the arrangements.

According to old-timers, the most money ever bet on a pigeon match at that time was in a contest between Kelly Ferrante, a bank teller from Hazleton, and Smokie Kurshock of Palo Alto, held in the Mahanoy City ballpark in 1947. Georgie Breen was backing Ferrante, Jackie McDonald and his group backed Kurshock.

Steve Salamander, a veteran of many years as a trapper and shooter, recalls the event. "I can't remember when so much money was bet on one match, and so much bet on one bird. It was a dirty and vicious affair. One fella borrowed eight thousand dollars on his house. Five houses were lost on the match."

Eddie Kelly birded for Kurshock and was promised five hundred dollars from Jackie McDonald if Kurshock won. Neither shooter was outstanding, but Ferrante won the match, killing 12 out of 25 while Kurshock killed 11.

There was bad blood between Jackie McDonald and Chet Hughes of Locust Gap. Jackie claimed he had been doubled-crossed in a primary election and nearly lost his place on the ballot. He vowed he would have his due. "I'm looking forward to the day when that Irish bastard pays his dues. I'll nail his emerald ass to the wall!"

Jackie systematically began his plan to settle the score with his one-time friend. He approached Cletus Coyne as to the feasibility of arranging a match between Cletus and Chet. "First of all, do you think you can beat Chet in a nineteen-bird match? If you don't, it makes no sense continuing the conversation."

"Hell yes, I can beat him! He's no pushover but I'll take him. I'll tell you one thing, if I'm gonna win, you better have Pete Petrole flying his black birds. We'll need all the help we can get."

"Don't worry about Pete. He'll fly his birds for me. You can count on that. I'll get in touch with him as soon as the match is set. In the meantime, I'll get Battler to arrange the match. Nineteen birds, two thousand a side and we'll kick that double-crossin' bastard's ass but good." Battler made the arrangements. The match would take place in two weeks at the Mahanoy City ballpark.

A huge crowd attended the shoot-off. They were treated to a day of entertainment, especially if they were betting on Cletus. Pete Petrole flew seven of his famous black birds away on Chet and Cletus won in a breeze. He killed 13 out of 15 and shot Hughes out at the fifteenth bird. Jackie had his revenge and Pete Petrole had pie a la mode for the first time in his life.

On the way home from the match they stopped for dinner at Charlie Simons' restaurant. When it came time for desert Jackie turned to the waitress. "I'll have a piece of apple pie, make it pie a la mode."

Without missing a beat Pete added, "I'll take the same. I don't know what the hell pie a la mode is, but if it's good enough fer Jackie it's good enough fer me."

The Petrole brothers, Pete and Rocco from Tresckow, a small town located a few miles southeast of Hazleton, were highly respected trappers and famous for their black pigeons. They had won many high-stakes matches with their birds. Many of the top shooters never signed an agreement unless they were assured of the brothers' services.

In 1945, at the Ten Pin Club, a match between Reed Middleton and Eddie Spitler was decided on the last shot. Sammy Lehman was backing Spitler and Jimmy Ryan and the Sophy brothers were backing Reed.

Pete Petrole was five feet two inches tall, low-key, soft-spoken, his outward appearance the epitome of humbleness. Inwardly, however, he possessed the heart of a lion and the competitiveness of Pete Rose or Mike Tyson. He had such confidence in the capabilities of his birds that he believed he could fly one away from any shooter in the world.

Pete had flown away four out of six birds during the match. Middleton was ahead by one bird as Spitler arrived at the mark for his last effort to tie the match. After a short conference between Ryan and Bill Sophy, it was decided that Pete should be the one to fly the last bird.

Jimmy Ryan approached Pete. "Pete, fly one of your black birds. It's getting dark and we think it can do the job."

"I don't know, Jimmy, there's so much money ridin' on this bird, I feel funny. What if it's killed? Look at all the money that's gonna be lost."

"Don't worry about the money. If it gets killed, it gets killed. I'll tell ya what I'll do. If you fly the bird away, I'll give ya a hundred dollars."

"OK, Jimmy, I'll put the bird in."

Pete explains his strategy. "It was gettin' dark and they were shootin' down grade. If the bird raised up it was a straight shot, so I put in a low-drivin' bird, straight and low. If it stays low he would have ta shoot down and he'd be short."

Pete's prediction was correct. Spitler shot down, missed the bird and lost the match. Another episode was added to the mystique of Pete and his black birds.

Pete was ecstatic with the results. He raised his hands high in the air and shouted, "Uff and druff my ass, he never saw the bird."

Jimmy Ryan gave him the hundred as promised plus another hundred for flying the previous four birds away. Ryan and the Sophys were happy and richer, and the Petrole brothers were sitting on top of the world.

The participation of the Petrole brothers as trappers was closely monitored by the gamblers. If the brothers were trapping in a match, they bet mostly on the miss. This gives an indication as to the confidence they had in the brothers' ability to fly birds away from most shooters.

In 1948, Pete was the main trapper for Dr. Frank Alimenti, a dentist from Hazleton, when he beat Vince Melany from Shamokin. In 1949, Pete birded for Jimmy Jones, of Scranton, when he beat Otto Meyers, of Scranton, for three thousand a side.

Georgie Breen backed Jones and won thousands on the encounter. Pete flew the last three birds away. Breen was ecstatic over the win. After the match, he held a victory celebration at the Petrole bar in Tresckow. He picked up the tab for the food and drinks, and at the conclusion of the festivities he handed Pete five hundred dollars.

"I don't know how you do it, Pete, but you have a magic touch around the trap." Putting his hand on Pete's shoulder, he continued, "I'm looking forward to more days like this. I won a lot of money today, thanks to you and your black birds. They're the greatest!"

In 1947, Pete birded for Harry Hoover, who was backed by Jackie McDonald and Battler Delago, when he beat Al Meiss at the Minersville ballpark. Two other trappers who played an important part in Jackie McDonald's success as a shooter were Steve Salamander and Tony Bee of Fountain Springs, a small village one mile south of Ashland. Because of their success their services were in great demand, and they kept at least five hundred birds in their pens at all times.

Early in his career as a shooter, Jackie McDonald seldom used the Petrole brothers. After losing a match because of their outstanding work at the trap, he became aware of their ability and realized they were a notch above the average trappers.

They worked hard to prepare their birds for a match. They brushed (trained) the birds daily and when the time arrived for them to fly in a match they were ready. The birds were trained to a point of near-perfection. When they were finally put in the trap, they were scared and nervous, which indicated they would leave the trap quickly and at a high rate of speed, and fly in any direction, left or right, high or low, according to the manner in which they were programmed by the brothers. It was this intense training and dedication that set the Petroles apart from the average trappers.

In a match between McDonald and Bill Bushbee, for one thousand dollars a side, Pete trapped for Bushbee and flew five out of six birds away from Jackie, who eventually lost the match.

He blamed the loss on Pete. "That son of a bitch of a Dago with his black birds, he really put the screws to me! From now on, he'll trap for me. I'll never shoot against that Wop bastard again." From that moment, he was Jackie's favorite trapper.

On one occasion they got their wires crossed, either by lack of communication or because someone with more clout stepped forward and secured Pete's services. McDonald and Delago had scheduled a match at the Brandonville Country Club on Sunday, September 8, 1948, with the understanding that Pete would be one of the trappers.

In the meantime, Jimmy Ryan had arranged a match for Shorty Bergen at Heckshersville and asked Jack Boyle, of Hazleton, to get in touch with Pete and ask him to trap for Shorty.

Jack Boyle was Pete's boss in the mines. "When Jack Boyle asked me ta do him a favor and trap for Shorty I couldn't turn him down. He always allowed me ta take off for hunting and never docked my pay. He always treated me good. I just couldn't turn him down. Maybe I was a little scared but I never called Jackie to tell him I wouldn't be there for the match. I hoped Jackie would win. Shorty won but Jackie lost."

Jackie let the word go out. "If that son of a bitch of a Wop ever shows up at my club, I'll shoot him."

When word got back to Pete, he made a hurried trip to Coal Castle to see Jimmy Ryan. "Jimmy, Jackie McDonald's mad as hell because I didn't trap for him last Sunday. He says he's gonna kill me! What'll I do, Jimmy? I'm scared!"

"Take it easy, Pete, I don't think Jackie has any intention of killing you or anyone else. Sometimes when Jackie gets mad he says some things he really doesn't mean. You go back home and I'll square things with Jackie. In the meantime, if I were you, I wouldn't go near the Brandonville Country Club!" In a few days

Pete received a call from Jimmy informing him that all was forgiven and he was back in the good graces of the Irishman.

A few weeks later, Jimmy Ryan brought to the fore the mysticism of Pete and his famous birds. He had arranged a match between Shorty Bergen and Tony Antonelli. He asked Pete to bring six black birds to the match. "We'll only use your birds if we need them. Just show up and scare the hell outta that Dago."

"Jimmy didn't use any of my birds but paid me fifty dollars just for makin' an appearance."

Pete was born in 1906 and began his mining career at the age of thirteen as a slate picker. When he was eighteen he became a laborer and at age twenty-six became a contract miner, the highest position in the mines, as well as the highest paid.

To become a contract miner, one had to have "papers," which had to be certified by the State of Pennsylvania and the Lehigh Valley Anthracite Mine, Inc.

He was proud of the fact that he worked in "the big vein," a vein of coal sixty feet high and forty feet wide. It was the largest and most famous coal vein in the anthracite region.

To supplement his income, in 1940 he opened a bar in Tresckow, a bar still in operation today. Being close to the pigeon scene, he took advantage of his access to the pigeons killed during the matches, buying them at the prevailing price of six birds for twenty-five cents. His wife made chicken broth or hor d'oeuvres which were served at the bar.

The preparation of the birds for consumption was a tedious task. After the feathers were plucked off, the birds were placed in a dish and saturated with alcohol and burned. This procedure singed the fuzz from their bodies. They were then cut into small pieces, soaked in salt water and vinegar over night, and the next day put in cold, pure water and placed in a deep freeze. Two days later they were cooked and packed in jars to be used as hor d'oeuvres at the bar. They were also added to spaghetti sauce and eaten by the family.

Pete was trapping for Jackie McDonald at a match being held at Jackie's club. At the conclusion of the match many patrons gathered at the bar for a few drinks. Pete, his brother Rocco and Gene Boyle were sitting at the end of the bar having a drink. Someone tapped Pete on the shoulder. He turned around and saw Jackie and a friend. "Hi, Jackie, how ya doin'?"

"Pete, you did a great job today, I'm proud of you. The Battler and I won some money from those farmers from the west end. By the way, I'd like you to meet a friend of mine from Fountain Springs."

Pete glanced up and saw a short, unobtrusive man, about five feet five inches tall, fit and trim, and dressed as if he just stepped out of *Esquire*.

"I'd like you to meet Mickey Mouse."

Pete never blinked an eye or moved a muscle. He thought it was another example of Jackie's Irish humor.

"Hello, Mickey, I'm glad ta make your acquaintance. If you're a friend of Jackie's, you can't be all bad."

"Hello, Pete, I've been looking forward to meeting you. You're one of my favorite trappers, and you handle those black birds like an artist. Jackie tells me that you're making him rich."

"Well, I don't know about that, but I'm always glad ta trap fer Jackie." After a few minutes of small talk the men left and joined their friends at the other end of the bar.

Pete met Jackie's friend on numerous occasions, mostly at the matches. He always took time to say hello and engage in a few minutes of conversation. A few years later, Pete was once again working as a trapper at Jackie's club.

During the course of the match Jackie approached Pete. "I have two free tickets for a Republican political rally picnic being held next Saturday at Watkins Grove in Fountain Springs. Senator Watkins is throwing a shindig. There's going to be plenty of booze and more food than you can imagine. Would you like to have the tickets? Maybe you and Rocco can make an appearance."

"That's real nice of you, Jackie. Sure, I'll take the tickets."

Pete and Rocco arrived at the Grove at 2:00 p.m. and proceeded to the pavilion, which was swarming with guests enjoying the sumptuous and delicious food and drink.

The aroma emanating from the heated pits where the steaks, chickens and hamburgers were being prepared started their salivary juices flowing. "Hey Pete, let's get a steak and a beer."

"Sounds good ta me, Rocco, let's go."

While they were enjoying their treat, they were joined by their old friends Joe and Bill Sophy.

"Ya know, Bill, I'm really impressed with this grove and picnic area. That Senator Watkins really knows how ta throw a party! He must be some guy. I'd like ta meet him sometime."

Bill took Pete by the arm and gently guided him toward the edge of the crowd. "There he is, Pete, right over there, the little fella."

"You mean that little fella with the bow tie?"

"Yeah, that's Senator Watkins. Would ya like ta meet him?"

"Just a minute, Bill, give me a few minutes till I clear my head."

"What the hell's the matter with you, Pete? Ya look like ya saw a ghost."

Pete was looking at the ground and slowly shaking his head in disbelief. He lifted his head slowly, puffed out his cheeks and blew out a noisy column of air.

"Jesus Christ, Bill, Jackie McDonald introduced me ta that man as Mickey Mouse! I've been callin' him Mickey Mouse fer the last two years. Everytime I met him I always said, 'Hi ya, Mickey!' He never blinked an eye and always answered, 'Hello Pete, how are you?' Holy Christ, Bill, I'm embarrassed. What'll I do?"

Bill looked down at Pete and paused a few seconds. A wide grin spread over his face. "Go up ta him and say 'Hi, Mickey.'" Bill doubled up in a fit of laughter. He put his hand on Pete's shoulder. "Pete, that's funny as hell."

After he recovered from his laughter, he gave Pete a gentle nudge toward the senator. "Pete, I'm sure the senator will be glad ta see ya."

When Senator Watkins saw Pete approaching he started toward him and extended both arms and embraced him. "Good to see you, Pete, I'm so glad you could make it."

Pete was in awe of his new-found friend. "I never knew you were a state senator and a judge. I never should call you Mickey."

"Never you mind, Pete, all my friends call me Mickey, and I consider you a friend." Pete and the senator remained friends until the legislator's death in 1978.

Pete and Rocco Petrole with their famous black pigeons and traps (*top*); Pete Petrole in his bar, 1990 (*bottom*).

37 Jimmy Ryan and County Politics

Jimmy Ryan was born in 1914 in Heckshersville, located a few miles west of Coal Castle and near Minersville. He rose from a humble beginning to become one of Schuylkill County's most outstanding citizens. He married Nellie Bambrick and had one son, James Jr.

He began his career as a door-to-door milkman. Eventually he expanded his business to include ice and coal deliveries. As his business flourished, he ventured into strip mining and founded the Schuylkill Construction Company. To coincide with his stripping operations, he built the Marlin Coal Breaker, which sized and washed the coal before shipment to consumers. The name of the company which operated the coal breaker was the Cass Contracting Company.

As he was on his way to financial independence, he became involved in politics. He was appointed a United States Marshal of the Eastern Pennsylvania District operating out of Philadelphia. While he was there, he made many political contacts within the statewide Democratic party. He mingled with the power brokers of the city and state. He was seen socially with Richardson Dilworth, mayor of Philadelphia, and United States Senator Joe Clark.

Bob Mulhall, of Coal Castle, recalls an event regarding Senator Clark when the senator made a hurried stop in Coal Castle.

"Every so often my dad would take me to Bergen's bar for a Sunday breakfast. On this particular Sunday, we were seated at a table near the center of the room, and the cafe was crowded with people eating breakfast or drinking at the bar.

"Jimmy Ryan and his entourage of eight people, including Senator Joe Clark, entered the bar. The patrons immediately recognized Jimmy and gave him a warm welcome. Jimmy held both his hands in the air to get everyone's attention. The gesture brought complete silence to the room.

"'Gentlemen, I'd like to introduce Senator Joe Clark.'

"The introduction brought a thunderous round of applause. In the meantime, Ryan and his friends had been given a large stein of beer by Agnes. Jimmy raised his glass in a toast: 'Here's to Senator Clark and the Democratic Party!' The toast evoked another thunderous ovation.

"Not to be outdone by his host, Senator Clark raised his glass. 'Here's to the good citizens of Schuylkill County, may they live forever. Gentlemen, the drinks are on me.'

"The place went wild! What a day! I'll remember it as long as I live.

"After the politicians finished their beer and were saying their good-byes, I heard Senator Clark say to Mrs. Bergen, 'Agnes, you have a beautiful place here. Jimmy has told me so much about you and your son James. Thanks for the hospitality and good luck in the future.'

"They made their exit and continued their trip to Shenandoah, where John Cuff, one of the leading Democrats in the county, was holding a political rally and picnic. Senator Clark was the guest speaker."

It was a state law in Pennsylvania that all bars and cafes be closed on Sundays, yet a United States Senator walks into a bar on a Sunday, buys a round of drinks for everyone and receives an ovation. It could only happen in Schuylkill County.

After a few years Jimmy Ryan resigned his position and moved to Coal Castle, his new residence. In 1950, he was elected Democratic Chairman of Schuylkill County. His party couldn't have made a wiser choice. He was a robust man with a warm and outgoing personality. The record he compiled as chairman would bear out the fact that he was a dedicated, energetic and astute politician. Among his Republican adversaries, he was respected and admired.

Within a few years, under Jimmy's guidance, the Democrats gained many of the major offices in the county. In 1960, he spearheaded the election campaign which resulted in the Democrats capturing the County Commissioner's office for the first time in fifty years. He demonstrated his astuteness in selecting the proper individuals who could motivate the electorate and win a victory in a contest where they were a distinct underdog. He selected two political unknowns to head the ticket. Ben Boltz was a successful businessman, Protestant, and Pennsylvania Dutchman who succeeded in bringing numerous Republicans into the Democratic column. His second choice was Joe "Socks" Holden from St. Clair, an Irish Catholic and one of the most popular baseball players in Schuylkill County.

Socks Holden was the star catcher with the St. Clair Indians of the South Anthracite League, which included teams from the west end of the county: Pine Grove, Valley View and Hegins were the entries. They were made up of the players who were Pennsylvania Dutch, Protestant, and Republican.

In 1934, Holden signed a contract with the Philadelphia Phillies and played under manager Jimmy Wilson, a member of baseball's Hall of Fame. He remained with the Phillies until 1937, when he was traded to the Baltimore Orioles. He managed in the minor leagues from 1940 through 1948. After he retired from managing, he became a baseball scout for the Detroit Tigers of the American League. Later, he was elected to the Major Leagues Scouts Hall of Fame. At this writing, he is president of the Holden Insurance Company. His son Tim, following in his father's political footsteps, is serving his second term as sheriff of Schuylkill County.

The friends Holden made during his playing days in the Anthracite League didn't forget him when they marked their ballots. He received the greatest plurality of any candidate in the history of the county.

38 James "Shorty" Bergen; Rol Holley's Farewell

James "Shorty" Bergen was born in Coal Castle, a small mining town located three miles west of Minersville. His father died when he was two years old, and his mother, Agnes, ran a small bar which served breakfast, lunch, hot dogs and hamburgers. Her place of business was clean and orderly with little or no trouble. Because she was a widow, her patrons never allowed anyone to step out of line or cause trouble.

Shooting pigeons was a way of life in the small community. Almost every evening during the summer and fall, the men, after finishing their supper, would gather at an area called the Island. It was located approximately three hundred yards behind the residence of Jimmy Ryan, the first citizen of Coal Castle.

It was an open field, and at the far end was a steep embankment about fifty feet high. At the top was an array of maples, oaks and a few evergreens.

The pigeon trap was set so that the contestants shot into the embankment and the trees. Behind the shooters was a rolling grassy knoll where small coal-burning homes dotted the area. Many of the residents, especially the women and children, observed the proceedings from that picturesque vantage point.

Katie Kaperna recalls some of her memories of the Sunday pigeon shoots in Coal Castle. "Sunday was a special day at the Island. There was great excitement and a carnival atmosphere prevailed. Seventy-five to a hundred men always took part, and they were either shooting or betting.

"We were never permitted to go near the shooting area, but when all the activities came to an end, we were allowed to proceed to where the dead birds had been gathered. Some days there were as many as four hundred birds. We wrung their necks, placed them in paper bags and cleaned up the area before departing.

"At times we took as many as twenty or thirty birds, which our mothers made into delicious soup. If anyone in the family came down with the flu or was feeling blah, they were given pigeon soup instead of the famous cure-all chicken soup. One thing for sure, the pigeons were never wasted."

Throughout the Depression, the poor people had an abundance of soup to supplement their meager food supplies. During the weekdays' shooting, there was very little betting and no drinking. If anyone wanted a drink they had to go back to the bar.

During the late forties and the early fifties the price of a bird and a shell was twenty-five cents. Each person took his turn to shoot and everything was low key.

Sunday mornings were a different story. Jack Mulhall, of Coal Castle, recalls the events that took place on most Sunday mornings. "Most of the shooters went to early mass, and the shooting of pigeons never took place until after the nine o'clock mass, after which the men proceeded to the Island.

"Prior to their arrival, a number of men who had attended an earlier mass dropped into Bergen's bar. They enjoyed a few eye-openers or miner's specials, to clear their heads before taking their place among the crowd either as shooters or spectators.

"The Protestants attended the Methodist Church, which conducted their services at nine o'clock. They were always in time to join in the festivities and enjoy a few brews at Bergen's before proceeding to the shooting area."

It was obvious to everyone who attended the shoots at the Island that Shorty Bergen was an exceptionally fine shooter. He stood five feet four inches tall and had a slender build. He is remembered as a quiet young man who seemed to possess an inner confidence. He never showed any emotion whether he killed or missed a bird. He wasn't superstitious, never fussed about his stance or the position of his head or feet and didn't possess any of the idiosyncrasies that were prevalent among many of the shooters of his day. A born shooter, he picked up the gun, took one sighting and was ready for action.

Jimmy Ryan didn't have the opportunity to observe Shorty as did many of the other men in town. However, Shorty's ability was brought to his attention and Jimmy was queried about the possibility of backing Shorty in some matches. He approached Willie Bergen, no relation to Shorty, who was the most knowledgeable man regarding pigeons and pigeon shooters in the Heckshersville Valley.

"Tell me, Willie, can this young Bergen kid shoot or are these fellas talking through their hats?"

"No, the kid kin really shoot. I think he's the best I seen around here in a long time. Do ya think ya wanna back him in a match?"

"If you think he's that good, maybe I'll go and see Agnes and see if she'll let the kid shoot."

"Good luck, Jimmy. Agnes keeps pretty close tabs on the kid, but if anyone kin convince her, it's you."

"OK, Willie, I'll give it a shot."

Willie was right; Agnes kept a close eye on Shorty. He didn't smoke or drink and she intended to keep him on the straight and narrow road.

Agnes was ten years older than Jimmy. They were lifelong friends and had great respect for each other. Agnes knew Jimmy when he was a young boy and watched him grow from his meager beginnings to a very affluent and powerful man in Schuylkill County, both in business and in politics.

He arrived at the cafe at three o'clock on a Wednesday afternoon, sat at the bar and ordered a beer. The bar was empty and quiet; Jimmy's tapping of his fingers on the bar sounded like a drummer warming up for a firemen's parade. Agnes placed the beer in front of her new arrival and never uttered a word. Jimmy took a sip of beer and looked across the bar and, in a slow and pronounced manner, began his spiel.

"Agnes, Jimmy's a pretty good shot, I thought I'd like to back him in a few matches. What do you think of the idea?"

"I knew that sooner or later you'd get around ta askin' me about James. Well, now that ya asked, let's talk."

"OK, I'll start by saying that Jimmy is a natural shooter, and a damned good shot. I'm sure he can win a great many matches and might make both of us a little richer. If he's as great as I think he is, he'll certainly help your business."

"I hear the men talk at the bar. They say James can really handle a gun and he's a terrific shot. I'm not worried about that part, but let's be honest, Jimmy, that pigeon and chicken fightin' gang are a pretty wild bunch. They do a lot of drinkin' and gamblin' and I don't want James caught up in that crowd. They can start him on the road ta hell. I hope you can understand my concern."

"Agnes, I understand what you're saying, but you must remember there's a lot of fellas who booze, gamble and carouse, but there are many people who follow the pigeon matches and never participate in those activities. People like Dr. Alimenti, P.S. Canfield, Harry Hoover, Bim Feeley, J.J. Maguire, you know them all. They're not boozers, and I can name many more. I'll tell you what I'll do, as long as Jimmy is under my jurisdiction at the matches he won't drink or gamble. What he does on his own time, well, I can't control his activities."

"I have great respect for you, Jimmy, and I know that you'll keep your word. I want you to promise me one thing. Never overmatch him so that he'll be embarrassed and hurt."

"Agnes, you have my word. I swear on my dead mother's grave!"

Jimmy Ryan took Shorty under his wing and protected him like a mother hen would. Shorty compiled a great record. Over a seven-year span, he participated in fifty matches and lost only eight.

Ryan secured the best trappers in the county: Eddie Kelly, the Hartman brothers, Al Rumberger, Willie Bergen, Willie Murray, the Lurwicks and the Petrole brothers. He had no trouble securing backers. The Sophys, Monk Miller and Jackie McDonald were ready to cash in on their new superstar.

Ryan handled his new-found prodigy as a diamond cutter would caress the Hope diamond. He knew Shorty would eventually confront the outstanding shooters in the area. He would develop him slowly, much as a fight manager would nurture a gifted but inexperienced fighter; nice and easy and never, never, overmatch him. Throughout Shorty's career, Ryan endeavored to adhere to this self-imposed principle.

Shorty's outstanding matches included ones against Guy Ditzler, Mark Motto, Sammy Lehman, Elmer Krommis, Fats Umbenhauer, Art Aestrack, Joe Brown, Sam Russell, Grant Dresher, Joe Piel, Charlie Simons, George Starr, Tony Bell, Nevin Shadle, Joe Bugeye and Al Edwards. The purses were usually one or two thousand dollars a side; between five hundred and two thousand spectators showed up for each match.

Jimmy Ryan and Dave Smith were good friends in and out of politics. They were both successful businessmen and traveled in the same social circles. One evening in 1950, while attending a political rally in Mahanoy City, they were sitting around having a few drinks with some friends, including Jackie McDonald.

Eventually the conversation got around to pigeon shooting. Jackie turned to Dave. "Dave, do you think you can handle Shorty Bergen in a match?"

Dave was an excellent shooter and never took Shorty seriously as an opponent. Jackie's question caught him off guard. He had been leaning back in his chair in a comfortable position with his arms folded across his chest. A surprised look crossed his face; he thought a moment before he replied.

"Ya know, Jackie, I never gave it much thought, but I don't think I'd have much trouble with the kid."

Jackie leaned back in his chair and looked up at the ceiling. "I don't know, Dave. Shorty's a pretty good shot, he might have a good chance of beating you."

"Jackie my boy, how much would you like ta wager on such a match?"

Jackie turned to Jimmy Ryan. "What do you think, Jimmy? Do you think Shorty can handle Dave?"

Ryan didn't hesitate. "I think it would be a great tussle, but I believe Shorty would win the match."

Jackie had the answer he wanted. "OK, Dave, how about a thousand dollars a side. How does that sound?"

"It sounds OK ta me. Why not make it two thousand a side, it would make the match a bit more interesting."

Jackie gave a quick glance toward Jimmy, who responded with a short nod of his head and a corresponding wink. "OK, it's a deal. Why don't we meet for lunch tomorrow to work out the details and draw up an agreement?"

The document was signed. The match would be held at the Minersville ballpark on Sunday, December 1, 1950, at 1 p.m., seventeen birds, trap and handle and the purse of two thousand dollars a side.

The announcement of the event caused great excitement throughout the county. Jack Richards, of the *Pottsville Republican*, picked up the story and made reference to the contest nearly every night in his sports column. The gamblers were always elated about any big match which brought people together. That's where the action was, so what else is new?

Ryan, McDonald, the north of the mountain boys and Georgie Breen were backing Shorty. The westenders, led by Sammy Lehman and the Sophys, were backing their hometown hero, Smith.

Georgie Breen and Jackie McDonald had great confidence in Shorty's shooting ability. "Ya know, Jackie, this kid is a good bet. Why don't we really stick it ta the Sophys, let's put a bundle on the lad."

"Why not, I'd like ta take a little of their moldy money. Let's get those bastards!"

It didn't take too much effort to put the bet in place. The match was a tossup, youth against experience. It was worth five thousand dollars to pick the winner. Jackie and Georgie thought they had put their money on the winner; only time would tell.

Both camps were after the services of Eddie Kelly as a trapper. It wasn't an easy decision for Eddie to make. He was friendly with both men and had trapped for them on numerous occasions. He finally made the decision to trap for his old employer, Dave Smith.

December 1 was a typical winter day in the coal region. The beautiful and colorful foliage of early October was long gone and only barren trees remained, their branches like ghostly fingers stretching upward to the overcast skies. The dark, unpainted fences surrounding the dusty infield and faded yellow grass would momentarily assume new life as a most provocative and explosive match lent excitement to the bleak day.

Two thousand people attended the event, all expecting a close match and all ready to back, with an abundance of money, their gut feeling as to who would win.

The match was tied after fifteen birds with each killing thirteen. Anyone wanting to bet on the kill had to lay three to one odds. The gamblers, as usual, had no sentimental favorites. They were betting on the kill, giving as high as four to one odds. They possessed great expertise at their trade. They were making money!

Bergen killed the sixteenth bird. Smith approached the mark as Pete Petrole put one of his legendary black birds in the trap. When the trap was sprung the bird flew straight and began to rise; Dave fired quickly, low and below the bird. It was a clear miss. The Bergen supporters went wild as their hero was one up and one bird to go.

Eddie Kelly went to the trap with one of Les Felty's birds. It was small and built for speed. Surmising their strategy, Shorty was prepared to shoot low and quickly. He took his customary one sighting and yelled "pull." As soon as the trap opened Shorty fired.

Kelly had pulled the trick he had learned from the Hartman brothers. He had placed the bird on its back, and instead of flying straight ahead as predicted, the pigeon rolled out of the trap and never took flight.

Shorty shot over the trap and the bird was home free, ready to fly another day. Dave could tie the match by killing the last bird. If that became a reality, it was agreed that the first man to miss in a shoot-off would lose the match.

The Bergen brain trust picked Pete Petrole to fly the last bird. It was getting dark and Pete's black bird was the logical choice. He tucked the bird in the trap and made his way back to the sidelines.

The usual taunts, swearing and noise were deafening as Dave arrived at the mark. He didn't waste any time, he looked toward the trap and yelled "pull." He let the bird go at least thirty-five feet before firing. It was a clear miss. The bird flew to safety amid the cheers and jubilation of the winners, and groans and ungodly epithets from the losers.

It was a great match and enormous amounts of money changed hands. Jimmy Ryan, Jackie McDonald and Georgie Breen hosted a victory celebration at Bergen's bar. Many of the pigeon men, in addition to the large investors, made their appearance.

As Eddie Kelly made his entrance, he was greeted by Jackie McDonald. Jackie put his arm around Eddie's shoulder in a friendly gesture. "Eddie, you're a born loser. Come on and join the celebration."

"You know me, Jackie, win or lose, I'm always ready fer a party. You kin buy me a drink."

That was just the beginning; the night was young. Much later, after Agnes ushered them out, they headed for Phil Laudeman's club where the party continued. Phil offered them the usual menu; plenty of booze, dice, cards, craps and chicken fights. It was a fitting ending to a great weekend.

On a cold, windy, snowy day in early December, Shorty and his mother were enjoying a late lunch. It was about 2:30 p.m., and because of the weather conditions, the bar was empty. The wind was blowing at nearly gale force, and there was at least an inch of snow on the ground. The weather forecast predicted a snowfall of six or seven inches.

Agnes expected very few customers, so she had a good excuse to close the bar early and catch up on her housework. If everything fell into place, she could possibly get a little rest.

She had prepared bean soup, a ham and cheese sandwich and a pot of tea for Shorty. After finishing the meal, Shorty leaned forward in his chair, put his elbows on the table and rested his chin between his hands.

"Mom, I think the match I have scheduled for December 16 will be my last. I'm getting older and I don't enjoy the matches as I used to. I think it's time to quit and devote my time and energy to other things. Mr. Ryan has been good to me, I hope he won't think I'm letting him down. What do you think?"

After a few moments Agnes looked at her son and nodded her head slightly in an affirmative manner. "James, you did very well as a shooter and you always conducted yourself in a respectable manner. Your dead father would be very proud, just as I am. If that's what you want, it's all right with me, but it's only right that you inform Mr. Ryan about your decision."

It was well known in pigeon circles that Jimmy Ryan held a tight reign on Shorty, as he had promised Agnes, "He will never drink or gamble at a match as long as I'm his promoter." Ryan never once wavered from his promise.

Shorty relates the final meeting between Ryan and his mother regarding the conclusion of his shooting career.

"Agnes, I want to thank you for letting James take part in the matches. He's a wonderful boy and you can be proud of him. He was one hell of a shooter!" He laughingly added, "He also made both of us a little richer." He gathered Agnes and Jimmy into his arms. "I'll never forget you two; you're wonderful."

At the time of this writing, James "Shorty" Bergen is head of the Schuylkill County Adult Probation Office and is scheduled to retire in 1992.

Dave Smith had one more important match in his career, that being his encounter with the legendary Rol Holley. One evening at Lurwick's, the bar was crowded, and Eddie Kelly and a few of his friends were seated at a table having a drink.

Rol walked in, accompanied by a friend. They sat at the bar and ordered a drink. Rol was an easy-going person who never engaged in arguments or fights in or out of a bar, but when he had a few beers under his belt he enjoyed needling Eddie about his shooting ability. Rol and his friend approached Eddie, who invited them to join him for a drink.

On this particular evening Eddie was the one who began needling. "Ya know Rol, I'll be the first ta admit that you're a great shooter, but I always thought my cousin Bunt Kelly could beat you in a fair match. You always got him liquored up and then you talked him inta believin' he couldn't shoot. But in yer heart, you knew that Bunt could beat ya if you two guys ever shot a match and ya were both sober."

Rol broke out in a fit of laughter and was joined by the others at the table. After the laughter had subsided, Rol looked at Eddie and waved a finger in his face.

"I kin beat Bunt Kelly in a match drunk or sober and I kin beat you with one hand tied behind my back."

Eddie jumped to his feet and stood over Rol. "I listened to yer bullshit fer the last time. I'll shoot ya fer a thousand dollars anytime ya want."

Rol was up to the challenge. He calmly looked up at Eddie. "OK, big mouth, yer on."

He turned and yelled to Jake Lurwick who was tending bar. "Jake, draw up an agreement so I kin shut this Irishman's big mouth."

The next day Eddie met Dave Smith and related the happenings at Lurwick's bar the previous evening.

"First of all, Eddie, you don't have a thousand dollars and second, ya can't beat Rol Holley. I know he's over the hill, but he's still a better shooter than you."

Eddie was surprised at Dave's frank answer. Now he was in a quandary as to how he could save face and get out of the match. "What do ya think I should do?"

"Don't do anything. If I were you, I'd stay out of sight for a few days. Maybe I'll see Jake Lurwick and see if Rol will take me on in a match."

"Do ya think Rol will take the match?" Eddie asked hopefully.

Dave hesitated a moment. "Well, he has a great ego, so I'm sure he won't turn the offer down."

Rol was a realist. He knew he was past his prime but his backers convinced him he could still take the measure of Smith. The Sophys jumped at the chance to back Dave. Sure, he had lost a close match to Shorty Bergen, but Rol was over the hill, so why not cash in and make a killing? No one was going to beat Dave Smith twice in a row.

Jackie McDonald, Jimmy Ryan and Georgie Breen were backing Rol. Once again there was a five thousand dollar private wager between McDonald, Breen and the Sophys. The match took place at the Salem Hill ballpark in Port Carbon, seventeen birds for two thousand dollars a side.

In spite of the fact that Rol was nearing the end of competitive shooting, he killed fourteen out of seventeen while Dave killed thirteen birds. It was Rol Holley's last match; he died a few months later. Two of his pallbearers were Eddie Kelly and Dave Smith.

James "Shorty" Bergen.

39 Eddie Kelly's Last Match

There was no doubt that Phil Laudeman's was the place to be on a Thursday afternoon. Hundreds of people were there each week to engage in their favorite pastime of shooting pigeons and attaining total relaxation.

Sam Russell, a local shooter, recalls an incident which occurred on one such afternoon. "I was preparing for a match. Willie Murray, Joe Tobin and Allie Sublosky accompanied me to Laudeman's. I shot twenty-five birds, then retreated to the sidelines to make a few bets and watch the action.

"We were unaware that Petie Joseph and the Sophys had arranged a match between Joe Valent, of Palo Alto, and Al Rumberger from Pine Grove. Phil Laudeman and Sammy Lehman were backing Rumberger.

"The match was for one thousand dollars a side, seventeen birds, trap and handle and each shooter had to shoot one-handed. The gun had to be held at his side until the trap was opened.

"No one had ever seen a one-handed match and you can imagine the excitement it generated. It added a new dimension to the usually exciting Thursday afternoons. The event confused the betters. Most thought a bet on the miss was a sure thing.

"To everyone's surprise, at the end of sixteen birds the match was tied, each killing eleven birds. Valent missed his final shot, and Rumberger killed the last bird and came away with the victory. It was the strangest match I had ever seen, and I have never heard of such a match since."

Eddie Kelly's career as a shooter came to an abrupt ending in 1947. He was at Phil Laudeman's on a Thursday afternoon; the time was approximately 5 p.m. He was putting birds in the trap for various shooters and was accompanied by two of his friends, Ricksey Kerticklus and Billie Berdean of Seltzer City.

Cletus Coyne and four of his friends arrived on the scene at 5:30, and it wasn't long before they were making bets along the sidelines. As Eddie finished putting a bird in the trap and proceeded toward the sidelines, the voice of Cletus rang out.

"Hey Eddie, do ya have a good bird I can shoot at, I feel lucky taday."

As Eddie neared his place along the sidelines he lowered his head, spit out some chewing tobacco and yelled at Cletus, "Just how lucky do ya feel?"

"I can kill your bird for a hundred bucks."

Without hesitating Eddie replied, "If ya lay me two ta one odds, ya have a bet."

"OK, Edward, get your bird!"

Eddie walked to the pens which housed hundreds of birds, located behind the main building. He studied the birds for a few minutes before picking a brown and white bird and gently placing it inside his shirt.

Eddie explains his method of choosing his birds. "I always look for a nervous and fidgety bird with a small body and big wings. They always get out of the trap fast."

"Cletus, since you're layin' two ta one odds, me and my buddies will take a bet fer a hundred bucks. How does that sound?"

"It's OK with me, here's my two hundred, let's see your hundred." Eddie produced the money and started to hand it to Cletus.

"Never mind, you can hold the bet. You won't have it for long!"

Eddie made his way to the trap and placed a jingler on the bird. When the trap opened, Cletus let the bird fly at least twenty yards before firing. The bird was hit, but not with the full load. It landed five yards inside the out-of-bounds marker. As the bird struggled to take flight, Cletus' bird catcher ran full speed toward the fallen bird, which was running along the ground and flapping its wings in a wild and furious manner.

Within a few seconds the catcher pounced on the struggling bird. Eddie Kelly was within five yards of the catcher and shouted, "Don't move the bird till we measure the distance from the trap. I think it's out of bounds."

The catcher looked toward Eddie as he gasped for air. "The bird's in bounds. It's a dead bird."

Eddie turned to his buddy Ricksey. "Go get Phil and bring a tape measure."

By that time, at least twenty people had gathered around the fallen bird, all waiting for Phil to make the measurement. When he had completed the task, the tape measured forty-one yards; the bird was out of bounds by one yard. It was a missed bird and Eddie and his friends won the money.

The catcher turned to Cletus. "I'm tellin' ya Cletus, the bird was in bounds when I grabbed him, I know it was in bounds."

"OK, Eddie, you heard the man, give me the three hundred dollars."

"No way do you get the money. You read the tape. It was out of bounds by a yard. It was a missed bird so we're keepin' the money! Come on, Ricksey, let's go inside and have a drink."

Eddie and his friends headed for the bar to celebrate, as Cletus and his friends hurled threats and verbal abuse at them.

As the second round of drinks was being finished, Phil approached Eddie and in a low voice whispered, "If I was you, Eddie, I'd get outta here quick. Cletus and his friends are as mad as hell. They want their money back or there's gonna be trouble."

Eddie heeded Phil's advice. He and his friends made a quick retreat toward the exit. Once outside they broke into a run and piled into Ricksey's car.

Cletus entered the bar and discovered that Eddie's party had made a quick departure. He raced to the door in time to see their car speed out of the parking lot. Ricksey was driving a new

1947 Plymouth and was confident he could outdistance anyone if he had a twenty-second start.

Eddie was doing his utmost to impress Ricksey with the gravity of the situation. "If those bastards ketch us, they'll not only get the money but they'll beat the hell outta us, so get this son of a bitch of a car on the road." Eddie didn't have to repeat the message. Ricksey was aware of the consequences if they were caught.

When he approached the end of the parking lot he didn't slow down; he accelerated the car as he made the left turn. It was a dirt road, which was to his advantage. As he gained speed, great clouds of dust rose from the road making it almost impossible for Cletus, who was chasing them, to maintain a high rate of speed. That's all the advantage Ricksey needed. Being a local boy he knew every turn in the road, and so he made a safe getaway.

When they arrived in Seltzer City, they drove up an old stripping road. This was their stomping grounds. It was the area where as youngsters they played and romped through the mountains. They knew every inch of the rugged terrain. They were as safe as if they were babes in their mothers' arms!

Cletus lost the battle, but he didn't intend to lose the war. He would bide his time, and sometime in the not too distant future he would gain his revenge. Eddie Kelly would rue the day he antagonized a member of the closely knit north of the mountain Irish clan.

Things remained cool between the adversaries for some time. They gave each other a wide berth whenever they appeared at the same pigeon match or chicken fight. They never met in a bar, so it could never be ascertained what would have happened if such an event had occurred.

Cletus, with the help of Charlie Simons, Battler Delago and Jackie McDonald, was patiently planning to lure Eddie into a match with himself. Jackie laid out the plan of the operation. "We must take our time and don't let Eddie realize how much we want the match. If we play our cards right, we can pull it off.

"Eddie's a great drinker, therefore the arrangements should take place in a bar. When he has a few drinks under his belt, he thinks he's the greatest shooter in the world. We'll nurse him along and make the purse plenty high. As you said, Cletus, we'll shoot the match in our own backyard, and before it's over that shanty Irishman won't know what hit him."

Cletus agreed with Jackie's analysis of the situation. "I think you're right. When we're finished with that jackass, he'll be glad to go back to his bootleg coal hole, and he'll go back broke."

Billie McCue, owner of a bar in Locust Dale, was selected as the person to approach Eddie, or his backers, as to the possibility of arranging such a contest. Chick Fetteroff, of Ashland, one of Eddie's chief backers, called Jake Lurwick about the proposition.

A meeting was set up at McCue's bar. McDonald, Simons, Monk Miller, Fetteroff, Kelly, Jake and Lamar Lurwick were in attendance. After much haggling and drinking an agreement was signed. The date was December 12, 1947. Twenty-five birds, three thousand dollars a side, trap and handle, at the ballfield behind Billie McCue's bar at 1 p.m., regardless of the weather.

In 1947, three thousand dollars was an enormous amount of money to bet on a match. It wasn't long before the gamblers jumped on the bandwagon and the purses were secured. The McDonald forces, together with Georgie Breen, Clemy Foulk and Jerome Cooper from Frackville put up the money.

Cletus was well fortified with good trappers: Steve Salamander, Tony Bee, Pete Oswald, Charlie Foose, George Backmer and Bob Felker, all from north of the mountain. Eddie had little trouble securing backers; the Hallahan brothers, the Sophys, Jimmy Ryan, Dave Smith, P.S. Canfield, Dr. John Canfield and the Lurwicks all gathered around him. The Petrole brothers, Hartmans, Lurwicks and Murrays were the trappers.

Eddie prepared well for the match. He was killing twenty or twenty-one out of twenty-five birds daily and his confidence was soaring. "Jackie McDonald and Billie McCue better sell a lotta booze the next few weeks, because they won't have too much money ta shove around after the match."

Eddie and his followers were in for the biggest surprise of their lives. The boys north of the mountain left nothing to chance or speculation. They covered all angles and were ready to spring the trap. The boys from the lowlands would regret the day they followed Eddie to north of the mountain.

The weather on December 12 was a complete surprise and an added advantage for Cletus. The temperature was 30 degrees and snow was falling. By the time the match started there were four inches on the ground. In spite of the inclement weather, five hundred people arrived for the shoot-off.

McCue did a booming business. When the match was ready to begin, the crews from both sides were well oiled and ready for action.

Both men were excellent shooters, therefore the gamblers were betting on the kill and laying odds. Considering the weather conditions, many of the betters jumped at the chance of getting odds on the miss. The gamblers were waiting for the suckers to make their bets.

From the moment Eddie stepped to the mark to shoot the first bird, the cards were stacked against him. He was not dressed properly; he wore an old overcoat, which he removed when shooting, a light white T-shirt, and no boots or galoshes to protect his feet from the cold and snow. Eddie had prepared well for the match, but he never dreamed the weather could be so cold and unpredictable.

The McDonald forces took advantage of the weather conditions. They flew only white birds. The snow, which produced a white background, made it difficult for Eddie to see the moving targets. Their trappers placed two sitters in a row, then a flyer. They continued this procedure throughout the match, two sitters then a flyer. Gathering all these facts, plus the wine and moonshine he was drinking, Eddie was in an impossible situation.

Another event was unfolding that did little to settle Eddie's nerves. Eddie noticed, when he arrived at the shooting mark and was preparing to shoot, that Jackie Hump, one of Cletus' supporters, had a revolver pointed at Eddie's head.

Dave Smith, standing behind Hump, stepped forward to reassure his buddy. "Don't worry about him, Eddie, I have a revolver pointed at Hump's head."

Eddie turned and looked at Dave. "That ain't gonna do me much good if he fires the gun."

Coyne won the match, killing thirteen out of twenty-five. Kelly killed twelve. Many people accused Eddie of selling out to Jackie McDonald for five hundred dollars.

"I never sold out in my life! My fingers were so cold I could hardly pull the trigger. With the snow, the white birds, the sitters and the booze, I just couldn't concentrate. I swear on my dead mother's grave that I didn't sell out! I don't think I'll ever shoot another match."

His encounter with Cletus was the last match of his career but he continued to be one of the most successful trappers in the county. As Cletus had predicted, Eddie went back to the coal hole broke, but not a broken man. No one, or no one incident, could break his spirit or his zest for life. He continued his life of pigeons, gambling, drinking, and his first love, attending the chicken fights.

40 Fixed Matches

Over the years, thousands of matches have taken place throughout the county, and millions of dollars changed hands. Most of the money eventually ended up in the pockets of the gamblers. Hence the inevitable question: have there ever been any fixed matches?

It is almost impossible to prove a shooter would deliberately miss a bird. In doing so, he would lose the match and line someone's pockets with tainted money. However, when professional gamblers are so closely associated with the sport, anything is possible. There were a few encounters which could fit into the tainted twilight zone.

In 1947, a match involving Skinny Gilbert, of Hegins, and a shooter from the Pottsville area took place in the Hegins ballpark. There was a great difference in the shooting abilities of the shooters. The Pottsville ace was an above-average shooter, whereas Skinny Gilbert could be classified as a poor shooter.

Anyone with an average amount of knowledge about pigeons could amass a substantial amount of money by betting on Gilbert's misses and the Pottsville ace's kills.

Eddie Kelly was trapping for Ace and he flew the first nine birds away from Gilbert. The Pottsville ace killed the first bird, then proceeded to miss the next eight birds.

Al Rumberger, from Pine Grove, was Gilbert's chief backer and had an enormous amount of money bet with Monk Miller and the Hallahans at odds of three to one. He and Eddie Kelly were betting heavily on both shooters' misses.

Rumberger turned to Eddie. "It will be a miracle if we win this match, Ace will have ta miss all his shots fer us ta win. I don't know if we kin pull it off. Ya better give Skinny some easy shots."

"Holy Christ, Al, I'm puttin' ducks in now. If they fly any slower I kin kill them with my hands. I just hope he kin kill a few."

Gilbert won the match by killing three out of fifteen; the Pottsville ace killed two out of fifteen. On their return to Lurwick's bar at the conclusion of the match, Eddie was approached by Jake Lurwick.

"Eddie, that match looked awful fishy ta me. Was the fix in?"

Eddie raised his head as he took a sip of beer. In a solemn and righteous voice he admonished the innkeeper. "Jake, I'm surprised at yer question, the Pottsville ace is as honest as the day is long. He just had a bad day." As he put down his beer glass, he gave Jake a slow wink of the eye. Yes, the fix was in! Eddie Kelly, Al Rumberger and the Pottsville ace did rather well.

In 1946, Joe Poolie, of New Philadelphia, and Sammy Lehman shot a match at the Ten Pin Club in Pine Grove for one thousand dollars a side, twenty birds, trap and handle. The men were excellent shooters and the match was considered a toss-up. The Sophy brothers and the Hazleton money boys, Georgie Breen and Gene Boyle, were backing Sammy. Poolie had no trouble getting the money up front.

Sammy killed eight out of fifteen. Poolie killed the first bird, then missed the next seven. Sammy coasted to an easy victory. A great amount of money changed hands, but most of it enriched the pockets of the Sophys, Breen, Boyle and Poolie.

Poolie shot very few matches after his encounter with Lehman. He had lost the public trust and was now paying the price. As a shooter he was ostracized. He continued to attend the matches but his participation was limited to trapping and betting.

The most controversial match in Schuylkill County took place in 1947 at the Mahanoy City ballpark between Bully Boyer, of Williamstown, and Al Martin, an outstanding shooter from the Scranton area. The purse was two thousand a side, twenty-five birds, trap and handle.

Al Martin was one of the best shooters in the state. Bully Boyer was an above-average shooter and not in the same class as Martin. McDonald, Coyne, Simons, Miller and Breen were the money people behind Martin. The Sophys, Hallahans and Lehman were backing Boyer. By the end of the twelfth bird, Martin had killed three.

Georgie Breen, accompanied by his one-armed companion who made all his bets and collected his winnings, was standing along the sidelines observing the action. By this time, Georgie realized the fix was in place and Martin was part of the arrangements. As Breen approached Martin, Eddie Kelly heard the following conversation.

"Look Al, I'm out five thousand and I want it back!" Martin killed the next five birds. Breen recovered his losses and then some. The one-armed man stuffed the money in the satchel and they quickly made their departure.

Eddie Kelly was the main trapper for Martin. He flew twelve out of twenty-three birds away from Boyer. He was promised the gate of one thousand dollars by Jackie McDonald if Martin won.

Boyer was leading by one bird going into the last shot of the contest. If Martin killed the last bird the match would be tied and there would be a shoot-off.

The pressure, tension and excitement mounted as Martin approached the mark. Thousands of dollars were riding on the last bird. The Boyer forces used everything calculated to unnerve and upset Martin. Two thousand people were screaming and cursing and waving their hands, handkerchiefs or any piece of paraphernalia they felt would contribute to a miss and score a victory for Boyer.

Martin came to the mark accompanied by his gun handler, Edgar Felty of Pine Grove. Sammy Lehman placed a bird in the trap and made his way to the sidelines. At the command of "pull" the bird took flight, but Martin never fired a shot.

At the exact moment the trap opened, someone along the right sidelines released a dog that started to run toward the bird, which was a least ten feet off the ground.

Martin explained, "I didn't shoot because I didn't want ta kill the dog."

The referee declared a missed bird, and the match was over. Boyer was declared the winner. A mini-riot ensued. Fights between the opposing forces broke out as the winners endeavored to collect their bets. The Mahanoy City police were called to restore order.

At the conclusion of the match, word got back to the McDonald forces that the Sophy brothers had put in the fix. They had given Al Martin's father five hundred dollars to throw the match. Battler Delago exploded, "If we find that old son of a bitch, we'll put him in the hospital for a long stay. He'll wish he was never born. He cost us a hell of a lotta money!"

Fortunately, the elder Martin was alerted that the McDonald forces were aware of the fix. It would be to his advantage to make a quick exit and go into hiding, if he didn't want to be confronted by a very angry mob of losers. He took the advice.

To the amazement of all, Martin overcame the bad publicity and stigma which usually follows a person who has been involved in such an incident. After a layoff of six months, he again entered the shooting arena and ended his career in 1974.

41 Bill Bushbee's Moonshine

Bill Bushbee owned a bar in Frackville where many of the citizens interested in pigeon matches, chicken fights, gambling and booze hung their hats. Bill was well known throughout the county and had a thriving bar business.

On one occasion, he teamed up with his friend Charlie Simons and went on a weekend drinking binge. They attended the matches at Phil Laudeman's, the Ten Pin Club in Pine Grove, Willie Murray's club in New Phillie and Jackie McDonald's Brandonville Country Club. At each stop, they drank, gambled and enjoyed the chicken fights. It was an enjoyable, carefree three-day binge.

Monetarily, they were well ahead of the game. They were on a lucky streak. Each had accumulated approximately ten thousand dollars.

When they arrived at Bushbee's bar at 3 a.m. on Monday morning, they were both pretty well oiled with liquor. They began playing cards and continued their drinking. When the card game broke up at 7 a.m., Charlie owed Bill thirty thousand dollars. Charlie returned to his home in Girardville to recover from his losses and also from his hangover.

A few days later, Charlie returned to Bushbee's bar. Bill was seated at a table drinking a beer. "Come on in, Charlie, pull up a chair and have a beer."

"I can sure use one. I'm just about over that drinking bout you and I had. That was some weekend!"

Bill placed a beer in front of his friend. "Here ya are, Charlie, here's ta yer health."

Charlie took a good-sized gulp, wiped his lips and looked across the table. "We certainly had one hell of a good time, but it's time I pay my debts. I want ta pay off my I.O.U.'s. I owe you thirty thousand dollars and I always pay my debts. I have it here in my jacket." As he reached for the money, Bill grabbed his hand and stopped him from taking the money from his inner pocket.

"Let me tell ya something, Charlie, I never welshed on a bet in my life and you didn't either. I want ya ta listen ta what I'm sayin'. We were both drunk when we were playin' cards. In fact I don't remember very much about the game. But I don't take money from my friends when they're drunk. Here's the I.O.U.'s and I don't want ta hear any bullshit!"

Charlie was taken aback by his friend's statement. "I don't know what ta say Bill. I don't remember much about the game either. I know one thing, when the game was over, I owed you thirty thousand dollars."

"Well ya don't owe it ta me any more. Now let's cut the bullshit and have a drink."

Six months later, Bushbee was closing his bar about 2:30 a.m. on a Sunday morning. Business was booming and the bar had been crowded. After he closed the doors, Mary Barrett, one of his barmaids, and his friend Yank Walker joined him for a nightcap in the kitchen. They were drinking the miner's special, a shot and a beer.

Bill walked out to the bar and returned with a dark brown bottle which he placed on the table. "I got some moonshine from Ringtown taday. Let's give it a try." Bill poured the drinks. They drank to everyone's health, including their own.

Yank finished his drink and walked to the door. "I had enough booze fer taday, I'm headin' home. I'll see you two in the morning." He closed the door and walked to his home, located a few blocks from the bar.

He had a most uncomfortable night, mostly because he had drunk too much liquor and then topped it off with the moonshine. At 7:30 a.m. he got out of bed, dressed and walked in the direction of Bushbee's bar. On the way he met his old friend Charlie Shuey.

"Come on, Charlie, let's go to Bushbee's and have an eye-opener."

"It's OK with me, I'm always ready fer a drink."

They arrived at the bar and entered the kitchen. The door was unlocked, just as Yank had left it a few hours earlier.

When they entered the room they found Bill and Mary lying on the floor. Both were dead! Yank was so overcome by the scene that he sat at the table in disbelief. He reached over and took the bottle of moonshine that was still on the table from the previous evening. He raised it to his mouth and took four pro-longed gulps and slowly placed the bottle on the table. Within three minutes he was dead.

The incident shocked the small town of Frackville, because the three victims were well-known and popular residents. It was the consensus of the police and the residents that the cause of death was the moonshine, the source of which was never re-vealed.

Reed Middleton and Eddie Kelly had been drinking with Bushbee a week before his death. They had a chance meeting in Frackville a few days after Bill's burial.

"Eddie, we can thank the good Lord that Bill didn't have any of that bad moonshine when we were drinkin' with him last week."

Eddie nodded. "We were damned lucky! I get the chills when I think about it. Let's go across the street and have a beer. Maybe we'll even have a shot of moonshine! Here's hopin' they didn't buy it in Ringtown!"

42 *Women and Pigeon Matches; Eddie Kelly and Pop*

Records show that few women have ever taken part in a pigeon match in Schuylkill County, either as shooters or trappers. The closest they ever came to a match was their participation in the activities which took place in the shooting clubs or bars before, during and after a match.

The owners of the clubs naturally made money on the drinks, but most of the revenue came from the extracurricular activities which the clubs provided. The gamblers were heavily involved in those activities. After all, that was the name of the game. Be where the action was taking place!

Billie and Ellie McCue owned a bar across the street from a colliery in Locust Gap, a small village west of Ashland. They had a thriving business, their patrons mostly miners, neighborhood people and pigeon enthusiasts, who not only enjoyed the friendly and relaxed atmosphere but also the added activities.

Many major pigeon matches took place at a baseball field located about five hundred yards behind the premises. The matches were always good for business.

Billie and Ellie shared the work load, tending bar and running the above-mentioned activities. Ellie could handle her liquor, smoke like a steam engine, chew tobacco and swear like a Lithuanian miner. She never gave any quarter or took any. She was a real hell-raisin' hard-drinkin' gambler and an enterprising business women. She was one of the rare women who was readily accepted in all the activities usually reserved for men only. In between chicken fights, she could be found in the pits shooting craps. Whenever she joined the activities no one batted an eye.

On one occasion, Ellie spent two days playing cards at the Ten Pin Club in Pine Grove. When she made her exit, she had thirty-eight hundred dollars in winnings. In 1947, that was a tidy sum of money to win in a card game.

In 1953, the State of Pennsylvania purchased the McCues' property to build a new road. Billie and Ellie were paid sixty-five thousand dollars for the real estate.

After receiving the money they lived like royalty. They attended pigeon matches, ate and drank with their friends, played cards, shot dice and never missed a chicken fight.

One of Ellie's friends asked her how she was enjoying her retirement. "Billie and me, we're havin' the time of our life! We're doin' everything we always wanted ta do. What the hell, we worked hard all our lives, now we're livin' like millionaires! We're on easy street. We're really livin' it up!" Within fifteen months both were dead.

Les Felty and his sister Roxie operated a bar at the bottom of the Vulcan Mountain, a few miles west of Ashland. Les was a good friend of Eddie Kelly. They trapped together and often attended chicken fights and were probably the heaviest drinkers on the pigeon circuit, spending many drinking hours together.

Eddie says, "I think Les could outdrink me. Whenever you went to his bar and bought a drink of whiskey, he'd buy you one. If you had five drinks, Les bought you five. It just went on and on. He drank between sixteen and eighteen quarts of Seagrams whiskey a week. Now that's drinkin'!"

Les spent some time in the hospital recovering from major surgery. His sister said, "Edward, you'll never know how much whiskey I don't have ta buy since Les has been in the hospital."

Roxie tended bar and it was she who made the business hum. She was good for business, had a pleasant personality and could adapt to any situation that arose at the bar.

Eddie Kelly puts it in simple terms. "If they wanted rough and tumble talk, she stayed right with them. If they wanted soothin' talk, she was there. She appreciated a good joke and her customers loved her. She was some gal!"

Vince and Jack Lurwick were on their way to a match in Pine Grove and stopped at the bar for a few drinks. As they approached the bar, Roxie gave Vince the wink and nodded toward Edgar Gibas, of Port Carbon, who was drinking at the bar. Vince took a seat next to Gibas, as Roxie filled his glass with some liquor.

"Look, Vince, she's fillin' my glass with blackberry brandy and she's chargin' me fer wine. Don't say anything, but she's makin' a mistake."

Edgar was trapping against Les that day, and by the time he left for the match, he was half loaded and his coordination wasn't conducive to making the best and proper decisions at the trap.

When they returned to the bar after the match, Vince asked Roxie about giving Gibas the brandy.

"He thought he was pullin' a fast one on me, but I fixed his wagon. By the way Vince, did he fly any birds away taday?"

"Not a one, Roxie, not a one." With a twinkle in his eye and a smile slowly spreading across his face Vince continued, "That wasn't very nice, Roxie, you didn't play the game on the up and up."

"I know, Vince, I know . . . here, have a drink on the house!"

In September of 1949, a match between Fats Umbenhauer and Elmer Williams, of Lavell, took place at the Ten Pin Club. Eddie Kelly was birding for Elmer, who was favored to win. After placing a bird in the trap, Eddie took his place on the sidelines and stood next to my father, P.S. Canfield, and my brother John.

Fats missed the bird and Eddie was ecstatic. "We're home free, Elmer, we'll win in a walk." Sammy Lehman put a bird in the trap and retreated to the sidelines.

As Elmer was preparing to shoot, Eddie turned to my father. "Do ya have a bet on this bird, Pat?"

"Of course, I have a ten dollar bet on the miss."

"You're makin' a mistake, Patrick. Elmer's gonna kill!"

As Eddie had predicted, Elmer blew the bird apart. My father and Eddie started to walk toward the shooter. When they came abreast of Elmer, my father pointed his finger in Elmer's face. "You had the gun up." The statement and gesture so unnerved Elmer that he didn't kill another bird and lost the match.

Eddie met my father a few weeks later. "You and your lousy ten-buck bet, ya ruined Elmer as a shooter! I don't think he'll ever be able to shoot again." Eddie was correct, Elmer never won another match.

My father always enjoyed Eddie's company. They both frequented the matches and both chewed tobacco. When at a match, Eddie always had a large chew in his mouth, but this never interrupted or interfered with his drinking. When asked how he could chew and drink at the same time, he always had a ready explanation. "It makes the booze taste better."

Except when he was working, Eddie enjoyed drinking. It mattered not whether it was bourbon or blended whiskey, moonshine or the famous miner's special. At the matches he was usually three sheets to the wind. In contrast, my father never took a drink in his life. He was a teetotaler.

When they met at a match, my father always "borrowed" a chew from Eddie. It was a simple ritual he cherished. Most of the time he had a package of chewing tobacco in his pocket; however, he always approached his friend.

"Jesus Christ, Pat, don't you ever buy a pack a tobacco? Ya have enough money ta buy the God-damned plant, yet yer always bummin' a chew from me."

"When I borrow a chew from you, Eddie, it always brings me luck."

"Yeah, you and yer damned luck. Enjoy the chew!"

My dad was a successful contractor, and his pleasures came from his family, his church, baseball, politics and the pigeon matches. The excitement and camaraderie of the matches, mingling with people such as Eddie, made the autumn afternoons a bit more enjoyable. It was the icing on the cake.

Pigeons and pigeon matches have played an important role in the entertainment and pleasure of residents of Schuylkill County. The matches can be traced back to the time of the Civil War and the era of Fred Coleman, 1894 to 1908.

The emergence of outstanding shooters during the twenties and continuing through the seventies, Rol Holley, Sammy Lehman, Brock Murray, Norman Erbe, Reed Middleton, Jake Lurwick, Harry Hoover and Shorty Bergen, to mention a few, and the success of the Hegins Labor Day Shoot have brought worldwide attention to the sport.

Hopefully the top shooters of today will carry this worthwhile and enjoyable tradition into the twenty-first century with as much enthusiasm and verve as their predecessors.

SECTION 5

If a bird in flight drops to the ground and closes his wings, the shooter can hold the gun to his shoulder but he cannot shoot until the bird is on wing again; but if it does not rise again within 10 seconds, the referee shall declare no bird.

SECTION 6

If a bird shot at and while in flight is interfered with by any person besides the bird catcher, it shall be declared no bird.

SECTION 7

If a bird hops out of the trap even though his 2 wings are tied, it shall be declared on wing.

ARTICLE VIII

If in the opinion of the referee the person at the scratch is balked or in any manner obstructed by any person other than his backers, he may order another bird to be trapped.

SECTION 2

Elbow shall be down below the level of the shoulder and gun below elbow until bird takes wing; otherwise, it shall be scored a miss.

5

A page from the "New Rules for Trap and Handle Pigeon Match for Schuylkill County."

Scorecard for use at pigeon matches, with advertisement, circa 1945.

	1	2	3	4	5	6	7	8	9	10	11	12	13	14	15	16	17

A twelve-year-old miner with miner's lamp.

Company scrip used by miners to buy food and clothing at the company store.